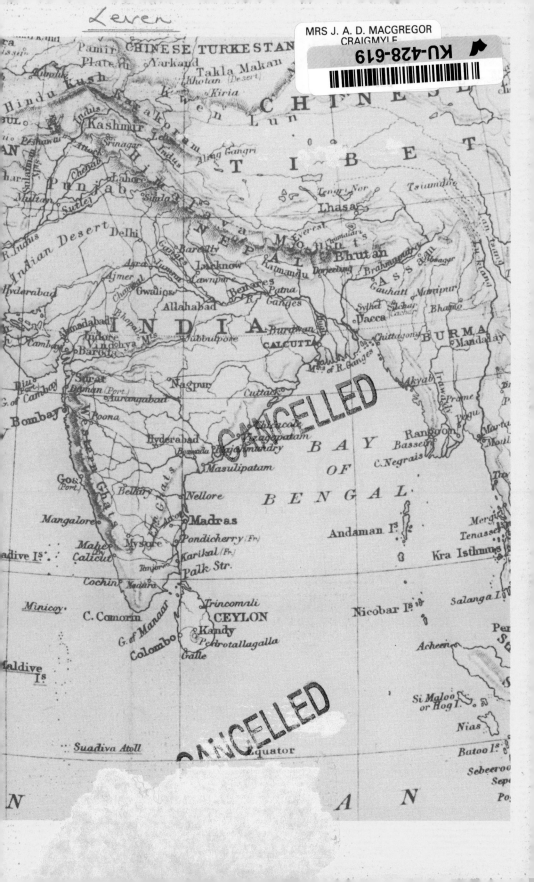

Lady Curzon's India

Lady Curzon's India

LETTERS OF A VICEREINE

Edited by John Bradley
with a foreword by Nigel Nicolson

WEIDENFELD AND NICOLSON
LONDON

Letters, journals and diaries copyright
© Lady Alexandra Metcalfe 1985
Text copyright © Professor John Bradley 1985

First published in Great Britain by
George Weidenfeld & Nicolson Limited
91 Clapham High Street
London SW4 7TA

ISBN 0 297 78701 2

Printed at the Bath Press, Avon

Contents

Illustrations

Endpapers: 'The Indian Empire and Surrounding Countries' (detail), from the *Imperial Gazetteer of India*, 1909 (British Library)

Government House, Calcutta

Simla, the Viceregal Lodge (British Library)

The Curzons *en route* to Sanchi

Akbar's tomb, Sikandra

The tomb of Itimad-ud-Daula

Viceregal visit to Lucknow (British Library)

Lady Curzon on a rhinoceros, Kashmir

The Curzons on the Viceregal launch, Calcutta

Lord Curzon with Cynthia and Irene

'Ringing the tiger'

Tiger-hunt in Hyderabad (British Library)

Viceregal visit to Hyderabad (British Library)

Lady Curzon at the Delhi Durbar

Alexandra at Simla

The Curzons' final departure from India

Unless otherwise indicated, the illustrations are reproduced by kind permission of Lady Alexandra Metcalfe

Foreword

These letters are of very considerable historical and human interest. They were written at the turn of the century by Mary Curzon, the wife of the most energetic and best-remembered of British Viceroys, mostly from India to her family in the United States, and others from England and other parts of Europe to her husband. Some of his replies have been added to complete the picture of their deeply touching relationship.

Lady Curzon was born in Chicago in 1870, the daughter of Levi Leiter, a self-made man who co-founded the famous emporium now known as Marshall Field. From Chicago the family moved to Washington during her childhood, and there she enjoyed a brilliant début as the loveliest, most charming and cleverest girl of her generation. She met Curzon in England in 1890 and married him five years later. In 1898 he was made Viceroy of India at the age of thirty-nine by Queen Victoria, and Mary became not only the youngest Vicereine in the history of the Raj, but fulfilled the highest role which any American, man or woman, ever occupied in the British Empire. She died in England at the pitiably early age of thirty-six.

When Queen Victoria was consulted about Curzon's appointment, she asked Lord Salisbury, 'Will Mrs Curzon, who is an American, do to represent a Vice-Queen?'. The Prime Minister, who knew Mary well, was able to re-assure his Sovereign that she would. She disappointed neither. Having youth and beauty on her side, allied to a capacity to enjoy herself and an instinctive flair for ceremonial occasions, she soon won over the Indian people, and, what was more difficult, the sahibs and memsahibs of the huge Viceregal staffs. She became a star. But so far removed were the Viceroy and Vicereine above any other servants of the Crown, that they could turn only to each other for mutual tenderness and consolation in the tribulations to which their high offices, and the climate, exposed them.

Mary's letters to her family describe her apprenticeship and developing confidence. She drew for them a picture of Indian life, at Calcutta, Simla and on their frequent provincial tours as far afield as Burma and the Gulf states, which has no parallel in the records of British imperial rule. She was seeing

India from the summit downwards, and was accorded every deference, every luxury, that the sub-continent could offer. Although her head was never turned, she undoubtedly enjoyed her glamorous role, culminating in the great Coronation Durbar at Delhi in 1903, and was able to express in her letters the humour of absurd situations that she was obliged to accept with dignity in public. They were not letters written for publication, and gain immeasurably from their unrestrained comedy, but never did she lose sight of the immensity of her husband's task and her own role in supporting him. Indeed, one can find in no other place a more intimate portrait of this remarkable man, who came to rely more and more upon her advice and love, particularly at the period of his quarrel with Kitchener, the Commander-in-Chief in India, which ended his Viceroyalty after six years of unremitting effort and achievement.

Mary returned to England in 1901 for her recuperation and to explain to its leading men Curzon's aims and plans, and relay to him their reactions. She was already a friend of all of them, from the King downwards, and her portraits of Edwardian society at its highest level, and of such politicians as Asquith, Balfour (who was half in love with her), the young Churchill and the Secretary of State for India, St John Brodrick, are among the most vivid and historically important in this book. Her letters from London are funny, gossipy, sometimes indiscreet, and always protective of Curzon's reputation. She did not only him, but the State, some service as his intermediary.

She came back to England a second time in 1904, for the birth of her third daughter (now Lady Alexandra Metcalfe, who owns the originals of the letters), and Curzon temporarily joined her there. She nearly died from a severe illness contracted in the unsalubrious Walmer Castle, but recovering, almost miraculously, she followed him back to India in the next year. By now she had achieved international fame and influence. Adulated in three continents, she remained unspoiled. One of her friends, Ettie Grenfell (Lady Desborough), wrote after her death: 'She was the best and most beautiful of all. There was no one like Mary. She had that innate dignity of nature that seems to set certain people quite apart, and one was never with her without feeling better and happier.'

Professor John Bradley has edited these letters with great skill. His selection of them from a vast archive has condensed Mary Curzon's life and character without distortion. In his Introduction, narrative links and abundant notes, particularly the biographical summaries at the end, he has added every explanation that a modern reader could desire for an understanding of this peak moment in the history of India, and of two people, Viceroy and Vicereine, who in their joint and separate achievements, and in their love for each other, formed a partnership which was brilliantly productive and, in recollection, intensely moving.

NIGEL NICOLSON

Prefatory Note

The journals, diaries and letters of Lady Curzon (1870–1906) constituting the bulk of the present volume are but a small portion of her extensive writings, which run to some fifty manuscript volumes of folio size. From these the editor has extracted correspondence relating specifically to the years 1898–1906, which cover the period she spent in India as its Vicereine and as the wife of George Nathaniel Curzon, Marquess Curzon of Kedleston (1859–1925) whose resignation as Viceroy was forced in 1905.

The initial section of the book consists of letters written from India by Lady Curzon to her family in America; these fall between December 1898 and December 1900 and reflect her early impressions of India and Indian life at various social levels. They are distinguished by wit and humour, insight and observation, and they describe in lively detail the durbars, levees, and drawing-rooms, the dances and dinners, the physical discomforts and gruelling journeys she experienced as Vicereine. The poignant deaths of so many British, young and old, did not escape her attention; neither did the vapid but often amusing snobbery of the Anglo-Indians (the British in India).

The second section of the book is composed of the letters exchanged between Lord and Lady Curzon when the latter returned to Europe for the spring, summer and autumn of 1901. These contrast sharply with the preceding correspondence and warrant attention especially for the picture they offer of Edwardian social and political life; they are populated by such figures as King Edward VII, Queen Alexandra, Balfour, Kitchener, Roberts, Milner, and the young Churchill. And in Lord Curzon's replies one sees the devoted husband and father behind the austere figure of the Viceroy. In fact, a more rounded picture of a man often slighted by the historian and biographer emerges from the 1901 letters, for one sees Curzon as the amused – if at times exasperated – observer of the Anglo-Indian scene. He pungently recounts a moment of social awkwardness or pithily describes a grim evening of amateur theatricals he is compelled to attend. And from the exchanges between the husband and wife there arises also a sense of deep, abiding affection that stands out in relief from the seamy vagaries of Edwardian London.

The third part of the book consists of two splendidly sustained pieces of writing by Lady Curzon: her Hyderabad Journal of 1902 and her Persian Gulf Journal of 1903. Both are individual in style – direct, often humorous, and rife with the colour and pageantry of the Viceregal progress. These are followed by sixteen letters from Lady Curzon to her mother, written in 1905–6, and by Curzon's moving letter of 19 July 1906 describing for Mrs Leiter her daughter's death.

Lady Curzon may not claim a high place in the august tradition of English letter-writing, for on occasion she can be trite, repetitious and even tedious; and she can relapse into such weary modifiers as 'fine', and 'magnificent' or such banalities as 'Ye Gods' and 'I laughed till I cried' – usages that pass muster neither orally nor on the printed page. But her lapses are outweighed by a spontaneity and freshness, an eye for detail, and a keen observation: consistently these qualities are manifest, as in her first impressions of Delhi and Simla, their reception in Bombay, the congealed formalities of protocol. Yet the key can change as she records with disciplined poignancy the death of a child or with vividness the exhibitionism of a Naga tribe or a visit to the Jama Masjid or a reception at Bhopal. And through her observation runs an individual American thread of awelessness that amuses as the absurdities of snobbism and pomposity are impaled.

Lady Curzon's writing is also marked by an extraordinary fortitude, a strength that grows as one considers the daily life, even for the most privileged, in Edwardian India. Swift-striking illness followed by sudden death, to say nothing of minor disorders, constantly beset the British living there. But what surprises and compels admiration is that Lady Curzon, although suffering a great deal, endured so much discomfort of this sort without complaint. She had a high, noble even, conception of her responsibilities as Vicereine – an awareness sharpened by the knowledge that as an American she was under particular scrutiny – and that she lived up to her obligations is apparent in letter after letter. Her clear, unencumbered records compel and engage, and they convey a charming personality and an individual way of looking at old things, old customs, old forms, with new eyes.

Following the simple theory that the least amount of editorial intrusion can be a satisfactory way of presenting a text, I have kept the editing to a minimum. Whilst following as closely as possible the original manuscript, I have nevertheless regularized addresses and dates and spelled out many of the numerals that proliferate in the original; and I have given abbreviations in full that might otherwise be confusing. For clarity's sake the odd punctuation mark is inserted, but Lady Curzon's Carlylean sense of capitalization, her ampersands, cavalier use of the apostrophe, and dashes are retained. Anglo-Indian terminology and a few linguistic oddities are clarified in square brackets within the text.

As the writings of Lady Curzon are the heart of the book I have not dealt with Anglo-Indian politics and touch only lightly on any problems besetting Lord Curzon during his troubled but productive Viceregal years. However, those military, political and social figures that recur are noted on their first appearance with an asterisk to indicate further information about them in the Appendix; others, often playing lesser roles, are briefly elucidated at the end of each letter. But no effort is made to annotate all members of the dramatis personae as many of them make mere fleeting appearances and little significance attaches to them, like the worthy Writzler who induced the Viceroy to enjoy mangoes, the Stouvells who raised a rumpus over the allocation of deck-chairs, and the Ruritanian Goanese officials who transformed a Viceregal visit into farce. To track them down would be to clutter the text with irrelevant details about many persons leading essentially grey lives.

Needless to say, the literature of India is immense, and I have plundered many a volume freely, but I owe a particular indebtedness to the following: Charles Allen (ed.), *Plain Tales from the Raj* (1975) and *Raj* (1978); E. J. Buck, *Simla Past and Present* (1925); Lord Curzon, *British Government in India* (1925); David Dilks, *Curzon in India* (1969–70); Michael Edwardes, *British India* (1967); Jan Morris, *Heaven's Command* (1973), *Pax Britannica* (1968) and *Farewell the Trumpets* (1978); Lord Ronaldshay, *The Life of Lord Curzon* (1928); Philip Woodruff, *The Men who Ruled India* (1953).

It is always a pleasure to acknowledge the assistance of others and in this case I am particularly grateful to Lady Alexandra Metcalfe, the last surviving daughter of Lord and Lady Curzon, who generously put her mother's manuscripts at my disposal; and to that I add my appreciation for her hospitality and for her patience in answering my questions. To Nigel Nicolson, whose excellent biography of Mary Curzon (1977) lighted many a dusky way, I am grateful for constructive criticism invariably tempered by genial interest and sympathetic understanding. To the following I am greatly obliged as well: Dr Richard Bingle of the India Office Library, Professor David Dilks, Graham Duff Esq., Lt.-Col. Peter Kidner, Glen Metzdorf Esq., Mrs. Audry Train and Dr M. H. Tweedy. And I owe a debt of gratitude to my editor, Linden Lawson, for her good-natured and informed assistance.

Introduction

With a newly aroused interest in Eastern life and thought, a growing awareness of a contracting globe and an increasing sensitivity toward racial problems, it is not surprising that the Indian continent is frequently before
Western eyes. Consequently, there have recently been many studies concerned with the countless aspects of India and its civilization; and to offer yet
another contribution perhaps requires explanation.

The primary justification is that the writer of the following journals,
letters and diaries – Lady Curzon, *née* Mary Leiter – possessed a refreshingly
original perspective upon India, where she lived as Vicereine during her
husband's stewardship from 1899–1905. As she moved in the train of Lord
Curzon she recorded for her family in America much of what she saw and
experienced, for she herself, the only American Vicereine of India, was born
in Chicago and brought up in Washington. It is likely, too, that no Vicereine
ever wrote as much about India as Lady Curzon; and from her extensive
manuscripts, mostly unpublished, can be extracted an impressive compendium of information and reflection on the Indian continent from an unique
point of view.

The forces that shaped Mary Leiter as she grew from child to adult derived
from years of stringent parental supervision followed by the brief but dazzling period when she became the brightest star in the Washington (and later
London) social firmaments. To clarify this one might briefly consider the
Leiter family and its rise to immense material wealth, an ascent accompanied
by a relative lack of vulgarity and ostentation. Perhaps the most notable
aspect of the Leiter saga is its freedom from that overweening pride and
arrogance common to so many robber barons and lesser parvenus of the
gilded age.

The American Leiters descended from a Swiss Protestant family –
Lutherans and Mennonites hover in the background – who emigrated to
the United States in the eighteenth century, finally settling in Maryland.
Levi Leiter, Mary Curzon's father, was born in 1834; he was indifferently
educated but, ambitious and independent, he was a constant reader of books

and was to be the possessor of an excellent library. By 1854, aged twenty, he was in Chicago, a city then fast becoming an immense, sprawling conduit to the west, working for a firm of purveyors of 'dry goods', which, Oscar Wilde notwithstanding, were not 'American novels'. Leiter's drive was incessant and by 1867 he was in partnership with Marshall Field to develop that extraordinary emporium that still exists and whose nearest British counterpart is Harrods. Marshall Field's, as the store was known, expanded far beyond the realms of 'dry goods' to embrace sales of furniture, clothing and all sorts of objects of superior quality. Over the years it became an extremely luxurious store, expensive in a way previously undreamed of in Chicago. Then came the great fire of 1871, but due to intelligent insuring Marshall Field's lost a mere half million dollars. Both before and after the fire, Levi Leiter had bought up a great deal of property and that, compounded with sensible investments in stocks and mining, ensured him an impressive fortune. Leiter did much to put Chicago back on its feet after the fire, both by gifts and donations and by persuading investors to put money into the city's future. In fact, this companionless man did much good, without fanfare, and he was rare among the millionaires of that era in his indifference toward the acquisition of political power.

In 1881 Leiter and Field parted company; in spite of their brilliant success in merchandising they had never got along well together. So Leiter sold out for two and a half million dollars, and later the same year – he was now only forty-six – the family moved to Washington, possibly to gratify the social aspirations of his wife.

In 1866 Levi Leiter had married Mary Theresa Carver, then aged twenty-one and the grand-daughter of a Connecticut judge. She had briefly been a school teacher and, if not particularly distinguished, was solidly middle-class. She has been variously described as pushing, arrogant, ambitious, proud, a bit of a Mrs Malaprop, and limited in intellectual capacity. An earnest Christian Scientist, described by her daughter Mary as 'of a high moral tone' and as 'peculiar but magnificent', Mrs Leiter was clearly a woman of parts. In addition to Mary Victoria there were two other daughters, Nancy and Marguerite (known as Daisy), and a son, Joseph (1868–1932). All appear in the pages that follow, for the girls visited the Viceroy and Vicereine during their years in India; and in 1904 both married Englishmen, Daisy[1] becoming in due course the Countess of Suffolk and Nancy (b. 1872) the bride of an Army officer, Colin Campbell;[2] both men had been aides to Curzon. Joseph was a rather expensive son, for his disastrous effort to corner the wheat market in 1898 cost his father ten million dollars. Yet the family seems devoted and certainly Mary Curzon writes with unbroken affection to and about them all. But so far as she had a favourite it was unquestionably her father.

A series of governesses supervised Mary Leiter's upbringing, but in

1886–7 she was allowed, under strict chaperonage, to go to New York where she studied French and German – her mastery of the former language far exceeded Lord Curzon's – and where she was initiated into the mysteries of science. She also attended a school for young ladies in Washington conducted by a Mme Cléophile Burr, and during her formative years there were several trips abroad, none of which was socially successful as the Leiters did not know anyone and Levi Leiter was too dignified to push himself and his family forward. It was not until 1890 that England and English society were opened to Mary with consequences that were to affect her whole life, for it was in that year that she met George Nathaniel Curzon. But her true education was really received at home under the moral and ethical codes of her parents. From the beginning of her life she was imbued with the 'old-fashioned' virtues, and these shone through her thoughts and actions. Only very rarely, and then in an understandably human way, did she fail those principles: an exceptional instance was her loathing of Kitchener, who played an important role in her husband's downfall.

The young Mary Leiter had a singularly American quality: to attempt definition is perhaps to court difficulty, although some of the elements implicit in it are clear enough. Elegance, dignity, charm, grace, freshness, poise, style – all these words come to mind as inherent in her form of Americanism and, undoubtedly, Mary Leiter possessed them all and carried them easily without vanity or pretension. But, above all, it was her independence of mind, the strength of her femininity, that set her apart as a special type of young American woman and it was this independence, fortified by an education superior to her European counterpart, that conferred upon her such distinction. In Mary Leiter this was additionally supported by a humour ranging from the sophisticated to the broadly farcical; it was always close to the surface and even when she maintained, under difficult circumstances, the dignity of her position, she broke easily into laughter when the solemn moment passed. With characteristic American irreverence she could prick the solemnity of pompous officialdom and the absurdity of exaggerated spectacle.

To the end of her life Mary Curzon was proud of her American heritage and background, and her letters often express her wish to return to Washington to be with her family and to absorb once more the American ambience. Yet her patriotism, if that is the right word, was not of the sentimental, flag-waving type; it was, as with many Americans, impressive, proud, and deeply felt. In such respects Mary Leiter is akin to Henry James's Isabel Archer of *The Portrait of a Lady*. For although Mary Leiter, unlike James's heroine, made a happy marriage, she was confronted with many of the latter's problems: adapting to a baffling new social milieu, sustaining a position within that order, keeping the envious at bay, parrying mindless condescension toward American life and, in particular, maintaining codes of conduct and principles of enduring worth and value. At very different but very high cost in each case the fictional Isabel Archer and the actual Mary Leiter accomplished this.

Yet Mary Leiter was not flawless, of course. True, the memoirs in which she fleetingly appears invariably present her as a paragon of beauty and intellect and to such estimates truth attaches. But through her writing runs a thread of innocuous vanity – chiefly over dress and jewellery – although it must be remembered that rarefied circles, British and Indian, attached great importance to colourful dress and rich adornment. Then, too, the question of snobbery arises: from her adolescence she delighted in the aristocratic and privileged societies with whom she mixed; but her pleasure seems artless, at times credulous, and rarely displeasing. More seriously, she did, it is true, tend to share the distressing anti-semitic prejudices of her 'set', although they were not of the virulent kind. In the balance, Mary Curzon emerges in a favourable light.

Various historians and biographers hint at her growing unpopularity in India, in particular Sir Walter Lawrence,* Curzon's able Private Secretary, who maintained that her success was limited and that with time she forfeited the admiration and respect originally granted her. Yet all this is couched in language so tentative that one questions not so much its veracity as the accuracy of observation it is based upon. Unfortunately, there were episodes that led to criticism of Lady Curzon, criticism of what some considered her poor judgement. Certainly, the inelegant occasion when her two younger sisters prostrated themselves publicly before the Viceroy in mock homage reflected badly upon their older sister. They were disciplined for this, but with so many British in India looking for faults in an American Vicereine it is hard to know how severely to take her to task for not bringing her sisters to a greater awareness of appropriate behaviour. Furthermore, with the constant euphoria of the press concerning her beauty, her carriage, her demeanour, her charm, and her general appearance – and taking into account the furtiveness of gossip in Anglo-Indian circles – it is impossible to unearth the 'growing unpopularity' of which Lawrence writes.

More than once Lady Curzon has been accused of such uninhibited admiration for her husband as to suggest weakness in her own character. Ironically, it was her countrywoman, the fastidious Consuelo Vanderbilt,* Duchess of Marlborough, who expressed surprise that Mary Curzon could so markedly subordinate herself and her personality to her husband. The Duchess further held that Mary Curzon subjected her own national characteristics to near oblivion. In view of the Vicereine's persistent adherence to her American heritage one may at least question Consuelo Vanderbilt's assessment.

* See Appendix for further information on names marked with asterisks.

When George Curzon met Mary Leiter in the summer of 1890 he was thirty-one, a rising patrician politician, a former student of Eton and Balliol, the brightest member of that witty, informed but none-too-serious group the 'Souls', and Conservative MP for Southport. He was as well by this time much travelled, and the acclaimed author of *Russia in Central Asia*. He had already become administratively addicted, obsessively diligent, and abnormally devoted to minutiae. His English, but not his French, was impeccable and although far from rich he was sought after by the opposite sex.

The engagement between Curzon and Mary Leiter was hardly a conventional one: they were unusually slow, even by the standards of their time, to reach an understanding. Between July 1890 and March 1893 (when they became secretly engaged) they rarely met or exchanged letters. More curious, too, is that in August 1892 Curzon was briefly in Washington whilst staying with friends in Virginia, but he failed to see his future betrothed. Again, in Egypt in February 1893 they were practically within hailing distance of each other but did not meet. However, in Paris the next month their engagement was agreed upon with the proviso, by Curzon, that it should remain secret for two years until he returned from a hazardous journey to the Pamirs and Afghanistan, a dangerous mission which prompted from Mary the following letter:

4 July 1894

VILLA MEDICI
LA BOURBOULE
AUVERGNE

Darling George:

Those three little words in your Paris letter – 'If I die' made me miserable enough for they acknowledge the possibility even the probability of such a calamity, so in case all these forebodings of trouble happen I thought I should like to tell you what I shall do if I do not follow the wise example of my Aunt who died within a short time of her love. This is a gloomy beginning to a letter but I shall never refer to it again & we are not likely to talk about anything painful if we have a day together in Paris. You know I shall not marry if you do not come back, do not smile incredulously for I am not likely to change my mind. You know I have not in four years (wh. are probably the most impressionable of a girl's life) in spite of immense pressure to do so. The worldly marriages have not the slightest attraction for me and I shall not be fond enough to yield to a personal inclination, so what I want to do is to be of as much help as I can to an organization of educated women who do a work very much like the one Mr Talbot is doing in the East End of London. They are religious, for that is what holds them together, but not in the sense of prayers & calls but in teaching & extending their wonderfully good work over an immense field, it is a kind of sisterhood [of] those who have irrevocably renounced the outer world & those who are associates. I have thought a good deal about it; after you decided to go, and after Springie[3] startled me one day by telling the dangers of the journey were almost insurmountable. I should renounce my large share in my Father's estate and only ask him for a sixth or what I needed in the work, and – this is what is difficult for me to write for I fear you may not understand it – I should love to do for your Kedleston what you and I planned to do together & release it from its debt – which is not likely to be done, is it George, by your brothers – it could be done so that no one but your Father or brother would ever know. Don't write and answer this – for I know you would never agree with me – you may even be vexed with me now, but it is a thing, in fact the only thing, I should love doing in case you did not come back for I should feel how great a satisfaction it would have been to you in a way had we done it together. I care very little for all my Father can give me save for what it can be to us – I shall never say a word of all this to you again – unless & when I write next time – there won't be a trace of sadness – but I am serious George *very* serious and my mind has an inherent faculty of not changing – save for you! for I have no will which would not yield to you.

Tear this up as soon as you have read it for I hate the thought of troubling you even for a minute & it is only a kind of cloud letter, for I shall keep a brave heart and believe & hope with all my heart & soul that you will come back safe to my arms.

Your loving
Mary

Their engagement was made public in March 1895 and six weeks later, on 22 April, they were married in the austerely harmonious Latrobe Church of St John's on Lafayette Square in Washington, some two hundred yards from the White House. Less than a week later they sailed for England and Mary Curzon, who remained steadfastly American to the end of her life, was not to see her native country again.

The events of the few years preceding Curzon's appointment as Viceroy in 1898 need not be rehearsed here; but evidence suggests that his wife was not happy during that time and that in several respects she welcomed the Indian appointment as a release from the stultifications of English upper-class life. It was one thing to be a rich, popular débutante and quite another to be a young foreigner in an alien society whose formalism one knew but slightly. Again, it was one thing to be a charming young American visiting the older civilization and quite another to be received at Kedleston as wife of the eldest son: on that first occasion Mary had also to face Curzon's eight brothers and sisters and to receive a scroll of welcome from the local tenantry. She was further required to run a town house, thoughtfully underwritten by Levi Leiter, and to deal with aggravating domestic problems. Curzon, of course, was too busy to take care of his wife, and her relations with Lord Scarsdale, her father-in-law, were not of the happiest as he was grotesquely ignorant of America and American life; and he also had the disagreeable habit of ceaselessly examining his tongue in the mirror.

Thus, aware of resentment toward her as an outsider who had carried off a fine matrimonial prize, homesick for her family and the familiar satisfactions of American life, and enmeshed in a political scene initially baffling to her, Mary Curzon's early married years in England were disconsolate and distressing. Her letters clearly demonstrate her feelings of isolation and neglect, feelings that bound ever tighter her family bonds. Some alleviation came through the birth of her two daughters, Irene (b. 1896)[4] and Cynthia ('Cimmie', b. 1898)[5] upon whom she doted. But it was with Curzon's appointment as Viceroy, terminating her English sojourn, that hopes and possibilities were generated for a new, happier life.

1 Marguerite Hyde Leiter, 'Daisy' (1879–1968), in 1904 married Henry Molyneux Paget Howard, 19th Earl of Suffolk and Berkshire (1877–1917). For some time one of Curzon's aides, the Earl was killed in action in the First World War.
2 Colin Powys Campbell (1859–1923) had been badly wounded at the siege of Chitral in 1895. He subsequently served with distinction as an ADC in the First World War overseeing Indian troops in France. He and his wife settled in California in 1919.
3 Cecil Spring-Rice (1859–1918), educated Eton and Oxford, Ambassador to the United States 1912–18.
4 She inherited the secondary title Baroness Ravensdale and died unmarried in 1966. Authoress of an autobiography, *In Many Rhythms*, the Baroness encouraged various worthy causes.
5 In 1920 she married Oswald Mosley and was MP for Stoke-on-Trent 1929–31. But her life was as sadly brief as her mother's, for she died in 1933.

PART I

Lady Curzon's letters from India, 1898–1900

The Anglo-Indian world waiting to receive the Curzons in 1898 was bound by resolute protocol and formality : precedence, rank, place, status and degree ruled the lives of the British in India with a stringency at times bordering on the absurd. From the moment Lord and Lady Curzon stepped aboard the liner bound for Bombay they were aware of the social strait-jacket into which they were thrust. In Charles Allen's lively and informative Plain Tales from the Raj *we observe the social differentiation of shipboard life : 'The military were separate, the* ICS *[Indian Civil Service] and government people were definitely on their own, and the planters, and then there were the others with children going out to join their husbands. The purser arranged the tables very carefully for all the different groups.' But social distinctions cut considerably deeper than through vocational categories. Repeatedly, memoirs and diaries reveal the decisive social separations effected between individuals and groups by accent, education, background, regiment, class, gesture and conduct. Many were the ways by which a man – and his wife – might be judged, filed and docketed as acceptable or unacceptable. At the top of the heap[1] stood, confidently, the members of the Indian Civil Service, at the bottom the box-wallahs, a disdainful term for businessmen and others unfortunate enough to be 'in trade'. Lest anyone lose his place in this bizarre social jungle a 'Warrant of Precedence', governmentally published and periodically revised, elucidated the right arrangement of guests at various functions so that one need never be flummoxed about putting an agricultural chemist above or below a sanitary commissioner at a formal luncheon or dinner. The refinements of this hierarchical order, the groupings and classifications, proliferate to the point of Gilbertian incredibility, and it is not surprising that, as she came to know British India better, Mary Curzon saw much to deflate.*

Certainly the ICS, *known irreverently as 'the pedestal mob', was an intimidating bastion of protocol. This select group, in Curzon's time some thirteen hundred, administered a country of three hundred million people and not, in spite of growing nationalism, without some success. The* ICS *was the bulwark of central and provincial government, for the chief positions in the web of Indian administration were filled by its members – all of whom, as Jan Morris aptly remarks, 'first went through the mill of the districts', where they might serve as commissioners, collectors, magistrates or any combination of those offices. It is generally agreed that the* ICS *was incorruptible ; but the Service has been scorned for narrowness, mocked for social snobbery, ridiculed for pompousness and in general considered fair game for the satirical pen. Yet there is another side to this Service ; for tales are told, especially about those removed from urban centres of governmental power, of humane and compassionate relationships forged between British civil servants and Indians. Many broke through the suffocating protocol and learned to overcome insular prejudices to reveal qualities of self-sacrifice, loyalty and trust that the wider experience, the common touch, developed within them. One learns of a commissioner purchasing rice at his own expense and doling it out as the starving needed it. Then, too, there was a delightful eccentric named Tawney who, called summarily to task for want of promptness, appeared at the next summons naked and 'borne shoulder-high in a tin bath-tub by four orderlies'. In the main, the ICS was a passable enough Service; and, aside from those who were unhealthily prejudiced, the majority appear to have been well-intentioned individuals who soldiered on in exile eventually to retire 'home', where they would be as alien, perhaps more so, than in India. It is regrettable, if understandable, that Lord Curzon could not, as his letters to his wife show, accommodate himself more easily to the ICS, and for that matter to the battery of ADCs who flanked him wherever he went as well.*

Mary Curzon received a Queen's welcome from the moment she stepped ashore at Bombay; but such a reception was rarely given to the lesser memsahibs (ladies) who went out as wives of junior officials in the Indian governmental system. Coming from convention-ridden, middle-class Britain, they were as socially constrained and hierarchically bound as the Indians and Anglo-Indians among whom they were to live. Whilst some may have been of the 'fishing fleet' – young women visiting India for several months hoping to acquire a husband (those unsuccessful and compelled to go home were unkindly known as 'returned empties') – most were fresh from England and faced daunting tasks of adjustment and re-orientation. For a start, the young memsahib was plunged into a climate so demanding that the physical shock was quite as severe as the psychological shock of the sudden extension of her social range, as she was thrust among people – black, white or of mixed colour – whose religions, customs, manners, thought processes and habits made excessive demands upon whatever slender sense of adaptability she might possess.

For the young wife the Indian adventure might begin with a long, arduous trip to a remote up-country station devoid of Europeans. As for living quarters, the bungalow would be poorly built, governmentally furnished, and the garden nondescript and discouragingly dust-ridden. True, there would be countless servants, each as conscious of his restricted obligations as the most fanatical trade-unionist, and of course a cook enjoying a small cut from the weekly household expenses. To add to the general discomfort and irritation there was the knowledge that a move might be required within a year or so and, come six or seven years of age, any children would have to be packed off to England. Furthermore, the physical business of living would be exacerbated by ants, civets, snakes, flies, kites (who would swoop down on the food) and other obnoxious animal life. Small wonder that advertisements for alleviation of physical discomfort were developed in the hope of making a cheerless life slightly less so. Thus were produced 'ladies air-tight patent-hat-boxes' (to stave off mildew), rust-proof corsets, spinal pads, and various cooling powders, with 'Rowland's Kalydor' as a last resort against freckles and sunburn. Not all prospects and living conditions were as bleak as this, of course, and there was always hope of advancement; but initial impressions of Indian Service life for the most privileged, let alone the under-dog, were hardly encouraging. It has been said, however, that the role of the memsahib gradually altered, and over the years she evolved from the perplexed mid-Victorian housewife into a rather more feline, snobbish creature so reviled in the work of Kipling and others. Many are the reasons for this, but paramount among them was the growing number of women coming to India, a number coincident with the shifting – often narrowing – imperial sense of mission. Even so, within the role Mary Curzon played in India she constantly demonstrated sympathy and understanding for the women, of all rank and colour, around her.

Grimly underlying all life in India were disease, illnesses hitherto unknown and sudden death. For many Indians (some millions are estimated to have died in the famine of 1899–1900) plague and famine were omnipresent, as Bishop Welldon* recorded:

India is never free from such maladies as fever, smallpox and cholera; perhaps it is never wholly free from plague and famine; but it is only at intervals that the gaunt spectres of plague and famine brood with deadly effect over whole provinces. Bubonic plague, as it is called, is not, indeed, afflicting to see; nor does a European in India, unless he is a doctor or a nurse, need to see much of it or to be at all afraid of catching it; but when it is virulent among the natives, it simply mows down whole families in a few hours.

But even if the European did not fall to the plague other inexorable illnesses, as Welldon notes, were at hand to carry people off with relentless rapidity. Frequently, too, ineptitude brought about death; and in the clash of cultures, misunderstanding, inadequate communications and mistaken instruction were all rife. The death of Lady Curzon's godchild in the autumn of 1900 illustrates the singular poignancy of death in India. The Vicereine wrote to her mother:

Tell the girls that Mrs Buck's baby of three months – my godchild – died suddenly on Sunday through neglect of the nurse & I went down to poor Mrs Buck & actually buried the baby. There was no one but another woman & me to put the dead baby in its coffin & Capt. Baker-Carr carried it downstairs. . . . We went to the cemetery – the coffin in a rickshaw – & the Father & Mother and I & Mr Kuber a friend behind & it was the saddest baldest most miserable funeral.

Again, as Welldon remarked, 'A European in India literally knows not in the morning what fate may be his before the evening.' Furthermore, burial, a rite made the more stark and forbidding by its immediacy, had to take place without delay to avoid rapid decomposition and spreading of infection. Even granting the elementary precautions of the time, the threat of death rarely receded until well into the present century; and to this the graves of so many young in the European cemeteries of India attest.

Lady Curzon's letters and diaries abound with allusions to physical disorders, which were endemic in others as well as herself. Sore throats, headaches, diarrhoea, pains, colds and complaints of simply 'feeling rotten' recur through her writings and are a register of the hardships of the European community. Thus it becomes clear that physical debility, climatic irregularities, unsettling food, dubious hygiene and uncomfortable living conditions took their toll among Anglo-Indians. Also, these 'minor' indispositions weakened and vitiated the systems of the sufferers, sapping their vitality and rendering them subject to more severe illnesses. This was certainly the case with Lady Curzon, whose early death sadly illustrates these facts.

Of Mary Curzon's India only a little remains. The statues of the Raj are gone, destroyed or huddled away in forgotten corners of cities or townships, the imposing buildings of the time house Indian government institutions, and those socially divisive clubs that remain are conducted along different lines. Simla is no longer a summer capital, the ICS a mere memory, and the memsahib more a citizen of the television screen than of the provinces of India. Similarly, the Curzons are long dead – although, when remembered, it is always with respect. Historians occasionally recall Lord Curzon as a man who missed greatness, although it would be a mean spirit who considered him unworthy of it. And Lady Curzon may be remembered by social historians as one of the most charming and gifted of a glittering circle. But her writings fortunately have not perished and through them something of the lost world of British India continues to speak.

The initial letters Mary Curzon wrote, commencing with the invitation to Windsor Castle in late November 1898 on the eve of the Curzons' departure for India, are so charged with youth and energy and optimism, so characterized by high hopes, that they render the final departure from India in 1905 high tragedy. The sequence opens with the awesome grimness of the Windsor visit and the low-voiced regal dinner followed by the inevitable royal summons, recorded in touchingly human terms, as the old Queen unbends to treat the future Vicereine as a daughter. Apparent, too, is Lady Curzon's growing awareness of their position, which is later underscored by their reception in full panoply at Bombay – an arrival dwarfed, however, by their appearance in Calcutta and their greeting by the Elgins,[2] by their early drawing-rooms and by Curzon's first durbars and receptions of maharajas in glittering formal dress. Thus the early letters pulsate with the grandeur and eminence of the Curzons' standing and their supreme, indeed royal, distinction.

Yet there are also touches of humour, reflections on the happiness of family life, and brief scenes of pleasing times at nearby Barrackpore[3] and Tollygunge; although protocol dictated that, when on duty, neither the Viceroy nor the Vicereine could relax even momentarily, Lady Curzon often broke through the stultifications of diplomacy. However, the endless entertaining – dinners for a hundred or more and receptions for many times that number – the incessant pressure of Indian problems, the constant effort to absorb some knowledge of the vast continent, and a relentless tide of house-guests all placed strain on the couple, who in the beginning rose to such varied demands easily and elegantly. Yet within their first weeks India made itself ominously felt as Lady Curzon ran a burning fever, suffered severe headaches and internal disorders that, though made light of, proved wretchedly debilitating. In sum, though, her first impressions – curious, eager, perceptive – carry the reader along as she adapts with grace and spirit to her new life.

1 The Viceroy and the Vicereine, like royalty, were supposedly beyond a social category, but they were ever the victims of covert gossip. As becomes evident, the Curzons were periodically attacked by the press, but then, as now, it was not always easy to discriminate between balanced criticism and journalistic irresponsibility.

2 Lord Elgin (1849–1917), son of an earlier Viceroy, was a relatively unobtrusive occupant of that office from 1894 to 1899.

3 Until the decision to remove the capital from Calcutta to Delhi (announced by King George V at the Delhi Durbar in 1911), Barrackpore was a 'happy rural seat' for the Viceregal entourage, a place where the restraints of office were loosened. Some sixteen miles up the Hughli (one of the mouths of the Ganges) from Calcutta, Barrackpore was a pleasing complex of parks, bungalows and classically inspired government buildings and residences. It boasted a menagerie, which in time deteriorated to 'two miserable bears', a condition many Anglo-Indians decried as 'the end of Empire'. Curzon's chapter on Barrackpore in *British Government in India* is one of the most readable in a most readable book.

[*November 1898*]   WINDSOR CASTLE

Darling Mamma & Papa:

We came here yesterday evening at 7 and were met at the station by a barouche and postilion & men sitting up at the back. We got to the castle & were met by Lord Edward Clinton, and conducted to rooms in Edward 3ds tower. Lady Lytton came in to see us, and while she was there the Queen sent for George & talked to him for half an hour. We then dressed for dinner at 9. When we were all assembled in the great corridor which is like a room, the Queen walked in assisted by her Indian attendant[1] and I had to walk forwards, kiss her hand while curtsying to the ground, and nearly remaining on the ground. She then put out her cheek for me to kiss which I managed to do although I had not expected this honour. She then went on and I had then to sweep curtseys to the Empress Frederic,[2] Princess Henry of Battenberg[3] and two other Christians.[4] By this time I was nearly dead and *quite* frightened and glad to walk into dinner. The silence of royal dinners is awful & no one speaks above a whisper & everyone tucks into their food. George sat between Princess Christian & her daughter & I sat between Lord Churchill who is Lord in Waiting and Sir Fleetwood Edwards – we had a heavy and excellent dinner & then returned to the great corridor & stood about until the Queen sent for us. She first sent for me, & asked me about my eye & my troubles with wetnurses – also spoke about the Indian native women, and about Khartoum & the Sirdar [Kitchener*]. She was very animated, and said 'When you have another child you must call it after me' & after a few more remarks she bowed her head & I backed away, and then she sent for George & I then talked to the Empress Frederic & Beatrice & Princess Christian until we went to bed. I stood until I was nearly dead. The Queen talked to the two other guests who were an admiral and a general and then went to bed & I again curtsyed & kissed her hand. We have been here all day. This morning [we] went to Frogmore & Eton, & this afternoon over the Castle and tonight we dine with the Queen again & we leave tomorrow. In the meantime my new wetnurse arrived from France this morning in my absence & everything at Carlton Gardens⁵ is in a state of fuss and excitement while I am here, but I can't help it, I shall get home tomorrow.

My eye is nearly well but it will be three weeks before the inflammation has quite gone. 6 o'c Later. We have just been summoned by the Queen. I will write later & let you know what happened. Later.

The Queen received me in a room all hung with miniatures & made me sit by her, and talked about babies, Indian life & every sort of thing – kissed me again when I left and told me to write her from Marseilles how we all were. Also to write to her from India. Then George had his audience and she gave him my Indian order which I can only wear after he is Viceroy. The order is very pretty indeed of diamonds turquoises & pearls .... George only gets his when we get out there. Nothing could exceed the Queen's wonderful kindness to me, and I was quite overcome. She is such a wonderful woman animated & keen & talks away – she produced a large pair of glasses & said 'I must put on my glasses to have a good look at you'. I felt shy. When George came in for his audience she said I must congratulate you for your wife is both beautiful & wise! Wasn't that nice. I write you all this *quite* privately and please don't send the letter to *any* but our own family. We begin to be treated like grandees. Station masters always meet us, carriages reserved, low bows & crowds staring & from nobodies we have jumped into grandeur. Later. Our last dinner was very nice. Lord Salisbury* & the French Ambassador were there. The Queen said goodbye to us after dinner & kissed me again & wished us good luck. So our great visit is over.

> Goodbye my darlings
> Your loving Mary

1 Known as the Munshi (teacher/secretary), his real name was Abdul Karim (1863–1909); he was a humbly born man and successor in the Queen's favour to the whisky-tippling John Brown. The Munshi was a 'pusher' and a generator of

political and social trouble at Court. As decisively as the Queen advanced this man, as fervently did her Court and ministers oppose him; and the ensuing combat was not untouched by humour. But the royal idiosyncrasy is nevertheless suggestive of the monarch's anti-racist attitudes.

2 Victoria (Vicky), 1840–1901, eldest child of Queen Victoria and the Prince Consort married Frederick Wilhelm of Prussia, later Emperor Frederick. She was the mother of Kaiser Wilhelm II.

3 Beatrice (1857–1944), youngest of the royal children and married to Henry, Prince of Battenberg (1858–96).

4 Yet another daughter of the royal couple, Helena (1846–1923). She became the wife of Christian, Prince of Schleswig-Holstein. She and her family were known as 'the Christians'.

5 Balfour's house, where the Curzons lived until they took a lease on 1 Carlton House Terrace.

26 December [1898]   SS *Arabia*

Darling Papa:

I wrote last from Marseilles where George, Mr Lawrence, Colonel Sandbach[1] Military Secretary, Lord Suffolk & Mr Meade[2] ADCs joined us and we sailed away in the teeth of a blow, ship pitching and nurses catting! The bad weather lasted for three days, and I was very hard-worked looking after everybody....

At Port Said where we took on coal we went ashore – all of us, and stayed during the coaling hours at the house of the P&O agent. ... After taking on a thousand tons of coal we proceeded through the Canal and stopped at Ismailia where we put off two hundred passengers – amongst them some people called Stouvell whom we made out by the names on their chair, but who became angry with us because the deck steward without our knowledge moved their chairs which were in front of ours, and the Stouvells became incensed – (we being quite innocent –) & they left a letter of introduction with the purser (which Mr Fry had given to George) & told him to give it to us after they had left the ship! It is the rudest thing I ever heard of! Do you know them, I hear they come from Chicago – well – our next stop was at Suez, and it grew hourly warmer and we began shedding our clothes and by the time we got to the Red Sea we were all in muslins & sun hats. My eye began to trouble me again & I had to lie in my hot cabin with bandages on it – fortunately it is better now but I am in black glasses. On Xmas eve we had a Xmas tree for the passengers and presents for all the children. I had brought the tree & all the trimmings & toys from London. The ADCs and I trimmed the tree in sweltering heat but we were paid for our trouble because the children were all wild with joy. I invited both 1st & 2nd class passengers & each child drew two numbers & got two presents which Irene and I handed to them. There were several infants like Cynthia & they all got rubber animals – & the boys had horns & tin soldiers & girls tea sets, dolls etc. You can't think how much pleasure that gave everyone and votes of thanks were passed & the Queen's and my health drunk amidst cheers.

Christmas day – Sunday – we landed at Aden – the beginning of our kingdom. As it was Sunday the official reception could not take place so we only went ashore in a state boat, white, rowed by eight blacks in red liveries, all our staff in uniforms, and lunched quietly with the resident general at Aden. We stayed on shore two hours, came back to the ship and sailed on our way again. George did not wear uniform – gray clothes & a gray top hat – I a white muslin white hat and blue spectacles! which I shall *not* wear at Bombay as I am saving my eyes for our arrival there.

It is very warm – about 80 on deck, punkahs [fans] are going over our heads, at meals I feel it a good deal in spite of thinnest clothes, and Irene is covered with prickly heat but is otherwise pretty well. Cynthia is enormous, & rolling in fat – she gurgles & laughs all day – fairly shakes with laughing at everybody and *never* cries – her fat peasant nou-nou with her huge frame & massive body marches about knitting with ribbons flying from her cap in the wind. She can neither read nor write nor does she know where she lives, but I have her address & have written twice to her husband for her beginning 'Mon cher époux'. She has a sweet face and looks like a Madonna and we all love her, and the ADCs & Mr Lawrence and Col. Sandbach practice their French on her. On Friday we land at Bombay, we go to the Governor's House & stay Friday night for a great banquet & reception and on Sat. we proceed in our train to Calcutta. I will send you papers of all the doings – George & I drive in a state carriage with four horses, postilions outriders & escort, and behind two Syces [attendants] running holding parasols over our heads – our drive is through wild masses of people for *five miles*, behind our carriage come all the staff & the officials sent by Gov. of Bombay & Viceroy to meet us, the procession is about five carriages – babies in one with a hood to keep off the Sun, all this time salutes of thirty-one guns will be firing & all the warships in the harbour cannonading – so it will be thrilling. I only wish some of my darlings were with me to see our triumphant entry. All England is interested in George's Viceroyalty and immense labour has been going on to double the telegraphic communications for the press. Harmsworth of the *Daily Mail* has two correspondents in this ship – one has come out to describe our arrival & the other remains five years as political correspondent. So we have the search light of publicity full on us!

I hope & pray for success in all the great work.

Mary

1 Arthur Edmund Sandbach (1859–1928). Educated at Eton and RMC Woolwich, he was Military Secretary to Curzon 1898–9 and in due course rose to the rank of Major-General.

2 Lieutenant the Hon. Arthur Vesey Meade (1873–1952), an Extra ADC to the Viceroy, who was to suffer severely in the South African wars. He later became the 5th Earl of Clanwilliam.

4 January 1899   GOVERNMENT HOUSE
                                                                                    CALCUTTA

My darlings :

I did not have time to write by the last post, as it left the day we got to Bombay, and I had only time to send a newspaper off as we were so rushed & hard worked. We landed at Bombay from the ship at 7 a.m. the Admiral at B., Lord Elgin's ADC, Capt. Baker-Carr[1] – and the Governor of Bombay's Military Sec. We went ashore in a big launch, and the landing stage was crowded with people and covered with red carpet ; in the newspaper description you will see the names of the various officials who were there. We spoke to them all, and received an address of welcome to which George replied in an admirable speech wh. you saw in the paper. At the end of the landing the state carriage was drawn up, and George & I got in to 'God save the Queen', and drove through seven and a half miles of packed streets – all the way lined with soldiers and police and bands at intervals playing 'God save the Queen' – we bowing & smiling hard.as ever we could ! Crowds cheered & cheered ; in the procession were guard of honour behind military escort then our carriage then more soldiers & two other four horse carriages with the suite. The babies, in [the] charge of the doctor, had gone straight to the Gov. of Bombay's house by a short cut and had none of the fatigue of the procession – our carriage was drawn by four immense horses with two postilions preceded by two grooms – & sitting up behind were two syces holding immense umbrellas over our heads though the day was cool & quite comfortable. We got to Malabar Point, the Governor's house, by 9 o'clock, & Lord and Lady Sandhurst met us on the steps, & George then reviewed the guard of honour, & I watched from a balcony. We then went to our rooms & balcony overlooking the sea & had breakfast by ourselves. The rest of the day spent quietly giving audiences and at 5 a state drive, George in front with the Governor in a four horse carriage & an ADC in waiting, escort of soldiers – & I in the next state carriage with Mrs Skeffington Smith who is visiting the Sandhursts & an ADC. We drove through Bombay again, & back at 7. At 8 the Sandhursts had a huge dinner of 112 people. We were fetched at 8.15 by an ADC and brought to the drawing room and Presented to all the guests. I went to dinner across a lovely garden all lit with lamps with Lord S. & George with Lady S. I wore white & my pearls & new tiara made out of the dog collar & looked as well as I could. After dinner we held a reception & 1400 people – English – Parsee – Mahommedan & Hindu filed past us as we stood on a gold carpet with immense golden chairs behind us – who should appear in the crowd but

Larz Anderson & his wife, also an American Consul & wife, friends of Mrs Bissell and Mrs Cleveland; at 11.30 it was all over. The next day we did nothing and at 5.30 went in state to the station – escort – state carriages – etc. and the crowds were enormous. The station is the finest one I ever saw in my life – troops here drawn up and red carpets everywhere and we marched to the special train to 'God save the Queen' & troops presenting arms & lowering colours to George. The special train is white and as long as the New York Limited, we each have a magnificent carriage just like an American private car. The babies & I filled mine with the nurses, and we had a fine cool journey & everyone flourished & was well.

The train & the line were guarded and at all the chief stations there were guards of honour & the head men, & if there was a native swell he appeared under a state umbrella with clashing cymbals, but this sight usually came off at 6 in the morning & was lost on us. The general traffic manager was on the train to look after the Royal family! At Calcutta we were met by the Lt.-Gov. of Bengal & Lord Elgin's staff and drove away in the royal carriage with body guard escort, I never saw such crowds as there were in the streets; if you think of the crowd at the Capitol on inauguration day & *double* and *treble* it you can think what it was all the way to Gov. House; we bowed & bowed & all cheered and it was a *marvellous* sight. At Gov. House all the swells in India were lined up the Grand Staircase & we marched up the broad red carpet; at the top was the Viceroy – he introduced George to officials & Col. Durand and Lord Elgin's Mil. Sec. introduced me – there were the four [*sic*] great Maharajahs Patiala, Scindia – Kashmir in *magnificent* jewels. No 1 had a breast plate of *enormous* diamonds & necklace after necklace. No 2 had emeralds to make your eyes water & No 3 had twelve rows of pearls as fine as Consuelo's *biggest*! My fine feathers paled before this magnificence. After introductions we went in the house & Lady Elgin received us in the throne room, & we went into a large drawing room where the wives of officials were introduced to me – then tea & then to our rooms. My bed room is so big you can just see from one end to the other! At 8 we dined en famille with the Elgins and to bed at 11.... Our military doctor Col. Fenn[2] seems nice & sees to all their [the babies'] food & their going out & coming in & relieves me of worry and care. I am thin again and well – my eye still troubles me.

I nearly freeze in my thin clothes & have to wear flannel jackets underneath. I keep the babies warm – it was only warm at Bombay. I will write more by next post. I am sending two newspapers.

Yr devoted
Mary

1 An Eton and Sandhurst man, Robert George Teasdale Baker-Carr (1867–1931) never rose above the rank of Major and retired from the Army in 1906.

2 Ernest Harold Fenn (1850–1916), an Army doctor on the Viceregal staff from 1898 to 1903.

My precious Mother & Nancy & Daisy:

George & I received all your letters to us yesterday, and he has asked me to write to you for you & the girls to read. I begin with his being made Viceroy. On Friday morning, as the two days before that, we were simply guests in the rooms you know as I described them in my last and the only function during those days was a banquet of 110 men which I didn't see as Lady Elgin came and dined in my sitting-room with me. At 9.30 on Friday all the Staff fetched George and marched two and two, he following alone, through the Marble Hall into the Throne Room at the end. There all the members of the Executive Council shook hands with him and the procession re-formed, they joining it, and proceeded back through the Hall to the Council Chamber in the north wing. There the procession divided, taking their places to right and left, and George walked up between them, turned round and faced the room, which was crowded with officials and Maharajas on either side of a passage roped off. I had come in with Lord Suffolk and taken my place at the end of the room. George stood under Warren Hastings'[1] picture while the Home Secretary read the Warrant, which took about five minutes. The Warrant proclaimed him Viceroy; that was all, there was no oath-taking and the whole proceeding was very simple. As soon as the Home Secretary had finished Lord Suffolk signalled to the Guard out the window, and the band played 'God save the Queen' and thirty-one guns went off; then the procession re-formed in the same order, Lord Suffolk and I bringing up the rear several paces behind, and we marched back to the Throne Room. While George shook hands with the Council I slipped off to the green drawing-room where we were to take leave of the Elgins, none of whom had been present in the Council Chamber. They soon came down *en masse* for goodbye – Lady Elgin, two unmarried fat girls and Lady E. B. Smith, who was very seedy, and Lord Elgin and their Staff. We had all round goodbyes and inspection of the babies, who were on the balcony, and then they departed, the members of the Council waiting for them to say goodbye in the Throne Room. George took them to their carriages, the babies, nurses and I went to the Council Chamber (now quite empty) to see them drive off, Lord Elgin still taking the right side of the carriage and taking the salute, George by his side modestly doing nothing and towering three feet above the small form of Lord Elgin. They drove to the landing stage by Prinsep's Ghat and there sailed off in an Indian Marine Ship, George on the return drive taking the salute. As soon as he came back we made a grand tour of the house and began moving and are still settling in the rooms vacated by the Elgins. The whole house is most inconvenient – that you know, as it is like Kedleston! I have a huge bed-room, half of which is curtained off to make a sitting-room, and as there is a balcony outside both are dark, and I have to do my hair with a hand mirror on a little upper balcony! Dressing in the evening with smoky candles is very difficult!

On Friday the Durands came to dine. They have been very unhappy with the Elgins and are glad to go home on leave. Saturday morning George received the Maharajas of Kashmir and Patiala. He sat on a throne made of silver with huge golden tigers for arms, and beside the throne to right and left were rows of chairs, a high silver one for the Maharaja. Behind the chairs stood red-clothed chaprasses [attendants] holding peacocks' tails, yak tails with silver handles and huge maces, quite twenty of them, and the big Hall was lined by the Guard of Honour. When the Maharaja arrived nineteen guns went off, and he marched up with his ministers and brothers, George advancing the necessary distance to the edge of the rug; he then led him by the hand to his chair, George sitting down on his throne (I was hidden behind a screen). Then began a lame conversation, George making polite remarks, then came the giving of *pan* – a kind of nut in silver paper – which was brought in a dish on a tray by a chaprasse, and George pressed a piece in the Maharaja's hand, and the Foreign Minister, Sir W. Cuningham,[2] did the same to the rest of the Maharaja's suite. Rose-water was then brought in silver flagons on a large tray and George put some in a golden spoon on the sleeve of the Maharaja, Sir W. Cuningham doing the same to the Maharaja's suite. After this they all rose to go, George again advancing to the edge of the carpet and shaking hands. The Maharaja of Kashmir was dressed in the uniform of an English general with the blue ribbon of the Star of India, but the Maharaja of Patiala, who came next and was received with only seventeen guns and only an advance half-way to the edge of the carpet, was dressed magnificently in pale blue robes and *covered* with jewels. Each Maharaja comes in the Viceroy's State carriages and escorted by the Bodyguard. There have been five of these Durbars, only varied by the number of guns and the splendour of the costumes. For the Maharaja of Benares there were only thirteen guns and George didn't advance at all to meet him. The whole of Monday George spent returning these visits to the Maharajas in their houses taken for the occasion; they received him in state, but as I wasn't there I can't describe. He returned from one visit with a huge tinsel chain round his neck – the ADCs and Secretaries also festooned in the same way. These decorations were promptly bestowed on Irene, who now prances about hung like a Christmas tree with tinsel garlands. After George's five calls on Maharajas he drove back to fetch me, and we went to a garden party given by the Lieutenant Governor of Bengal. We drove in the State barouche with outriders and escort, and at the garden party walked round with the Lieutenant Governor and his wife being introduced to everyone. It was bitterly cold, as it has been since we arrived, and everyone was shivering, but very pleased to see us. There were Natives galore who surrounded George, so that he couldn't meet nearly as many English as I did. Many of the people were charming and the party was quite beautifully managed, and we were delighted. At 6 we drove back and had an hour before dressing for dinner. At 8.15 the two ADCs-in-waiting come and fetch us and walk ahead of us to the drawing-room where the dinner guests are arranged in a kind of horse-shoe. George goes first and shakes hands with them all, and I come after him. I should say that as we come to the door one ADC says 'Their Excellencies' and all the guests bow. After shaking hands all round and getting back to the door through which we entered George takes his lady into dinner and I go in with my man. Last night Mr and Mrs W. A. Gladstone,[3] Mr and Mrs Ritchie[4] – she was a Miss Thackeray, cousin of Mrs Richmond Ritchie,[5] who was also a Miss Thackeray – Count Clary, Vicomte d'Humières, Lieutenant Liennass and Count Stenbel. These four had brought letters respectively from Sir A. Bigge,[6] Rennell Rodd,[7] the Empress Frederick and Lord C. Beresford.[8] They were all very nice. After dinner I have to walk out of the room alone, preceded by an ADC, the ladies coming behind. The men smoke, and when George comes into the drawing-room we all get up and stand till he sits down, and have to jump up every time he does. We each sit and talk to guests, ADCs bringing up relays. Today we are having a quiet day, at least I am. George is receiving deputations, and tonight 40 to 50 people dine here, all officials.

On Sunday we went to the Cathedral, which was rather an ordeal as the Viceroy's seat is an odd box with two large Gothic chairs in full view of the whole congregation, and as every single creature spent his time gazing at us it was pretty trying, and as the service consisted of long anthems and every sort of elaborate music we got tired, and I was so glad to get out that I nearly committed the awful crime of climbing into the carriage before George. It is difficult to remember always to allow him to go through a door first, and he never thinks of it, but I manage to usually. The custom is for the Viceroy and his wife to walk side by side, but when we march through big crowded rooms I think he should go first. . . .

I have finished this in pencil as it is such a long letter, and the house pens are *so* bad!

We are all well and working hard – George with official work and I very busy with the house, as the House Steward and Captain Adam,[9] who manage the household, are both ill, so all the arrangements come on Colonel Sandbach and me for dinners, entertainments, etc.

Yours very affectionately
Mary

PS. Will you send this to any of the family you wish as I can only write this one letter this week.

1 (1732–1818), first Governor-General of British India (his appointment extended from 1774 to 1785), he began his career as a 'writer' with the East India Company. He rose steadily but ran foul of home influences upon Indian matters as early as the Regulation Act of 1773 which 'established the influence of the crown, or rather parliament, upon Indian affairs'. It is said, too, that he incurred the displeasure of pompous politicians by failing to greet them in a 'ruffled shirt'. In 1788 political chicanery brought about a trial for Hastings' impeachment for 'high crimes and misdemeanours'. This dragged on until 1795 when a verdict of 'not guilty' was brought in; but like many before and since, the guiltless accused was ruined by legal costs (although some restitution was subsequently made). Always controversial, Hastings was a parliamentary scapegoat but an insatiable worker, a brilliant, honourable administrator and, in sum, one who served India and his country with immense distinction. Hastings and Curzon, both victims of lesser persons, had much in common.

2 (1848–1928), Secretary to the Foreign Department 1894–1901.

3 Possibly (allowing for a slip of the pen) William Buckley Gladstone (1856–1922) and his wife. He was educated at Eton and Trinity College, Cambridge. An elusive figure, he is vaguely alluded to in Cambridge alumni records as 'in business in Calcutta in 1899'.

4 Gerald and Margie Thackeray Ritchie – the latter was a cousin of the novelist's daughter.

5 Anne Thackeray Ritchie (1837–1919), daughter of the novelist and a writer in her own right. She was the wife of Richmond Ritchie (1854–1912), who had a distinguished career in Indian affairs in England. Secretary to the Political Department 1902–10, he was trusted and admired by Curzon, whose secretary he had once been.

6 (1849–1931), later Lord Stamfordham and Private Secretary to King George V. It was his distressing duty in 1923 to inform Lord Curzon that the King would not be sending for him to follow Bonar Law as Prime Minister. It was Stamfordham who suggested Windsor when the royal family changed its name in 1917.

7 (1858–1941), a friend of Curzon's from Oxford days, a member of that forum of intellectuals known as the 'Souls' and in time Ambassador to Sweden and to Italy.

8 (1846–1919), a former senior naval officer. Perhaps remembered, if at all, as the central figure in a notorious scandal of the 1890s involving the Prince of Wales, Lord Randolph Churchill and several others. Needless to say, it concerned 'crim. con.', a Victorian expression for adultery. Even a passing glance at the scandal suggests the appropriate name of one of Beresford's commands – the *Undaunted*.

9 Frederick Lock Adam (1867–1907), badly wounded in the South African fighting (which may account for his early death). He also served briefly as Military Secretary to Curzon's successor, Lord Minto.

My precious darling Papa:

I received a beloved letter from you which has made me so happy. I feel such a long way off from everybody as we only have one post a week, and then my letters are limited to yours and Mamma's, as the world is a busy place and only my own think constantly of me and write faithfully, friends write once in six months! I am getting used to the new life – and it is all very wonderful. George is treated *exactly* like a reigning sovereign. Every-one bows & curtseys – ADCs precede him – the only difference is that he has a great deal more power than most kings, and ruling India is no sinecure – and a Viceroy has it in his power to be a *very* great force, or he can be a cypher. Great things are expected of G. as ever since the days of Lord Dalhousie[1] there have been good but not great Viceroys and the whole of India has awakened to the belief that G. will do great things. The Hindu is very superstitious, and many things which have happened since our arrival have meant prosperity. Firstly rain fell all along our journey from Bombay & the weather is cooler than it has been for many years. Secondly in many places the crops have been splendid. Thirdly in Bombay two little cows – you know they are worshipped by the Hindu – joined our procession and ran in front of the state carriages, & this incident was very popular. Then we look so young & happy & bow & smile unceasingly when we are out & this pleases everybody. The other day a soldier in the fort had his arm blown off by a cannon firing a salute to one of the native rajahs who came to see George and we went to the Military Hospital to see him and this pleased everybody, so that now when we go out there are crowds & cheers everywhere. The Elgins were quiet shy people who never did anything so all our doings are in direct contrast to theirs, consequently popular. On Satur-day we went to the races in State. Body Guard outriders & five state carriages, we drove up the course in state like Ascot, got out and went to our Royal box from which we looked at the racing & were stared at the whole afternoon. There were five [*sic*] English guests staying with us: Mr and Mrs Verney, Lord De Brooke's eldest son, & Lady Cecilie, & Mr Goff & a Mr Green. They with all our staff made up the procession. When we left the races they cheered us & gave me a special cheer. Last Thursday we held a drawing room – at 9.30 we were escorted to 'God save the Queen' into the throne room – where all the high officials were grouped either side of the throne – the throne was covered with a perfectly *magnificent* solid gold carpet which was laid over it, the ends coming far out on the carpet of the room – on the dais [?] were two immense chairs, one of silver with gold tigers behind G. A smaller one for me. We stood in front of them and all the entrée ladies filed past making two curtseys – they then took their places to the left of the throne beside their husbands who were already there – as each lady came up her name on a card was given to the ADC who handed it to the Military Secretary & he called out her name – she then proceeded to curtsey to G. who bowed solemnly & then another curtsey to me & I bowed & smiled. We did not shake hands with anyone – just bowed – the ladies were beautifully dressed and did their bows far better than I should have done them – trains & feathers are optional, but *many* wore them. After all the entrée ladies had passed the public entrée were admitted, all the ladies looked very well dressed and it took the private & public entrée just an hour to pass; after they had all passed we marched upstairs to the Great ball room preceded by the staff and followed by the private entrée who had remained throughout the drawing room in the throne room. The rooms were crowded as all the husbands of the ladies had joined them upstairs and there ensued a kind of evening party, we sitting in big chairs which were arranged in a semi-circle & in about three-quarters of an hour ADCs bringing up a steady stream of people for G. & me to talk to. When the time came to go we marched out of the room & retired to well earned bed.

I wore a white gown – with white flowers embossed in velvet on it – it was simple but lovely but as the absurd American papers have been printing foolish accounts of imaginary bejewelled dresses covered with real stones the Calcutta paper next day commented on the extreme simplicity of my dress. The American papers do their best to make me ridiculous and I send some of the absurd cuttings – do be very careful *never* to repeat anything I write about the Queen or anybody. I am so *terrified* for fear of things coming out in the press in England which make people laugh at me.

On Saturday we had a dinner party of 20 – and a Mrs Hallowes whom George knew at Oxford sang after, G. is *always* meeting Eton & Oxford pals, and I hear constantly when we are meeting new people – 'Weren't you at so & so' or 'I remember you at Eton'. The high sheriff of Calcutta, a Mr Gladstone, he knew as Billy Gladstone at Eton, and every kind of official or man of business in Calcutta seems to have had the advantage of being at school with the Viceroy! All this is immensely popular. We have unearthed a Mr Pelham who is at the head of the telegraphs & he is a sort of connection of G's & is coming to dine on Friday. To-night we have a dinner of 60 – people to lunch both today & tomorrow who have brought letters – a Miss Cavendish Taylor & her brother, tomorrow a French Count de St Maurice & his American wife, and the day times are filled seeing people and arranging all the functions, so life is no sinecure.

I never knew a more inconvenient house than this – and the distances are perfectly awful, you know the plan so you can imagine the distance between my room in one wing, and the children's at the other end of the square.... Sunday morning we all went up the river on a launch to Barrackpore – it took us 1½ hours and we landed at a little pier and walked a long way under a bamboo arbour up to the house which is very like an English country house – and the park – which alas! is open to the public who pour into it and destroy all privacy – is lovely. Lord Canning made a rolling country out of a flat plain and planted perfectly splendid trees so that with a stretch of imagination we could imagine ourselves in an English park afflicted by drought as the grass is all brown. After lunch I took G. to drive in a tiny little pony carriage drawn by wee little ponies – the body guard had to go with us and you can't imagine anything funnier than two immense horsemen carrying lances, then a pony trap in which sat the Viceroy, entirely filling it – I perched up driving two little specks of ponies – sitting up behind were two red liveried servants, and riding behind more immense body guards – we felt that this cortège was so absurd that we drove once round the park in a cloud of dust & then slunk home by a garden path & saw Lady Canning's[2] tomb, which is beautifully placed by the river. Luncheon & tea we had under an enormous banyan tree, and as huge kites swoop down and carry off all the food on your plate native servants stand about with great sticks wh. they wave at them. Monday morning we came back to Calcutta by launch, all – especially Irene – having loved our Sunday, and rested for all our labours this week.

Darling – I finish this in pencil as I have not been well. Chill & headache, but shall be better long before you receive this.

I will write all about our State ball. The weather is *better* and I brought *no* warm clothes. The babies flourish bless their hearts.

Goodnight my beloved
Yr loving Mary

1 James Andrew Brown Ramsay, 10th Earl and 1st Marquis of Dalhousie (1812–60). He served his country ably, if autocratically, both at home and in India (1848–56) where, as Governor-General, he annexed the Punjab, suppressed disturbances, extended education and instituted many other improvements. Due to his prickly personality, his loneliness (because of his wife's premature death) and his deteriorating health (he left Government House aged forty-three, on crutches), Dalhousie 'instilled a great dread of himself into the official mind'. It is perhaps fitting to note at this point that Governor-General was the title of the Crown's senior representative in India until the 1857 Mutiny, after which the East India Company transferred Indian affairs to the British Government. After that, the term Viceroy became appropriate.

2 Charlotte (1817–61), the devoted wife of Lord Canning, 'Clemency Canning' (1812–62), Governor-General during the Mutiny of 1857; she died a characteristically swift Indian death. Canning, who survived his wife by only seven months, kept a daily vigil at her graveside, where a light constantly burned. Her early death is the more poignant when it is recalled that Lady Canning bravely endured a period of estrangement during an earlier time in their marriage.

2 February [1899]   GOVERNMENT HOUSE
                                                                CALCUTTA

My darlings:
   This is my journal for you all.
   Thursday, the 26th January 1899. I wrote all day, and after the post had
gone George and I walked about the garden, which out of range of the
naked eye becomes a barren wilderness. At 8 we had a dinner of 63, meeting
in the Throne Room before dinner and dinner was in the Marble Hall. It
went off very well and was a beautiful sight: uniforms add so enormously
to the general effect out here.
   Friday, the 27th January 1899. I went to two hospitals and to a Nurses'
hostel this morning. Colonel Fenn and Lord Suffolk went with me, and
Colonel Harris, the Head of the Medical College, took us all over that
Hospital, and Dr Joubert took us over the Eden Hospital, and Miss Taylor
took us over the hostel for Nurses who are training for the Dufferin Fund.[1]
The streets between Government House and the Medical College Hospital
were crowded to see us pass. It was very hot indeed, and the beautiful cool
stone-floored wards of the Eden Hospital were wonderfully comfortable.
   Miss Dick and Miss Bakewell of Pittsburg came to lunch, also a Russian
sent by Sir N. O'Conor whose name we can none of us remember or
pronounce, and two Frenchmen introduced by Princess Raziwill and one by
Lord Reay. At 5.15 we went a new drive to Tollygunge. After dinner I
went to a Fancy Dress Ball in the Town Hall, given in aid of the Women's
Friendly Society: I wore an Empire gown. Lord Suffolk and Mr Meade and
Colonel Sandbach went with me and the Committee and the Stewards met
us at the carriage door. They were Sir William Cuningham, Sir Patrick
Playfair,[2] Captain Adam, Mrs Gladstone and Mrs Jenkins. They gave me a
bouquet and we marched in procession upstairs, where all the swells were
standing in two lines through which I walked bowing. At the entrance of
the Ball-room the band played 'God save the Queen', and my procession
and I went up the Ball-room to a dais, on which two immense chairs were
placed. After dancing the opening quadrille with Sir William Cuningham I
sat up on it and talked to people, Lord Suffolk, Mr Meade and Colonel
Sandbach making a kind of guard behind me and bringing up people. At 11
I went to supper with the Lieutenant Governor and after supper went away,
the band again playing the 'Queen' as I went. Some of the costumes were
exceedingly pretty, and the room was immense and the ball beautiful. *One*
woman was dressed as a black cat *&* had a long tail over a white satin skirt
covered with rats!
   Saturday, the 28th January 1899. Bourne *&* Shepherd, the photographers, came at 11.30 and took up the remainder of the morning taking
photos of the babies and me. After lunch we went to the races – staying

only for three – and while there the Commander-in-Chief[3] and Lady Lock-hart and Sir Simon and Lady [illegible] came and sat in our box. At 5.30 we drove to the station and came down to Barrackpore by train. A storm came up suddenly and it poured with rain, which will do wonders for the garden.

Sunday, the 29th January 1899. Barrackpore. Everything looked lovely and fresh this morning after the rain, and the air is delicious. We sat under trees and read and wrote – real *dolce-far-niente* existence, which is as grateful to us over-tired people as water to a thirsty man. George gets quiet hours for work and I get plenty of time for the children, who are flourishing. They drive out in a landau with three nurses and two red liveried men on the box and two standing up behind, and when they go out in the morning in their rickshaws there are an army of attendants, including the Viceroy's policeman who usually carries one or two broken-legged dolls. Cynthia is beginning to make noises and says 'Dadada', and knows what she wants and grunts and scolds till she gets it, as it often happens to be a lighted candle or a bottle of ink.

Monday, the 30th January 1899. We only came back from Barrackpore after lunch, and as the tide was against us we were nearly two hours on the way, and I was just in time for my tea party. After the ladies had gone I looked at Jeypore enamels. We dined alone with that portion of the Staff not dining out.

Tuesday, the 31st January 1899. At 10 we looked at our hacks; they have just arrived from England. Sir William Cuningham came to lunch. At 3.30 George received an address from the Calcutta Trades' Association, and re-plied to them in an admirable little speech. The deputation sits about in a horse-shoe round the throne, and when they have assembled George walks in, preceded by his ADC-in-waiting and Mr Lawrence. The President of the Association reads an address to George, who is seated in Tippoo Sahib's* howdah-chair on the throne. When he finishes he hands the address to Mr Lawrence: then George stands up and reads his reply. After this the Chair-man presents everyone, and George (still sitting if the body is a Native one) shakes hands with each: after this he leaves and they disperse. The Calcutta Trades Association gave him a magnificent casket. He has about a dozen and a half now of coffin-shaped caskets and cylinders of silver, like drains, which contain the rolled address. They are all much the same and none very fine. At 4.30 we went to polo, and saw a match between the Gloucester Regiment and a Calcutta team. The Maharaja of Kuch Behar played very well.

Bishop Welldon dined at 8.15, having come here straight from the train. He went in to dinner with me, and after dinner had a talk with George in his study. When we were alone we had great jokes with him about his legs! in their Bishops stockings!

Wednesday, the 1st February 1899. We drove out to the Bodyguard lines at 4.45, Colonel Sandbach and Captain Adam with us, and for the first time

Ali Khan, the Afghan who went with George to Kabul, and whom George sent for to come and act as Orderly to the Viceroy, rode beside the carriage. He is a captain in the Guides Cavalry and a good stout specimen to look at and he bumps along beside the barouche with his sword drawn and adds picturesqueness to the cortège. At five to six we got to the Cathedral for Bishop Welldon's enthronement. The trumpets sounded and the organ played as we arrived, and the whole congregation rose as we were conducted straight across the Cathedral to our throne-like pew! I never felt more shy in my life. The procession to the chancel of choir and clergymen was splendid, and at the end came the Bishop, following the verger holding a tall gold crook. The Bishop advanced slowly up the aisle, and when he got opposite us he made George a low bow, which he was not in the least expecting, but had fortunately presence of mind enough to return. The service was magnificent and began with the Archdeacon taking the Bishop by the hand and conducting him to the throne, which is hung in purple. As Welldon's robes were flaming red over a white surplice it was very brilliant. At the end of the service he made an address. . . .

Your devoted
Mary

1 Lady Dufferin, wife of the first Marquess of Dufferin and Ava had, during her husband's Viceroyalty (1884–8), initiated a programme for developing medical aid for Indian women.

2 (1852–1915), a businessman, sometime Vice President of the Bengal Chamber of Commerce. He was also briefly Sheriff of Calcutta and served, in the 1890s, on the Viceregal Legislative Council.

3 Appointed Commander-in-Chief, India in 1898, William Stephenson Alexander Lockhart (1841–1900) was a Scot of unusually wide experience in Indian life and in military matters. Amir Sahib was the respectful title given him by native tribesmen.

13 February [1899]   GOVERNMENT HOUSE
                                                       CALCUTTA

Darling Precious Papa:

I hope all my journal letters which I have addressed to you & Mamma & the girls will reach you and that their [Nancy and Daisy] coming abroad will not necessitate their [the letters] having to be forwarded to *them* & that thus you will not see them, as I write my daily account of all I do *especially* for you and Mamma and I sent a package of photos by a Mr Simmons from Cleveland addressed to Mamma. They were the proofs and I did not want to wait for the photographs to be printed so I sent them at once, and as soon as I get the phs. too I will send a separate set for you and Joe in Michigan Avenue.

I will have every possible comfort arranged for the girls and they will come straight to Simla and there it will be beautiful and cool and I will do everything to give them a happy summer. And I think there is no one on our staff who will be a matrimonial danger and I won't allow any flirtations as here I am a kind of Queen of Seringapatam and can't have flirtations in my court! George and I are so bottled up that we can never go to any private house to an entertainment but *whenever* the girls go to a dance I will have them chaperoned by Mrs Dawkins,[1] or Lady Young the wife of the Lt.-Gov. of the Punjab,* so they will always be in good hands. The babies are sweet beyond words and very well indeed. I go to Simla with them on the 6th of March. I have my room filled with your photos, the big one of the Bonica portrait, the two Venetian ones *&* two Linden Lodge ones so whenever I look up your beloved face looks at me from every table. I do not know if Mr Choate[2] will take our house, he has offered 1900 pounds and we ask 2000 gs. as we want to pay off the debt. Our lift in Mr Balfour's house he is going to take from us at a valuation. The Bradley Martins have got a house in Mayfair so we have lost them and I am not sorry as I can't bear her.

I keep well here though I feel the heat and am now sitting under a punka. We are in mourning for Prince Alfred of Edinburgh[3] and have to be until the 9th of March. The other day I had to be in mourning for the Bulgarian Princess, and it seems very odd to walk about in the garb of woe for people I have never seen! I am posting you two letters this week my darling Papa.

Your loving
Mary

1 Louise Dawkins, wife of Clinton Edward Dawkins (1859–1905), a Cheltenham and Balliol man who served a short term as Private Secretary to the Viceroy as well as in other significant capacities. Polesden Lacy, a house of unusual beauty, was the Dawkins' English home.
2 Joseph Hodges Choate (1832–1917), American Ambassador to the Court of St James 1899–1905. He took the Curzon's London house in March 1899 and subsequently, in April 1904, rented Balfour's town house in nearby Carlton Gardens.
3 Queen Victoria's grandson (1874–99).

16 February 1899   GOVERNMENT HOUSE
                                                                  CALCUTTA

Darling sweet Papa:
Thursday, the 9th February 1899. Post day is always very busy for we arrange to do as little as possible until six o'clock when our letters are all taken. One post in and one out in the week crowds all the joy of receiving and the rush of answering letters into one short day as, in spite of resolutions to

write, one puts it off weekly until Thursday comes, and then the burr of pens sounds in every room.

The Lonsdales[1] arrived at 4.30. Captain Marker[2] met them, and after post had gone they came and saw us on George's balcony. At 8 we had a dinner of sixty and I sat between Lord Lonsdale and the Count of Turin, who talks a *pot pourri* language, scarcely intelligible and made up of French, Italian and English. I asked him where his brother, the exploring Duke of Abruzzi, was. He said 'Oh! He is walk to *Pole*.' This conveyed nothing to me, but it dawned on me that he was walking to the North Pole! and this is actually the case. We had a small dance of 500 people after dinner and danced in the opening Lancers with Lady Woodburn and the Count of Turin.

Friday, the 10th February 1899. Lady Lonsdale and I saw some Delhi jewels this morning, and this being Council day Mr Chalmers stayed to lunch. One or more of the Councillors usually stay if the Council has been a long one. We said goodbye to the Count of Turin after lunch as he goes to Darjeeling at 4 o'clock. At 4.30 the Nepalese Envoys came to fetch George on his return visit to the Maharaja. They came in their State carriage and wore their wonderful bejewelled bird-of-Paradise head dresses and their semi-English uniforms, the trousers of which seemed pulled on over their full Native petticoats, so their figures were none too graceful. George shook hands with them and then got in his carriage, and with the Staff in uniform and thirty Bodyguard and the whole state show, and thirty-one guns going off, proceeded to return the visit.

At 5 he came back for me and we went out to drive. In driving home by the river I was much astonished to see a fat Native without clothes driving in a landau with both windows closed: his brown skin glistened through the panes of glass and I can't conceive what possessed him to go driving in this state. We had a dinner party at 8 – the Bishop, the Caselees, and others.

Saturday, the 11th February 1899. At 3 we went to the Calcutta University Convocation. We went in State and the route was crowded. When we arrived we were met by the Vice-Chancellor Sir F. Maclean, the Lieutenant-Governor, Sir Edwin Collen and the Bishop, and while George was being robed in a hot dark blue velvet robe I was conducted up a long aisle through a dense throng of Hindu and Mahommedan students. Mr Lawrence and Captain Marker walked behind me and the Registrar walked in front of me. A stage-like arrangement, with the Viceroy's throne in the middle of it, had been arranged, and in the front row of the audience an enormous silver chair – the one kept at the Foreign Office and used on State occasions – had been placed for me, with chairs on either side for Lady and Miss Maclean and Mr Lawrence and Captain Marker. The Viceroy's procession marched up, and he and the Vice-Chancellor and the Bishop and the Lieutenant Governor sat down in their majestic chairs, and the ceremonies, which were tedious and consisted of giving degree to students, began. This took nearly an hour, as there were great waits between the batches from the various Universities. Four ladies got degrees, which were all conferred by the Vice-Chancellor. After all the odd-looking scholars had been made BAs George rose and made his speech, which was very fine, as he spoke with great authority and decision: even those who could not understand it must have been impressed. He spoke for nearly 20 minutes, after which the Vice-Chancellor spoke for 30, and we were pretty tired when the Convocation 'By order of the Chancellor was declared closed'. George then climbed down the dais and I out of my chair, and I walked behind the Chancellors and Governors until we got to the robing room. The Audience was one great stare, as I seem to be as the 'Englishman' put it 'The first Consort of the Viceroy who has attended a Convocation'. The drive back was hot and the crowd undressed and stolid, and only children under ten clapped.

Sunday, the 12th February 1899. The Lonsdales and I went to the Cathedral at 6. At 8 we had a small dinner party, everyone in black, as we are in mourning for the Princess Ferdinand of Bulgaria until tomorrow.

Monday, the 13th February 1899. George went shooting at 7 a.m., and I had a glorious morning as the mail came and I devoured letters and papers until lunch. At 4 Lady Lonsdale and I went to see Hamilton's jewels and then to the Garden Party in the Fort, where George joined us, driving straight from the *Maud*, which he sailed home on from his shoot. The Garden Party was given by the Gloucestershire Regiment and we stood and walked about. It was very formal and stiff as no-one knew quite what to do, and we walked about doing our best to remove the gloomy formality.

At 8 we dined with the Chief Justice and Lady Maclean.

Tuesday, the 14th February 1899. It has begun to be hot and I have punkahs going in my rooms. Lord Elphinstone has come to stay, and he drove out to the Gymkhana at Tollygunge with Lord Lonsdale and Lady Lonsdale, and I went next in the barouche with Captain Meade. I enjoyed the Gymkhana, but we were all miserable over Captain Patterson, one of our ADCs, getting a bad fall and breaking his toes.

Wednesday, the 15th February 1899. Lady Lonsdale and I went to church at 10.30, and this afternoon I had my first Dufferin Fund Meeting of the Central Committee. Mr Rivaz,* Mr Chalmers and Sir A. Trevor – all Members of the Viceroy's Council – Sir Patrick Playfair, Sir William Cuningham, Mr Risley[3] and Colonel Miley all came and sat round a table covered with papers and with me at the head of it and Colonel Fenn on my right conducting the business. I began the proceedings by making a modest speech of twenty words, saying I was not very wise about the management of the Fund and looked to my Committee for counsel and advice. This seemed a successful opening and we then proceeded to business.

Now that Lent has begun I have less gaiety and more hospitals to occupy my time. So you will now begin to receive budgets about my good works.

Goodbye my darling Papa.

Ever your loving
Mary

1 Born in 1857, the 5th Earl of Lonsdale succeeded to the title in 1882 and died in 1944. Famous for his sporting interests, he was the force behind the Lonsdale library, an immense compendium of field sports.

2 Raymond John Marker (1867–1914), eventually to rise to Colonel. ADC to Curzon (1899–1900), then to Kitchener (1901–2) and soldier in India (1902–6), Marker played a role in the Kitchener/Curzon controversy of a sort that incurred the hostility of Lady Curzon.

3 Herbert Hope Risley (1851–1911) of the ICS was a distinguished scholar of Indian ethnography who became Secretary of the judicial department at the India Office and was appointed KCIE in 1907.

23 February [1899]   GOVERNMENT HOUSE
                                                                    CALCUTTA

My precious Papa:

My journal has been quite silent this week as I was seized last Thursday with a bad attack of fever – my temperature flew up to 106 & I thought I was dead but I wasn't! The pain of the fever was awful as the high temperature lasted 36 hours & my poor poor body was burning up – with this I had a violent headache & bad diarrhoea, and for a week now I have been struggling with the miserable after stage of this devilish *fiend* fever. We have had a Consultation today & the Drs say I am better but as weak as a December fly. My engagements have all gone to the wall & I shall not be up to much before I go to Simla.

It is the suddenness of things in India which sweeps one into a heap – well one minute, half dead the next, & as you know I have a talent for quick attacks and recoveries & long before you have my account of this I shall be well.... I can well stand fever & pain while my daughters are so happy & well – George is too – and I pray that you are so my blessings are manifold. I can't bear to think of you fighting your splendid battle alone – & oh! I hope while I keep the girls that Mamma will stay with you my beloved darling Papa.

Your loving loving
Mary

The hill-town of Simla is another theme of the Curzon papers, for the behemoth that was British government in India moved to this salubrious spot to spend March to September of each year following a visit in the 1820s by an earlier Governor-General, Lord Amherst. At various times Lady Curzon (for instance in the summers of 1899 and 1900) and the Viceroy (in 1901) recorded their impressions of Simla and environs, he in a particularly lively manner.

All writers on Simla seem entranced by the beauty of the place. Located in the foothills of the Himalayas, the views were panoramic, the botanical life profusely coloured and the climate favourable both for convalescence and escape from the oppressive heat of the plains. Simla was free from traffic: only the Viceroy, the Lieutenant-Governor of the Punjab and the Commander-in-Chief of the Army were permitted vehicles in the town proper, so that the tonga or rickshaw became the chief means of getting about. As for housing, there were the customary cavernous residences like 'Snowden' and 'Barnes Court' for senior staff. Not for nothing was Simla known as 'The Abode of the Little Tin Gods'. Scattered among the adjacent hills and nearby townships were bungalows and chalets for lesser fry; many bore such suburban names as 'Daisy Bank', 'Hermitage', 'Primrose Hill' or 'Woodbine Cottage'. Similarly, there was a gothic church, a Masonic lodge, a Catholic church, several schools, shops selling British goods, bespoke tailors, and consular representation from various countries. On the face of it Simla seemed a thriving community.

So full was the social life that it is miraculous that government, even with Curzon at the helm, operated at all. The community bristled with dinner parties, balls at the Viceregal residence (where the staff ran to hundreds), dances, concerts, polo, dogshows, gymkhanas, cricket, croquet, football, hunting, golf (at nearby Naldera), camping and – most curiously – there were even opportunities for people to study French literature and the fine arts. There were races at adjacent Annandale, picnics galore and of course an active club-life marked by the usual social discriminations. Simla was especially addicted to the theatre and the talents were such that productions were given of The Scarlet Pimpernel, The Mikado, The Belle of New York, Cavalleria Rusticana, *and something called* Tuppy. *Simla had its own theatre,* The Gaiety, *likened by one devotee to 'a tiny jewel of a theatre in a small German principality'. Simla was a lively spot.*

But Simla society presents a dubious picture even when drawn by the ever conciliatory E. J. Buck, whose Simla Past and Present *is a highly readable and informative account of how people lived there. Buck is distinctly cool in his appraisal of the place and considered it 'undisciplined', which is possibly a euphemism for lax behaviour; and his point is substantiated by Maud Diver's* The Englishwoman in India *(1909) :*

> *That the Simla woman (by which is meant not all women in Simla, but the typical devotee of Simla society) is frivolous, and free and easy both in mind and manners, is a truth which her most ardent admirer could not deny. One plea, at least, may be put forward in her defence – namely, that if former generations of her type helped to make Simla what it is, the tables have now been turned, and it is Simla which*

makes – or rather mars – the woman of today. Moreover, in a country where men and women are constantly thrown together under conditions which tend to minimalise formalism and conventional restraint, where leave is plentiful and grass widows – willing and unwilling – abound, it is scarcely surprising that the complications and conflicting duties of married life should prove appreciably greater than they are elsewhere.

It would appear, too, that the social snobbishness practised elsewhere acquired an even sharper edge in Simla where, despite the relaxation of behaviour, the strict protocol was observed over the most trivial activity, where orders of precedence were meticulously adhered to and where, in the totally unsuitable surroundings and climate, the full gear of Victorian middle-class England appropriate to the social occasion was worn. Similarly, the heavy multi-course Victorian meals – including mulligatawny soup and weighty pudding – were the order of the day. To many it must seem absurd – to some curiously moving.

8 March 1899   VICEREGAL LODGE
                                                                SIMLA

Darling Papa:

Yesterday I received your letter and also one from Mamma containing her plans so I have written her by this post to Paris & now to you. I came up here with the children on Sat. We all stood the journey well though the drive straight up mountains for 58 miles to Simla is trying as the horses have to change every four miles. Simla is a funny place and so hilly & such narrow roads that only three carriages are allowed & those belong to us, the Lt.-Gov. of the Punjab and the Comm.-in-Chief. Everyone else goes in a rickshaw pulled by men & when they come to Simla in carriages they have to leave their carriages before reaching Simla & either walk, ride or go in rickshaws. You never saw such mountains; they go for miles in all directions & you see nothing but the tops as our house is sitting on a mountain 6000 feet high. All the little houses in Simla are clinging to the sides & while the back of every house is flat against the hillside the front is supported by tall poles; it is impossible to imagine a quainter spot. All the government buildings are slipping & slithering down mountains – the hill men pull the rickshaws very fast, two go in front & two push behind you & you think every minute you must go head over heels as you spin down hill like lightning. When I think of your timidity on mountains & how often we have laughed at the way you shied away from precipices I can see your hair bristling on end at Simla thoroughfares!

This house is like a big American country house, but not so well planned as there are no servants' rooms at all. My maid & the nurses are all in the best guest rooms & Best & Daisy's maid will have to be hung up on hooks! I have brought two beautiful horses for the girls & they each have a rickshaw with four royal liveried jampanis [bearers] to pull them. I am so happy that Mamma will be with you so soon my darling Papa. I can't bear to think of you alone so much.

Your loving & dear Mary

30 March 1899   VICEREGAL LODGE
                                                                        SIMLA

Precious Mamma & Papa:

The girls are safely with me. Sweet Nan was taken ill at Aden & was far from well when she landed. Mr Lawrence brought her up here with a trained nurse and she is wonderfully better and is going to get up to-day – she needs feeding up after the bad food on the journey and I am ransacking the country to get delicacies for her; it is a very worrying time for me what with Nannie ill, & my wetnurse with gastric fever and Cynthia vaccinated & my second nurse ill, & I have toothache till I cry. I am never out of sickrooms though the house is full of guests, Lady Lonsdale & her cousin, and I have to organize and arrange and plan until I am dead with fatigue. It seems that I can never have ten days in which to rest & recover from my bad fever in Feb. but I go working on & am happy because Nancy is so much better & the wetnurse & Cynthia turned the corner – Cynthia is the best & most most patient baby I ever knew – Daisy is well & constantly with me & I do all I can to make her happy. India is a risky place to get your relations out to and I must get the girls warm flannels & flannel nightgowns which I find they are not provided with. The danger of chills is great; I am lending them my things now – their thin batiste things are useless here. Their maids will quickly make them things. I rejoice to see how nice Marie is. I feared a Holden & find a dear little woman; both maids are kind to the ill wetnurse & they cheer her up. Daisy has her breakfast in bed with me & I cuddle & I spoil her & feed her up. I hope they will be happy. We are quiet now but in another month the gaiety will begin.

I will write a long letter next time. Goodbye my sweet precious Mamma and Papa.

Your devoted
Mary

12 April 1899   VICEREGAL LODGE
                                                                SIMLA

Sweet darling:

The girls are very well and happy and have made great friends with Lady Lonsdale who is still here; he [Lord Lonsdale] came last week and they are leaving on Friday. They have stayed about seven weeks with us which is somewhat of a visitation! but both are very nice and make no trouble. George is here and working hard – he never takes any rest but it is his way to grind while others play and I am glad to say he keeps well, and he goes to bed at midnight which is a great thing and he sleeps well. Nannie and Daisy both look much better than when they came and are so dear and sweet. Nannie is killing and keeps us all laughing – she calls all the Captains Majors and the Colonels Captains and mixes up their names to our great delight. The doctor's name is Colonel Fenn & the Military Secretary Colonel Sandbach and she calls them both Major Fennbag. One of the ADCs had a pair of very short breeches for riding on yesterday and she asked if he had grown out of his *pants*! They all delight in her, and clamour to sit by her at table as she is so funny and sweet. Daisy is very sweet too & everyone likes her and she has annexed Captain Meade, quite a harmless youth on the Staff. She writes to and hears from Craig W. and both she & Nannie spend hours writing letters and they promise me they write to you and dear Papa.

I am very very sorry they have not brought their strings of pearls – they would be as safe as mine and I do not like them to wear those huge sham rows as they are very vulgar and they need their own nice ones. I shall lend them mine whenever I can spare them. They have plenty of lovely evening clothes and only lack sufficient plain day clothes – just coats and skirts – these they are having Julie & Best make of cloth I have got them, so they will soon be well equipped. Simple clothes are the most useful for India.

The babies are well and send their love to beloved Gagni. Irene remembers you perfectly and talks constantly of you & Granpie. Cynthia blooms. Good-night my beloved mother.

                                                  Your devoted
                                                  Mary

3 May 1899   VICEREGAL LODGE
                                                                SIMLA

Dearest darlings:

I have been in bed four days with fever & cold & am up today for the first time.

Daisy and Nannie are sweet beyond words to me and I never knew two more darling girls. I love them so & they are such comforts to me. The little cloud is all past[1] and Daisy is so sweet and a thousand times more attractive because she is dignified & not flirting. I am so proud of them both and they help me with my tea parties & are just as sweet and dear and pretty & smart as they can be. They are now as anxious as I am to keep up the dignity of this position. I told them we were the first Americans they had ever seen out here and we could just show them how nice and quiet Americans could be. They are dining out a good deal and Mrs Dawkins is going to take them to a dance next week.

I can't write any more just now. I am much better but still cough & raise a good deal – no blood but mucus. I shall be all right again soon, it is only a fearful cold.

George is up again – we aren't a very robust pair I fear. Good night beloveds.

Your loving
Mary

1 Presumably a reference to the unfortunate episode involving Lady Curzon's sisters, newly arrived from America. Apparently ignorant of the exacting protocol, they (as noted earlier) misguidedly prostrated themselves in mock homage before their brother-in-law on a ceremonial occasion.

20 May 1899   VICEREGAL LODGE
                                                                      MASHOBRA[1]

My darlings:

We have come out here again to spend Sunday in the delicious peace and quiet of these mountains. We sat under trees all morning, Irene digging and making a garden. Capt. Wigram[2] dug it & outlined it with stones while Irene planted trees & flowers in it, and Capt. Adam, Capt. Marker & Capt. Carr cut out paper animals which we stood up in long lines on the road to the Ark which was seated on Mt Ararat. It was a great success and Irene [was] perfectly delighted & running from one to the other to see the newest elephant. Cynthia is blooming. I sent both babies out here on Friday, it does them so much good.

Last Thursday George and I held our first garden party. When most of the guests had arrived we walked out to 'God save the Queen' between two lines of people all bowing and curtseying. Two ADCs walked in front & led us to a tent furnished with carpets & chairs under which we stood and shook hands with 500 people, the girls walked about and talked to everyone they knew. Nannie wore her gray cloth with turquoises & I wore gray crêpe de chine, while Daisy wore the lace dress she got of Pagnier....

I am better again; it is my liver that gives me such bother. You know I always was liverish and out here it is worse – and I go up and down and am ill & well in turns. . . .

We go to Simla tomorrow & leave the babies here. All your London letters came late this evening. I am so grieved that you do not say any more about the house in London. You write it is so bare! I think you may have bought some furniture & put in the most unfurnished parts!! Did you!

Nannie and Daisy are well & sweet, they love Mashobra. Goodbye my beloveds.

Your devoted
Mary

1 An agreeable retreat five miles from Simla.
2 Clive Wigram (1873–1960) or 'Wigger' was to become 1st Baron Wigram of Clewer. ADC to Lord Elgin in 1895 and to Curzon 1899–1904, he subsequently served George V as Assistant Secretary and Equerry 1910–31 and as Private Secretary and Extra Equerry 1931–5. Perhaps Wigram deserved to rise, for his passion for committee work seems unquenchable; he appears as constable here, governor there, and committee-man everywhere. But he found time to marry the oldest daughter of Neville Chamberlain.

15 June [1899]   VICEREGAL LODGE
                                                        SIMLA

My darlings:

We have been camping in the woods for three days and only came back yesterday. We enjoyed ourselves oh! so much sitting under the trees and sleeping in tents. The dear girls were very happy, we just adore them and George and I constantly say whatever shall we do without our sweet ephelies – ephelie means *elephant* according to Irene & as they are very fat & we have great jokes about their sleeping like elephants Irene calls them 'Aunt Elephies'. Daisy has gained fifteen pounds and is huge; her sit-upon is perfectly enormous and she is bursting out of her clothes! She is too big for looking her best in the race as she is almost buxom, but this shows you in what grand health she is – Nancy too is plump and sweet, but not so colossal as Daisy. I on the contrary am *very* thin, but I am pretty well. The babies are too sweet for words to describe. Irene is getting more affectionate and worships me much in the same way that I did my 'Muvvini' when I was little – do you remember, precious Mamma.

George is well, but rather bothered as our expenses have been so terrific that we are 12,000 rupees behind, but in time we shall pick up I hope. Even here George keeps & sees to all the accounts and works like a slave; it is no use begging him to work less as he will work till he kills himself in spite of all the begging not to in the world. We have one of our big dinners tonight, and next week a dance. The girls fly about a great deal but I go nowhere and have nothing to do. The staff run the house so I have no care or worry.

I will write more next time.

Your devoted
Mary

21 June [1899]   VICEREGAL LODGE
                                                                                SIMLA

My dear Papa:

I have put off writing this letter[1] to you ever since we came to India, but as we are in a tight place I feel that I must tell you of it, and I will write you a full statement of our affairs.

The expenditure which we have been forced to incur in coming out and starting in India – i.e. fares, freight, insurance, *stores*, wine, horses, carriages, harness, exclusive of any item of personal outfit either in George's, the babies' case, or mine – is £9719.4.6 (and this in another three months will be increased by £1000 by expenditure on a new pair of carriages & harnesses, the present ones having to be replaced). To meet these charges we received £3500 from the government and £500 from you – that is £4000 in all – and before we shall have discharged our debt we shall have had to find £6700 ourselves of this by forestalling the whole of George's & my joint income up to Nov. next. We managed to pay £3700 (for which cheques were furnished yesterday), remaining £3000 in debt.

The heaviest expenses for us have been stables which we took over & we have paid Lord Elgin £5500 in full – neither George nor I have made one *single* expenditure of a personal nature & the whole of this sum has been the public expense of our coming. We were told by our predecessors that the outlay in starting would not be less than £10,000 & it has been proved true. Other people who have come here have had capital to draw upon but we have had only our income. The expenses of Reigate and Four Carlton Gardens we have paid outside of the sums I mention & out of the few hundred pounds. If the £2000 are more than you can help us out at present *of course* you will tell me. The girls are very well & full of life & spirits & gaiety. I am quite alone at Mashobra as I have a kind of bloodpoisoning which has covered me with spots & blisters & I am not fit to be seen, but I hope to be well soon.

Your loving
Mary

1 This letter is of interest both because it throws light on the Curzons' financial affairs and also as an indication of how certain monetary transactions were effected between senior diplomats.

6 July [1899]   VICEREGAL LODGE
                                                                                    SIMLA

Dearest dear Papa:

We are all well and happy and we live in a deluge which never stops for more than a few hours. You think you know what rain is but you really don't until you see the floodgates open here and the earth fairly drowning under the fury of the downpour. The choice in India is between violent heat, or *Torrents* of rain. The girls have mackintosh clothing and go out in all weather, & they go [on] immense walks. We do everything for their enjoyment that mortals can, and I think they enjoy themselves. The society is not so fascinating as London or Paris or Washington but there are very many pleasant people and at all our dinners I arrange the girls' places myself.

The babies *bloom* and love their aunties – the 'Aunty' is sometimes dropped and Irene calls 'Nanzy' whenever she wants her. She is allowed to sew on a corner of Nancy's embroidery & this is a *great* treat! Irene sends kisses to Grandpie.

Your loving
Mary

With the waning of the Simla season Lady Curzon, in the autumn of 1899, accompanied her husband to parts of India hitherto unknown to her, and the novelty of that experience is communicated in her letters and journals home. Initially writing of Delhi, about which she was 'wildly excited', she dashes off no more than a hectic series of impressions – of the Mutiny monument, of a native sword dance, of a social gathering; but her telling description of the Jama Masjid (Great Mosque) powerfully evokes the variegated hues and bizarre glitter of the barbaric Mogul world, whilst her account of the Red Fort (of Delhi), with its marble canopies, splendid thrones and fragile carvings, is most delicately perceptive. Sharp, though, is her reaction to the tasteless transgressions of the British who have erected ugly barracks nearby and thus intruded an unsightly symbol of the conqueror into an impressive dynastic scene.

After Delhi, the Viceroy embarked upon a dangerous and extensive visit to plague- and famine-ridden areas in the Punjab, Rajputana and Bombay; Lady Curzon rested briefly at Simla but rejoined her husband at Bhopal for a tour of

Central India, a progress marked by imperial formalities of course but also tempered with relaxed interludes. At Gwalior, for instance, Lady Curzon's spontaneous levity breaks through the gravity of that occasion as she comments on Mahratta shrouds and the fanciful colouring of horses even as she is herself the victim of a farcical collapsing chair.

Perhaps the signal aspect of the Central India tour arises from the attention drawn to the spiritual and primitive sides of Indian life, which are juxtaposed so dramatically as the Curzons visit Muttra, Brindabah and other places associated with the god Krishna; whilst memories are evoked of the colourful savagery of the Mogul emperors (notwithstanding Akbar himself) as Mary Curzon leads us through Fatehpur Sikri and Sikandra, where the Emperor is buried in ornate splendour. Her two visits to the Taj Mahal are swiftly passed over because, for her, it defies description, and possibly, as many modern tourists find, satiety has taken its toll. But, curiously, Cawnpore, scene of incomprehensible butchery, is given scant attention.

By mid December 1899 the Curzons were back at Government House in Calcutta and, as the letters show, their more customary life had re-asserted itself. Lady Curzon's sisters Nancy and Daisy departed in the New Year; the receptions and dinners were in full swing, and yet a certain flexible domesticity is evident as we see the ADCs playing with the children and Mary Curzon herself fussing over maids, over press vilification and over her family avoiding 'fast Americans' in Paris. Indeed, it is apparent that when stationary in places like Calcutta or Simla she tends to move fleetingly across a variety of subjects whereas when travelling there is a tendency to concentrate on a particular experience, to amplify a description of a place, an individual, an occasion. The variation – conscious or unconscious – is noticeable and modulates her prose, bringing a change of tempo that works against stylistic monotony.

29 October 1899   [DELHI]

My sweet Ephilies:[1]

... At 9 we got to Delhi – a guard of honour of Afridis drawn up & 'God save the Queen' as G. appeared on the platform and Mr Fanshawe[2] the Commissioner bursting out of his uniform and Gen. Blood[3] & his staff smiling & saluting – while George reviewed the guard of honour I stood still & talked to Gen. Blood and gave the crowd in the station a fine opportunity for a stare. As soon as presentations were over we got in the barouche and drove through crowded streets. Mr Fanshawe and Capt. Baker-Carr in our carriage and an escort of Bengal Cavalry and an artillery team pulling the carriage. The bodyguard had on their new uniforms and looked magnificent and George's Afghan orderly rode by the carriage looking very fat and uncomfortable. It wasn't a bit hot and I was wildly interested in everything as to see Delhi for the first time is an epoch in life.

We are staying at Mr Fanshawe's house which is pretty and filled with things he has collected all over the world. After breakfast George received a deputation and after it three nawabs. After lunch we siestad for an hour and at 4 had a grand drive round. The escort in front drowned us in dust but had to be endured. After our barouche came a killing carriage of canary yellow lined with raspberry with silver lamps three feet long supporting silver birds. This has been lent by the Maharaja of Patiala & the staff drive in it & look very sheepish! We drove down the Ridge & went to the Flagstaff tower[4] and the Mutiny monument and saw where the batteries had been placed in the Siege of Delhi. We then drove to the [Kudsia Gardens?] & thence to the gap in the walls through which Nicholson[5] and his men got into Delhi and then followed the narrow lane down which he went with his men fighting all the way until he was killed. Then we went to his tomb and all leaned against the newly painted rail. I don't know why they always paint rails one must lean on, & seats one must sit on when the Viceroys travel. We departed from the cemetery with gridiron bars on our chests, & drove home to rest a little before dressing for dinner. At 8, twenty-eight swells came to dinner and I went in with the Bishop of Madras & on the other side of me Gen. Blood. I forgot to say he went with us on the drive this afternoon & was very nice but not as good a mutiny guide book as Mr Fanshawe who was excellent. After dinner I talked to the ladies & when the men had finished smoking we went up on the roof of the house to watch an Afridi Khattak Sword dance. It was strange & weird as they wore flowing white garments & swung round a bonfire in a huge circle waving swords in dangerous proximity to their neighbours' heads and as they grew more & more excited kerosene was poured on the flames & the band grew so excited that the players turned summersaults over their drums and danced too. There is an activity in native bands which I miss in ours!

After the band & the dancers had exhausted themselves and their audience as well we went to bed. In the morning we went to the famous church to which the mutiny officers were going when the Sepoys shot them down. It is a very pretty classical church – the chaplain was quaint and preached a very odd sermon and said Goodbye to his congregation saying he would not meet them again officially. Our private opinion is that he is about to be locked up. He has made a great agitation about our going to the Jumma Musjid on Sunday & he is cracked I think. . . .

Your devoted
Mary

1 See Lady Curzon's letter of 15 June.
2 Herbert Charles Fanshawe (1852–1923), from a well-known ICS family, who

ill-advisedly became involved in a controversy with the Viceroy. He 'retired' in 1901 and subsequently wrote a book on Delhi as well as a handbook on India.

3 Bindon Blood (1842–1940) of the Royal Engineers, a veteran of Zulu and Afghan wars, who retired in 1907. In his *Four Score Years and Ten* Blood is insensitively critical of Curzon's judicially compassionate attitude over the fatal beating of an Indian by members of the 9th Lancers. Blood's perspective makes chilling reading.

4 The 150-foot tower that became a place of retreat for civilians, the sick and the wounded, during the siege of Delhi, one of the most savage encounters of the Indian Mutiny of 1857.

5 John Nicholson (1822–57), a legendary hero of British India respected for his commanding personality and for fair if rigorous justice. Pacifying and retaining the loyalty of the Punjab, Nicholson was a major figure in the relief of Delhi, where he was fatally wounded. He was one of those rare, quasi-mystical figures of past imperial Britain, of whom Field Marshal Roberts wrote in his *Forty-one Years in India* (1897): 'Nicholson impressed me more profoundly than any man I had ever met. I have never seen anyone like him. He was the beau-ideal of a soldier and a gentleman.' Like most unusually gifted people, Nicholson was an intractable subordinate.

[30–31 October 1899]   VICEROY'S CAMP
                                                                       [DELHI]

Darling Ephilies:

I think I left off my last letter after church on Sunday so I begin with our going to the Jumma Musjid in the afternoon. There was a great crowd as we drove up to the steps which are the finest I have ever seen and 150 feet long. The Mosque dignitaries met us, they were eight venerable Mohammedans all in stocking feet, and they conducted us up a long tongue of red carpet which reached from the north door of the Mosque which was the King's and is now only open for Viceroys down to the street. You walk into a courtyard the size of Grosvenor Square with lovely pink sandstone colonnades on the right & left & in front the most beautiful mosque in the whole world – its face is white marble framed in the beautiful rose red Delhi stone – & the three domes are of pale yellow marble glistening like gold and the minarets are pink with enough white to make them look very light. This façade is absolutely beautiful. We put on flannel shoes to go inside the mosque, which was the first time that it had been done since the Mutiny as ever since '57 the English have trodden the marble with nailed boots. The Governor of the Punjab had wished to start the wearing of shoes from the doors & in the great courtyard but George decrees that they need only be worn in the holy of holies so that is some satisfaction to the Mahommedans and not a great trial to the English as you can see everything from the courtyard. The inside [of] the Mosque is all white & black marble and the bow window towards Mecca is polished to look like mother of pearl. While George went up the minaret I sat & waited looking with perfect delight at the beautiful colours which the sun gave the golden domes. The harmony of colours all in natural marbles is perfect. From the Mosque we went to the Fort[1] and drove in the Delhi Gate where Sir Bindon Blood met us. We first went to the hall of audience which is in the same deep pink stone as the outer walls & Gates of the Fort – it faces the Great Gate of the Fort and is open on three sides and the roof is supported by rows of beautiful pillars some double & some single – at the back is the inlaid marble canopy throne of the Mogul Emperors wh. is a great platform with a marble canopy over it & the famous peacock throne used to be here but was carried off to Persia long ago by a Persian conqueror. The whole of the throne was decorated by Italian workmen imported by Shah Jahan[2] but much of the beauty has been destroyed by the vandals who have picked out the precious stones. We then went to the King's palace which is the loveliest dream imaginable. The private hall of audience, open on all sides with carved lace marble screens looking on the river, is colonnaded and the floor, the roof, the pillars & the King's throne are a vision of delicate inlaid glistening marble & soft gilding & delicate carving. The King's apartments & the baths beyond are white marble,[3] too, all inlaid from floor to ceiling and these are so fairylike that the pearl mosque just beyond the baths seems almost severe and chaste in white simplicity after the brilliant beauty of the palace – it is all quite small, and just as exquisite as you want it to be. I laughed with satisfaction and joy as it all surpassed anticipation, but the ghastly monstrosities of modern barracks of yellow brick three stories high fairly crushing all the beauty is a rude reminder of the present masters. All the other conquerors have beautified Delhi but the British have disfigured existing beauty and invented the most frightful iron & brick modernities to stand alongside the splendour and beauty of the past. . . .

Your loving
Mary

1 The Red Fort – to be distinguished from the building of the same name at nearby Agra. The Delhi fort is some 3,000 by 1,800 feet and is a dazzling reminder of Eastern opulence. Curzon was responsible for its refurbishment, as he was for other Indian buildings of aesthetic and historical importance.
2 (1592–1666), Mogul emperor, the fifth of his dynasty, who succeeded his father as ruler in 1627. His way to the throne was unusually bloody – even by Mogul standards – for he reputedly had all male contenders in his path removed. His love of beauty was as developed as his murderous propensities and his court was a centre for goldsmiths, silversmiths and other artisans.
3 Carved in the marble are the words: 'If there is a paradise on earth, this is it, this is it, this is it.'

Darling Papa:

... My train got into Bhopal at 9.45 [25 November]. The station was beautifully decorated and crowded with people. Colonel Barr the agent for the Viceroy in Central India came into my carriage, and said if I would get out the Begum who is ruler of the State would receive me, so I did so, and he took me into a little tent arrangement on the platform, all hung with lovely silks and carpeted with gold, inside which stood a tiny little woman entirely wrapped up in green moire silks, with two gauze holes for her eyes to look through. She took my hand and sat me down, and I talked to her while Mrs Barr interpreted. Presently we heard signs of George's train, so I went out to meet him, and jumped in his carriage and found him looking well after his long tour of famine and plague. As soon as he got out of his carriage the Begum advanced to meet him, and welcomed him to her State. The bands played and we drove off – George and I in front, and the Begum in a closed carriage behind. The way was lined by Imperial Service Cavalry; and when these gave out the army of the State, aged veterans with orange beards and trousers, holding out rusty muskets stood about three feet apart, and behind them the most wonderful crowd of Natives, camels, elephants, in every rainbow colour; all Native bands playing a kind of 'God save the Queen' and trumpets shrieking royal salutes. It was impossible not to laugh at the grotesque show – the splendour and the squalor and the pic-turesqueness of it all. We drove under arches and banners, and there seemed to be innumerable flags carried before and behind us. We had 1½ miles of this before we reached the Residency, where Mrs Barr met us and showed us our rooms. Nothing else happened until 3, when George received the Begum in Durbar, and after I received her with Mrs Barr as interpreter. She came in a gray hooded gown, and looked just like a little old spook. She took up her mask while she talked to me, and she has a sad bright little old face. She only stayed a few minutes as she had to go back to receive our return visits.

At 4.30 I went to the Lansdowne Hospital with Colonel Fenn, and all the way there Colonel Fenn and I were in fits of laughter, as all the bugles gave us a royal salute, troops presented arms and went through all their tricks.

At 6 George started on his return visit to the Begum and ten minutes after him I did. We drove through the Native town, which was illuminated, to the Palace – not a wonderful building but big – which was a flame of light. It was bewildering, and the world seemed entirely made of myriads of lamps – the grass, the trees, the palace, the flowers, everything was ablaze. George had not finished his visit, so we sat in the carriage, Mrs Barr, Captain Marker and I, gazing at the wonderful sight. Presently George came out, and was escorted to the door by the tiny Begum, this time in a white spook attire. She met me at the door and took my hand, and to my utter surprise led me to a dais, on which sat the Viceroy's chair of state. This she motioned me into, while she sat in a less grand chair on my left, and Mrs Barr on my right: the big room – all ugly chandeliers and candelabra on the floor and pillars wreathed in paper flowers – reeked of attar of roses. We talked a little, and I admired the magnificent gold carpets with which the whole room was covered. She presently garlanded me with flowers, and sprinkled me with attar, and gave me the inevitable *pan*, a kind of nut to chew and then, with all her nobles, in the gorgeousest clothing I ever saw, we started a tour round the illuminated gardens. Captain Marker was waiting outside, and his face was a study as I emerged hand in hand with the tiny masked Begum, and we walked in procession through the hundred thousand twinkling lamps. Under a shamiana [canopy or large tent] she had her presents to us displayed: one is a pretty ivory house for George, and for me a little brougham big enough for two Shetland ponies, made entirely of *mirrors* and lined with green velvet – it is too funny. I eventually tore myself away and flew back to dress for the big banquet of sixty given for us by the Begum. It came off in a huge tent, all hung with gold brocade, and after the ices the little Begum came and sat between George and me, and made a speech in Urdu. It was the climax of the Begum's day: to see the tiny veiled woman standing and making a speech proclaiming her loyalty to England; to which George replied proposing her health. The tent in which we sat after dinner was furnished with magnificent gold carpets, and silver and gold chairs and howdahs, so that the effect with the electric light was beautiful.

Sunday we rested as I had a headache, and George had work. At 3.30 the Begum's daughter came to see me. She is at daggers drawn with her mother, so George could not receive her. Great purdah arrangements had to be made for her, and Mrs Barr received her at the carriage and brought her in to me. She spoke little English, and was hideously dressed and very plain as her teeth are destroyed by betel nut. George went to see the Fort at 4.30, but I stayed in to nurse my head for another dinner party. The same officials – General and Mrs Jeffreys, Colonel and Mrs Barr, Major Newmarch, Captain and Mrs Bruce and Sir Howard Melliss – dined, who were here last night, and we had one in the same tent of gold brocade, and a shockingly bad dinner prepared by Peliti, the Simla caterer. . . .

Tuesday, 28th November 1899. We went one hour by train last night to Sanchi, where we slept, and this morning went to see the Tope, a Buddhist temple. A dozen elephants in gorgeous howdahs and hangings were ranged by the platform of the station, and George and I got on the hugest. As the elephant had to climb up hills and steps, we swayed in our howdah like a skiff at sea, and I laughed till I cried. The procession, brought up by Garland on an elephant, was fine. The Tope was curious and the gateways very fine. I was carried back to the train in a golden dhoolie [covered litter], as it has begun to be hot, and the elephantine scenic effect was quite as fine without me on the top of one.

We went through an interesting part of Central India, as there were many interesting ruins which we could see as we flew along. We arrived at Gwalior at 5, and were met by the Maharajah and all his male relations, and the English guests whom he had invited for the visit – dear old Father Lafont from Calcutta was there. George drove in the first carriage with the Maharajah, and I in the next with Colonel Barr. The State carriages were *magnificent*, and the whole way was lined with troops, and no sooner had one band stopped the 'Queen' than another broke out in a different key. The crowd was picturesque, and everything intensely spick and span: this was intensified by the down-at-the-heel look of Bhopal, from which we had come. This Maharajah Scindia is enormously rich, and was covered with jewels. The palace we are staying in is gorgeous.

This is my weeks journal *&* in my next I will write a full account of Gwalior.

Your devoted
Mary

[From the Journal]   [GWALIOR]

Wednesday, 29th November 1899. This morning at 11 the Maharaja paid his state visit to the Viceroy. He came with an immense escort of his own troops and runners ahead of his carriage carrying silver pikes with tigers' heads on the ends. He was covered with jewels, and all his male relations made a fine show with Mahratta hats, which are shaped like a Chinese junk with the prow sticking high over one ear and the stern over the other. Each carried a vast bundle of coloured muslin.

At 11.20 I went with Captain Marker and Mrs Barr to see the school for Native girls which the Maharaja has endowed and housed in the old palace in the Native city. Troops lined the whole way. Some were very old irregulars holding pikes and wearing orange trousers and beards of all colours. Bands were all along the line playing 'God save the Queen', and the bugles tootled salutes. Mr Johnston, the Maharajah's ex-tutor, met me at the carriage, and took me into a cool white marble courtyard surrounded by cloisters. A dais with a silver canopy stood at one end, with a crystal chair on which I sat gingerly. Several ladies were present, and I was told the Maharani was behind a curtain looking on opposite. About 60 native girls of all sizes, dresses, and shapes, proceeded to sing me a song of welcome and then do an English drill. It was droll and graceful, as they did it with Native music, and the silver anklets on bare limbs, gauze attire, and frequent view of the leg, made a very Oriental rendering of dumb-bells and crossbars, [also] the slow graceful swaying & flower wreathed sticks & drowsy cadences of Indian guitars. After they had done their drill and heaped garlands of flowers at my feet, Mrs Barr and Mrs Heyland, the lady who is teaching the little Maharani, took me over to see her. She and her mother-in-law and their ladies were huddled behind screens and sitting on stamped velvet Maple chairs. I shook hands and sat down and tried to talk to them all. Such jealousy exists between Mother-in-law and daughter-in-law that any too frequent remarks to the latter were resented by mamma by a good kick to her daughter-in-law under the chair, which I saw and so devoted my attention to both. The Maharaja's only wife is a dear little person about seventeen, with a bright pretty face and the tiniest little form. She is not much bigger than Irene, and was married at eleven. The mother is a huge, fat, cake-coloured lady. Both were dressed in gauze draperies and wore very fine jewels. The little Maharani had the most splendid nose ring of pierced diamonds. I presently went away and promised to come and see them after dinner.

After luncheon we went to the Gwalior Fort. The Maharajah met us at the base of the rock and had 18 elephants to carry us up the 300 feet, but we preferred dhoolies as they were quicker, so we went up thus, the Maharajah riding by me and the Staff on the elephants. The Fort is on the top of a flat hill, 300 feet high, 1½ miles long and half a mile wide. It is called the Windsor Castle of India, and the Hindu Palace Fort is very fine, and the temples beautiful. We drove about to see them in pony carriages which had been sent up for us, and we had tea on a fortified terrace overlooking the old Gwalior city and the new city Lashkar, where the present Scindias have built their town. We climbed down again and drove home to dress for the great banquet of a hundred given for us by the Maharajah. He received us, but we dined without him. After the dessert he came in with all his nobles to make his speech. A Mahratta custom is to carry your shroud about with you, so as to have it handy for sudden death, and as they came into the Banqueting Hall carrying immense bundles of pretty colours, I thought they had brought their bedding in preparation to listening to long speeches! But Colonel Barr explained that they were only keeping their shrouds handy. What a good idea for English political meetings when death seems preferable to a few words more....

Thursday, 30th November 1899. At 8.30 we went to the review, George riding and I behind in a carriage with Colonel Pears and Colonel Fenn; down a mile long avenue to the Parade ground we drove through two lines of Mahratta Sirdars dressed in all colours and sitting on horses *painted* to their taste, and wearing garters, head-dresses, necklaces, and every ornament a horse *can* wear. The nobles sat on silk-cushioned saddles and by the side of everyone who was a sufficiently great swell stood a man holding a giant umbrella of red or yellow satin on the end of a long stick. The effect was *killing*, and I never saw anything so amusing. Around the saluting point all the great swells were assembled. The Maharajah, in the uniform of an English Colonel, was caracoling about, and on his right was his grandfather sitting on a white horse painted in orange *stripes* and covered with tinsel and silk cords, feathers in his hand and garters on his knees. A great umbrella was held high over horse and rider. I took a photo of them, to the old man's great joy. The elephant battery was imposing, & all the elephants salaamed with their trunks in the air. Kipling says only a Viceroy sees this royal form of salute....

Friday, 1st December 1899. At 8 this morning we were ready to start for the tiger shoot, but we only got off at 9, and drove 25 miles to a camp which the Maharajah has had pitched for us. All the way out troops surrounded the carriage and galloped 200 yards either side, and great precautions are taken for the Viceroy's safety, as a plot was supposed to exist to kill him; so there are guards everywhere. The camp, where we arrived at 10.30, is the prettiest thing I have ever seen. A quantity of lovely trees, flowerbeds and fountains; and the tents built round three sides of a square are marvels of comfort and beauty. After breakfast we drove 3 miles further, and then went over rough ground on elephants to a deep gully where the tiger drive was to be. There we got into a castellated tower – George, the Maharajah, Captain Baker-Carr and I in the main tower, and Mr Barnes, Captain Marker, Mr Lawrence and Colonel Fenn in two little round towers the other side of the nulla [ravine or watercourse]. We waited for hours and no tiger came. We did not make a sound and the tension of expectation was very great; and when my Camera cracked & the chair I was sitting on collapsed it sounded like the earthquake in a china factory, and my whole soul apologised for the outrageous action of the furniture & I was seized with a *fou rire*. We had food in our little tower but the opposite party had none & after 8 hours of famine showed signs of emaciation so with wonderful aim George threw a fine plum cake across the chasm which was caught in silent gratitude by six hungry [hunters?]. A tiger broke back and the beat began anew, and about 5 there was a crunching and a growl, and a flash of yellow dashed before us, and George fired and missed him: the fraction of a second, and as the tiger galloped past, George shot him in the back and Captain Baker-Carr fired, and all was over and the tiger *gone*! It was so sudden and thrilling that my eyes were falling out and my tongue tied. Then began an elephant beat to try to send back the tiger, and just as we were despairing there was a furious growl and a rush, and again the tiger rushed past. This time we could not see him for the thickness of the jungle, and we had to remount our elephants and go back to camp without the tiger, but we knew he was badly wounded and we should get him tomorrow. We walked back through the jungle in the dark & found the camp illuminated and a perfect fairyland. As we had only nibbled sandwiches, dinner was our first real meal since morning.

Saturday, 2nd December 1899. We started in at 10 – George, Mr Barnes,

Mr Lawrence, Captain Baker-Carr, Colonel Fenn and I. The Maharajah,
Captain Marker, and Colonel Crofts have been out since 6.30 in search of the
wounded tiger. We got in to Gwalior at 11.20, and I went to say goodbye to
the Maharani, who received me and spoke English and played the harmon-
ium. On my way back to my rooms I looked out and saw the Maharajah in a
barouche drawn by four horses, and in the barouche two immense dead
tigers! It was a sight! He had gone out and got George's wounded tiger and
another, popped them in the carriage and driven 20 miles in two hours, and
there he was triumphant and dusty with his two tigers! We were all photographed as soon as the Maharajah had changed his dress, and the tigers were
included in the photo so we looked as though we had shot them arrayed in
frock coats & chiffon! At 12.45 we went in the Maharajah's new light
railroad to the station, where there was a crowd in a tent and the Maharajah
made a speech, and then George answered and opened the light railway. We
then proceeded to our own train and said goodbye to the wonderful Maharajah, who is the kindest, most thoughtful host, as well as the greatest
genius for organising & to dear Col. and Mrs Barr who have made our visit a
perfect delight. We were delighted with our visit and he pleased because we
were; and we all were happy and grateful for our Gwalior delights.

4–12 December [1899]   LUCKNOW

Darling Papa:
  Monday, 4th December 1899.   This morning at 9.30 the girls, who arrived
last night, Captain Marker, Captain Baker-Carr, George and I went by train
to Muttra, which is one of the holy cities of India. There was a public
reception there, and the Jodhpur Lancers, who are living in the 9th Lancers
lines during their absence in South Africa owing to the famine in Rajputana,
made the most picturesque escort. Colonel Maharaja Sir Pertab Singh[1] rode
by the carriage. We had lunch in the Collector's house, where we are staying,
and after started off to drive through the town. It is very picturesque, and the
carved stone lattice balconies are beautiful. After going to a mosque, which
seemed out of place in a Hindu sacred town, and to the spot where Krishna[2] is
supposed to have been born, we drove to one of the ghats, and got on board
an immense raft carpeted with a huge red rug, on which sat two silver chairs
with less grand ones around them. George and I sat on them, and we floated
down the river, and saw the temple steps leading to the river crowded with
the most picturesque Hindu crowd. Priests came off in boats and brought us
offerings of sweets and flowers. The great man here is a rich Hindu banker.
He has built temples and spent untold sums on them. He and his son went
about with us. Sir Pertab Singh and Major Turner came to dine, but I was
very tired and dined in my room.

Tuesday, 5th December 1899. This morning at 9 we drove to Brindaban, eight miles away. Krishna spent his childhood here, and left his sacred footsteps in some stone which is duly worshipped. We first drove to see a new temple which the Maharaja of Jeypore has spent fourteen lakhs [one lakh = 100,000 rupees] in building. He will not complete it, as his priests tell him he will die when it is finished. We then went over a grand old temple built in 1575 by a Jeypore Maharaja, and much mutilated by that bigot Aurangzeb[3] in the last century. The crowd in the great open space in front of the temples was enormous. We next went to see the car of Juggernaut which comes out on great festivals, and then over the new temple built by [blank in MS]. A municipal address was presented to George in one of the temple gardens. We then climbed up to a roof to get a view, and the heat was awful. . . .

Thursday, 7th December 1899. I could not go to the Hospital this morning, as I was too unwell. George went to pay visits to the Maharajas of Bharatpur and Dholpur, who came to Durbar yesterday. He afterwards went to the Jail to see carpets, and then back to Camp at 1 to receive six small Rajahs in Durbar. At 2.45 we started on a long drive to Akbar's[4] city, Fatehpur Sikri. It was a 24 mile drive, and I thought it would kill me, but I was determined to go. The drive was through a fine avenue of trees the whole way, and we had changes of artillery teams, so we flew along, and I felt much better in spite of my remains of chill. We got to Fatehpur Sikri at half past five. George and I are living in the Palace enclosure at Akbar's Prime Minister's house, which is a beautiful eight-roomed red sandstone house *exquisitely* carved. The girls are living in the house Akbar built for his Christian wife. It is decorated in crude frescoes: one is supposed to be the Annunciation, another the Garden of Eden, but your imagination has to supply most of the pictures. After dinner, which I had in my room, we went to see the mosque illuminated: it was magnificent, and Sulim Sheikh Akbar's holy man's tomb was absolutely beautiful seen by moon and lamps. The marvellous open work, glistening marble and the mother-of-pearl tomb I shall never forget.

Friday, 8th December 1899. All the morning we marched round Akbar's extraordinary palaces, temples, baths, summer houses, zenanas [apartments for women], astrologers' roosts, halls of audience, and Sulthanas' houses. Akbar's bedroom, or the palace of dreams, the pavilion, or palace of the winds, are one more amazing than the other. The whole of Akbar's life can be traced, and the place is an immortal monument to him. The town has been deserted since Akbar's day, as the water supply was bad and his successors would not live there. So all but the palace enclosure has perished, but all the houses inside that are in almost perfect preservation. The girls went back to Agra at 12, but George and I stopped on, going everywhere with Mr Smith the Archaeologist who is restoring parts of the palace. . . .

Saturday, 9th December 1899. After lunch we drove 8 miles to Sikandra, where Akbar is buried in the most *magnificent* tomb, which is an immense erection of three stories of carved red sandstone, and the fourth is a jewel of carved marble; and at the top, with the sky for a canopy, is the great Akbar's cenotaph (his body is below), a jewel of marble work, and at the head of it a marble column in which the Koh-i-noor used to be set and shed its radiance on the tomb. The climb to the top was a grind, but we got up. In the gardens of Sikandra the Agra residents gave us a garden party under the biggest shadiest trees I have seen for a long time.... George presented Sir Pertab with his CB and made him a charming little speech. He took me in to supper, and talked the funniest English, which I could not understand. The Maharajas of Baratpur and Dholpur came and the [illegible] was covered with gorgeous pearls. He brought his two little boys: the one of six was a little dear; he was very sleepy and lay down on the sofa and went fast asleep, and remained oblivious to the noise of the party for the whole evening. His pagri, or turban, which was a mass of jewels lay on the floor by his side, & I stationed a guard over him as we all went to supper and left him alone fearing his emeralds the size of eggs might vanish in the night.

Sunday, 10th December 1899. Soon after breakfast Captain Baker-Carr took me to Itmad-ud-daulah's tomb. He was Jehangir's[5] father-in-law as Noor-Mahal was his daughter-in-law, and when he died she wanted to build him a silver tomb, but she was told that so precious a tomb would be defiled by vandals, so she built it of marble instead, and made it one of the most beautiful things in Agra.... This afternoon Captain Marker and Captain Baker-Carr and I went to the Taj.[6] I had seen it once but it is so exquisite that we went again, and climbed a minaret. No words of mine can give any idea of the Taj. It is the most divine creation of a building in the whole world, and it quite silences my meagre descriptive powers by its appalling beauty. After dinner, on our way to the station, we went again to the Taj, and saw it by faint moonlight. It seems more lovely and ethereal in this light. At 11 we got in the train and slept on board, and left for Cawnpore at 6 on Monday morning.

Monday, 11th December 1899. We got to Cawnpore at 11.30 and drove to the Mutiny Memorial Well. The solemnity of it was marred by the most garrulous guide. The figure of the angel is dwarfed by the immense screen which is built round the well into which the women and children were thrown,[7] but the whole monument and fine gardens are effective. George and I parted here, he going to the Government harness and leather factories, and I to the Dufferin Hospital. After seeing it I went to the Ghat where the English in boats were shot by the Mutineers,[8] then to the Memorial Church, and back to the train, and at 2.30 we left for Lucknow. The horses in my carriage ran away, and nearly ran over a level crossing, over which a train passed just as the horses were pulled up: so it was a very narrow escape. I was not frightened but Col. Fenn nearly had apoplexy & I stood on the front of the carriage and got a hold of one rein which the coachman had dropped....

Tuesday, 12th December 1899. We spent the morning going over the Residency which is very harrowing. Several Mutiny veterans were standing on the lawn, and George looked at their medals. . . .

This is all for this week darling Papa. I am hard worked as you see but am alive & pretty well. I fear Mamma will have gone when this reaches you.

Your loving
Mary

1 (1844–1922), Indian statesman and soldier who relinquished his rule in 1911 as Maharaja of Idar to assume the regency of Jodhpur. He was pro-British and it is said that when the First World War broke out Sir Pertab 'would not be denied his right to serve the King-Emperor in spite of his 70 years', and he actually came to France and commanded the Jodhpur Lancers.

2 The form taken by Vishnu (the solar god) and widely worshiped in northern India.

3 (1618–1707), a Mogul emperor whose name, with unintentional irony no doubt, translates as 'ornament of the throne'. Inhumanly biased in religious views, Aurangzeb reigned for forty-six years, many of them spent in rapine and bloodshed. A measure of his filial piety is evinced by his eight-year incarceration at Agra of his father who, however, was allowed the amenity of a harem in his seclusion.

4 Jellaladin Mahommed Akbar (1542–1605), another Mogul emperor. Reputedly wise, merciful and conciliatory – rare adjectives for rulers of this period – Akbar was also a land reformer and patron of letters. He died at Agra and is extravagantly entombed, as Lady Curzon records, at nearby Sikandra.

5 The son and successor of Akbar and the father of Shah Jahan.

6 Plans for the Taj Mahal were initiated by Shah Jahan upon the death of his favourite wife, Mumtaz Mahal ('the chosen one of the palace'). Curzon was instrumental in the conservation and refurbishment of the Taj Mahal and donated an exquisite bronze lamp inlaid with gold and silver to be hung there.

7 The site of perhaps the most atrocious carnage of the Indian Mutiny. A short, brilliantly evocative account of the killing of June–July 1857 appears in Jan Morris' *Heaven's Command*. Cawnpore became emblematic of the primitive despoliation of Victorian womanhood and of the atavistic propensities of suppressed 'natives'. Morris notes that the well and the angel have disappeared and that, in 1971, no 'hush of elegy' hung over the thriving city.

8 The ultimate in betrayal, as in horror, was the slaughter of some five hundred soldiers in the very boats to which they had been taken in 'safe conduct' for egress. About a hundred women and children were separated from the rest and later butchered on the afternoon of 15 July 1857 and their remains hurled into what became the Memorial Well.

15 December 1899   GOVERNMENT HOUSE
                                                      CALCUTTA

Precious Papa & Mamma:

Thursday, 14th December 1899. I stayed in my room and wrote to Her
Majesty, and did all my mail letters, and at 1 went down to see Lady MacDonnell, who is the most sympathetic delightful woman.

At 3 a Rani, who is in strict purdah, came to see me. Her Sedan chair was
brought to the door, and she popped into the drawing room, wearing huge
Turkish trousers of bright pink, a white jacket, and at least 60 yards of bright
blue gauze wound about and dragging behind her; and on her head a very
quaint silver ornament, four arms of a Dutch windmill, eight inches across,
fastened on her forehead, and two wreaths of silver flowers forming a kind of
hat. Her hair was parted up the back, and bunched amidst the silver roses on
the top of her head. She spoke a little English, and I asked her how long it had
taken her to come in her litter, expecting her to say five minutes, but she said
twenty years! She said to Lady MacDonnell that her health was poor, and
Lady MacDonnell asked her from what she was suffering. She replied, 'Me
inside out'. The trial of looking grave was terrific, and as soon as she had gone
we roared with laughter. I forgot to say she had white silk gloves on, with
rings on each finger over the glove. . . .

                                                      Your loving
                                                      Mary

11 January 1900   GOVERNMENT HOUSE
                                                      CALCUTTA

My darling Mamma:

I think this will get to you before the girls. They left me very well and I
have had telegrams to say they had got to Ceylon well & safe. I am glad
because the weather is so awful & it tried Daisy very much indeed in
Calcutta. She will tell you that she wanted to die it was so hot & miserable &
muggy & she suffered poor darling from neuralgia terribly. When you come
out to visit me it must be to Simla. I honestly think the climate in the plains
would kill you. . . .

I am pretty well and very very busy – never a day without various duties
and the constant entertaining is slavery but we go through with it gladly as it
is a duty. . . . Irene is very well & sweet & everyone loves her. Everard
Baring[1] our new Military Secretary and all the ADCs make love to her & she
shows calm indifference to them all. My new nurse is very nice indeed & the
only trouble which can befall me now is that one of them should marry which
would be terrible. My maid is too plain to marry but all women somehow do

marry out here as they are so few. I have written to tell Mrs Talbot you and the girls are in Cairo and also Lady Rodd. If they ask you to anything address their envelopes The Hon. Mrs Talbot and Lady Rodd and Mrs Talbot will I hope be nice to you – she is one of those chilly critical British women but nice – don't let any one of them draw you about me as all English women are ready to pounce as my being here excites such jealousy in many hearts. I hope you are well my darling & that the sea has done you good. I wrote you to Naples.

Your ever loving
Mary

1 The Hon. Everard Baring (1865 –1932) of the 10th Hussars was the Viceroy's Military Secretary until 1905. In 1904 he married Lady Ulrica Duncombe – known to her friends as Mouche – who appears later in this book.

8 February [1900]   GOVERNMENT HOUSE
                                                      CALCUTTA

My darling Papa:
   We are very sad today as the Commander-in-Chief Sir William Lockhart is dying I fear, and he is a true friend to us so we feel his illness very much. You will hear long before you receive this if he has pulled through. . . .
   I am going through an awful scathing in the papers & in society for 'giving my sisters undue importance'. The world is a miserable carping place & even such papers as *Vanity Fair* have raged at the 'royal rank given a Vicereine's sister'; is it not cruel to think one can't be human about one's own family! It will all be forgotten I hope before long and don't let the meanness of it distress you as I fear you must have seen it in the American papers. I am going to send the babies to Simla the end of this month as the heat is very great here. I cannot go with them as my duty is with George unless they need me and then I would fly at once.
   Goodbye for today my precious darling Father.

Your loving
Mary

9 February 1900   GOVERNMENT HOUSE
                                                      BARRACKPORE

All my *Darlings* & specially twenty-four year old *Nan*:
   I have written you so much of our doings and entertainments that I am going to devote this to accounts of ourselves & our daily habits. We are getting used to Indian customs and peculiarities. Everything is wonderfully peaceful and tranquil and no one is ever in a hurry. Everyone has a quantity

of attendants and each of these has his special occupation and his caste only permits him to do that *one*. One man heats your bathwater, another brings it & a third pours it into the tub – a fourth empties it and he being low caste does the objectionable things which no drains necessitate – quite a different lot wait on you at breakfast and there is a waiter for every person at table. The result is that the waiting is *admirably* done – and they all glide about in red livery & bare feet and a dinner of a 100 – or one of 8 – are wonderfully smooth and perfect, and the immense number of native servants in the house are all under the head English steward named Hillier who came out with Lord Lansdowne,[1] he literally does everything – he is steward, butler, and housekeeper and an invaluable man. George and I each have a high caste attendant who sits outside our doors & attends us wherever we go. My swell's name is Ramdas, and whenever we drive out he sits up in the rumble behind the Great barouche & behind him stands a Syce – two postillions in front two outriders, eight body guards & one officer & a policeman so it takes eighteen people besides the ADC *in* the carriage to take a Viceroy out. Irene and Cynthia have quite an army and every one does nothing, but it is part of the magnificence. Last night we dined at the Comm. in Chiefs – we arrived with an ADC and the Military Sec. & the Comm. in Chief & his staff met us at the carriage door & conducted us into the house while the band played 'God save the Queen'. We shook hands with all the guests, went in to dinner & sat at the head of the table. I had to make the move to leave the table, & for all the fuss & ceremony we might as well be monarchs. The society in Calcutta is very pleasant and the Anglo-Indian is full of interest – but Calcutta is just like any other modern capital excepting that it has *nothing* to interest the tourist and no sightseeing, so there is nothing for anyone to do besides society. I go over hospitals and schools and houses, and I see all sorts of people in audience and I am getting used to everyone curtseying.

Some *awful* people *insisted* on being asked to the ball at Gov. House last Thursday, a Mr & Mrs Jack *Latta* of Chicago. They got the American Consul to write and say they expected to be asked just as though I were the wife of an American Minister abroad upon whom they looked as a creature paid to entertain them. They appeared, Mrs Latta wearing an immense Scotch plaid *day* dress *turned* in at the neck. I had seen her at polo with the same dress in the afternoon. If I am overrun with such people I shall have to tell the Consul that only those who bring letters to me or are known to me or whom he recommends *can* be asked to Government House. For this last ball there were Mr & Mrs & Miss Bucknell, Col. & Mrs Dick & Miss Bakewell, Mr & Mrs Latta – Mr Simmons of Cleveland – Mr & Mrs Anderson; all but Mrs Latta were civilized but her Scotch plaid with each plaid over a foot square in green & brown & red I shall never forget! Gen. Patterson the Consul is very nice *indeed* and his wife is pretty and charming. Calcutta is a destructive place for clothes; it is much dirtier here than London and there is just as much smoke –

my white dresses I can only wear three times & I am sending a box off to Boidin soon. The heat is not bad at all, it is just beginning to be a little warm but the house is *cold*, and I wear flannel all over me, and always carry a wrap: it is a great place to wear capes and wraps in. Irene is very well and sweet and Cynthia is an *angel*. I sent you a photo by Mrs Anderson which we had taken in Bombay – and I have told the Private Secretary to have every paper sent you that describes our doings and also to send you the weekly picture paper called *The Empress*. Garland my maid gets on well out here and seems happy and now has found French pals in some little sisters of the poor who come from Brittany. She has ample milk for Cynthia, who is the fattest fairest little butter ball you ever saw – she loves me, and always takes my *face* in both her hands and bites it all over so that I have a regular bath. Irene always wants to be loved and cuddled just as much as Cynthia, though in old days she never used to have time to be loved.

The ADCs are devoted to her especially Lord Suffolk and Captain Marker; they often go and have tea with her or bring her birds or pets. Lord Suffolk shewed her the little bears the other day & lifted one up for her to pat when the miserable beast began a cascade of various descriptions all over the floor. This was the last of the bears.

I shall go to Simla the beginning of next month or just as soon as it gets warm here....

1 The 5th Marquess of Lansdowne (1845–1927), Viceroy of India 1888–94, Foreign Secretary 1900–5. Opinions of his abilities were decidedly mixed.

27 February 1900   GOVERNMENT HOUSE
                                                            CALCUTTA

Darling Papa:

We have been intensely glad to hear of Lord Roberts' victory as it lifts a weight of care and anxiety off our Indian shoulders.[1] All England's enemies wait to pounce in a moment of weakness and we have been fearing the Russian who was getting bold while he watched successive disasters – and now gallant little Lord Roberts has gone out and lifted England from the most dangerous dilemma she has ever been in. While all the other generals were being beaten & outgeneraled he has defeated Cronje who is the ablest fighter of them all.

Our famine and plague are as bad as can be and I don't know what will become of India if rain does not come next summer, it will mean total annihilation of whole provinces – in Rajputana where the flower of the Indian race comes from they have had no rain for three years – their wells are dry, 96 percent of their cattle dead – their fowls & animals dead too, & they are living in millions on relief works. The English won't let any one die in India and nature brings scourge & every disaster which they battle with one after the other – in olden days this enormous population was kept down by barbarities such as burning widows – infanticide – wars – snake bites – & wild animals & famine & pestilence. Now every one of these things is combated and people are *made* to live with the result that there are more than the soil can support. It is a problem!

The babies are well & write me every day. Simla is a fine place for them and very cold and bracing now. We are going to Assam this week and I will write you from there & tell you all we do. I am drinking cocoa now so you will be convinced, darling Papa, that I have at last struck the elixir of life! God bless you.

> Your devoted
> Mary

1 Roberts' defeat of the grimly indomitable Boer, General Piet Cronje, at Paardeberg (near Bloemfontein) in February 1900 was a significant victory in the South African war.

27 February 1900   GOVERNMENT HOUSE
                                                              CALCUTTA

Darling Mamma & Nancy & Daisy:

I was rejoiced to get letters from Mamma & Nancy this week. The boon of letters grows greater every month. I live so isolated a life that my only comfort is letters from my darlings. I haven't the babies to make me happy now and I miss them terribly....

Yesterday I had a hard day – I went to the women's friendly Society meeting where I bought rubbish and heard a report & a speech then the Dufferin Fund meeting, a report of which I send you, and then a dinner of seventy people in the evening and complete weariness to me of soul & body after it all. My life is real hard work I can tell you.

Take care in Paris to keep out of the herd of Fast Americans who will swoop down on you and don't ever let Daisy & Nancy dine at restaurants. The only times I *ever* went to a restaurant was to *Voisins* with you & once to Bignon's to a private room with Papa to dine with the Jack Gardners![1] Restaurants are so fast in Paris & in these wicked days girls must be so careful. I have written Daisy a long loving letter about Paris & how this year of all others to keep her level head screwed on the right way.

If you spend all your money sweetheart & put your jewels in pawn (! ! ! !) just cable me & I will get the Indian treasury to buy them. The girls know how awfully I need a brooch or some stomach adornment and if you see any windfall [?] I will sell some Viceregal belongings and make a plunge and buy it. I shall never be a swell again and my 'busam' is yearning for 'jools' – paste not scorned.

Capt. Marker started for South Africa & only got a few miles in his ship when the war office ordered him home to London so he is now going there poor man. Goodbye my darlings – I have such a headache I can't write any more.

Your loving
Mary

1 Jack Gardner was a wealthy, clubbable New Englander of impeccable lineage; but it was his wife, Isabella Stewart Gardner (1840–1924) who illuminated – perhaps electrified – whatever she touched. Social Boston gossiped maliciously about 'Mrs Jack' but it seldom refused her invitations, and she was encircled by such Yankee intellectuals as Henry Adams, Charles Eliot Norton and the James brothers (William and Henry). Whistler, Sargent and, in particular, Bernard Berenson assisted in building her splendid art collection, which was finally housed in Fenway Court, Boston's only palazzo and a wonder to behold. Stories of her eccentricity are legion.

Although Lady Curzon as recently as October 1900 wrote that 'I get wearied by this incessant entertaining six months in Simla three in Calcutta and three on tour', she once more accompanied her husband in that same autumn on his exacting six-thousand-mile journey around the south-western Indian peninsula, a progress that took them through modern and medieval India as well as to the deteriorating remnants of Portuguese imperialism in Diu and Goa. Tours of this sort were continuously undertaken and enjoyed, particularly by Lord Curzon, for they appealed to his interests in politics, archaeology, architecture, philosophy and society. Lady Curzon quite naturally shared many of these concerns, but her presence on the tours may be partly attributed to her sense of duty and to her affection for the Viceroy.

Her account of the south-western tour, which commences with their departure from Karachi, is lively for it is an entertaining mixture of the hilarious, the grotesque and the embarrassingly inelegant that so often characterizes Indian life : the guns fail to fire properly, language barriers occasion absurdity, local authorities appear in Ruritanian garb and lack of dignity reduces one episode after another to the level of farce. Yet occasionally a serious note is struck, as in the visit to the Renaissance churches of Old Goa or the synagogues at Cochin.

On this particular tour the Viceroy frequently visited places demanding expenditures of energy beyond Lady Curzon's strength, so she would often rest whilst he pursued a special obligation or interest. Near the end of the south-western tour Lady Curzon, understandably exhausted, elected to return to Calcutta from Madras by sea whilst her husband progressed up the east coast by train. Their separate arrivals in

Calcutta were followed shortly thereafter by the death of Queen Victoria in January 1901. Six weeks later Lady Curzon sailed for an extended stay in Europe.

6 November 1900   VICEROY'S CAMP
                                                          [*en route* to Goa]

My darlings all:

We left Karachi on Tuesday morning after a night of great dissipation, as Mr James gave a kind of evening garden party. Conjurors were eating fire and cutting out their tongues in one place – air balloons going up in the flower beds – and fireworks going off on the lawn. We spent the entire evening, until nearly 12, roaming about from one show to the other, until I was dead beat. The next morning I had a blinding headache, and in spite of it had to smile, and handshake, and say goodbye to everyone, as we boarded the *Clive*, which was moored alongside an elaborately decorated wharf. The yards were manned and bands played and the crowd cheered, and there was the usual red carpet and flowers and 'farewelling'. We got under weigh about 9, and had a long very hot day sailing down the coast to *Kutch*, where we anchored next morning. . . .

We stopped next at *Diu*, a small Portuguese town on the coast which was captured by a Portuguese pirate in 1526. This gallant warrior sailed into Diu harbour and invited the Governor of the town to come aboard his ship. The innocent agent of Akbar did so, and as he was returning to shore his Portuguese host shot him in the back and then took the town. In those days Diu was an important trading centre, and the Portuguese proceeded to build a very fine fort and several large picturesque Renaissance Churches, but as a seeming vengeance for the dastardly method of capturing the town, it has dwindled into an insignificant little hole with no trade and no shipping, and it can't be reached by rail, or sea, unless the Governor comes in a gunboat! So life at Diu must be a living death. The Governor, who is a sickly Portuguese, came in a dilapidated barge to meet us. He was in fullest dress and knelt on one knee when he bowed over my Viceregal hand! George, Mr Lawrence, Major Baring and I went off with him in his barge (which we were told was not seaworthy) and we sat under a blue and white awning which rested on our heads. The sea was rough, and as we rowed along the walls of the fortress George's thirty-one guns began going off in our ears. The guns were so old that only luck prevented them from bursting, and the wads of the charges flew round our heads. On shore a phalanx of Goanese signors met us wearing evening clothes and billycock, or obsolete opera hats, and we had to look grave while our sides were bursting with laughter. The Governor's wife also met us. She was a Portuguese from *Shanghai*, and she *spoke* English, *looked* Chinese, and *fanned* herself like a Spaniard. A band played 'God save the Queen' in a Diu rendering, the Diu army performed feats on a bugle, and we then started to process through the town on foot, as no horse could live at Diu. George walked ahead with the full dressed Governor – I behind with the Governess and another tiny woman, who spoke no known language and fluttered a fan whenever I addressed her with my smile. All the brilliant staff and the black Marquises straggled along until we reached the *Palace*. The army in the meantime had passed us at a quick march and was playing 'The Queen' when we got to the door. We stopped only a moment in the bleakest palace on earth, then processed to the Fort – I still supported on either side by the hopping ladies, who perspired fearfully and fanned like mad. They implored me to get into a palanquin [light litter], which I did to spare them apoplexy, and I was thus carried to the Fort. The Diu army again passed us at a quick march, and as we entered the ruined fortress bugles brayed, dogs howled, and the tired ranks presented arms with shaking knees. We went all over the Fort, and I even walked around the castellated parapet, jumping over the gaps just to make the little ladies die of fright, as they came too, and skipped over the chasms into the arms of the brilliant Staff with heartrending little screams. After the Fort we walked to the Jesuit Church, in which was some splendid old wood carving; then back to the palace, where we sat on high-backed chairs and drank the health of the King of Portugal in tea made of straw and sweet champagne. It is impossible to describe the amusing scene in the audience room of the palace with all of us sitting in a row. George was so hot that his collar had gone, and he was fanning himself with an immense red satin fan. Immediately facing him sat the little lady who couldn't talk. I sat next him, and in front of me was the Governor's wife. Major Baring, Mr Lawrence, and all the rest were ranged down the room *fanning*; no one spoke except the two little ladies, who jabbered to *each other* in Goanese. We were all bordering on hysterics when the Governor, after a thirty minute wait, flew into the room followed by tea poured out – filled with milk and sugar – in mugs on trays. We drank it in solemn silence, and I looked as though I had lost an aunt, while the Staff retired to the balcony and dissolved in laughter. We then formed in procession again and walked to the beach, the army for the last time doing quick march past us, and when we were about to embark the Governor explained that the army was in a state of collapse and could barely salute, as it had never in its life had such a long march. Our whole walk had not been three quarters of a mile! We bade farewell to Portugal and were rowed to the *Clive* in the moonlight in one of our own boats, and we laughed the whole way and all agree that the Diu visit is our crowning spectacular farce....

Yr devoted
Mary

My darlings all:

...*Monday, November 12th*. We sailed into Goa harbour this morning at 8. It is one of the most lovely harbours I have ever seen – a perfect three quarter circle with high hills all round. Marmagao is a place consisting of one old house turned into a Railroad station, and four gaunt red iron sheds looking into the sea over the heads of a few Goanese asleep in some timeworn railroad trucks. The line goes along the coast here, and we watched for George's train to appear through telescopes. While waiting, Portuguese officials in rusty full dress uniforms kept coming off in barges to pay their respects, and I was fortunately on deck at 8, as Colonel Fenn, Captain Baker-Carr and Captain Wilkinson couldn't speak French, and the officials could not speak English. So I spoke to them in French, but this was hopeless, as their French is unlike any I ever heard. Just when we were despairing the State Secretary appeared, in a barge rowed by twenty men in red, with high silver helmets on their heads glistening like teapots in the sun; came alongside; and after much yelling came on deck. He was enormously fat, wore evening dress, a 'dicky' tied with tapes to his disappearing collar, and a dilapidated top hat. He was surrounded by a Staff, and they all sat round me in a circle, while I talked to the fat man, who claimed the intimate friendship of M. de Soveral[1] – but I had my doubts as to the intimacy when he said that Soveral was so great a friend of the Prince of Wales that he always called him Albert Edward! This man wanted to spend the morning on the *Clive*, but his perspiring personality was more than I could bear, so I stretched a point and said I *saw* the Viceroy's train arriving so he rushed to his barge to meet the train which wasn't due for over an hour, and I stopped on the cool deck, while all the rest went ashore later to wait for the train, which arrived at 11. The Governor of Goa had not turned up by some mistake, and George had to sit in his stifling carriage for 20 minutes until he came in his launch from across the bay. Then there was an official reception in a tent on the shore, which I watched with a glass, and then George came on board to wait for two hours before the luncheon in the station, which is called a Palace. I did not go ashore as the heat is frightful. After lunch I went on board the Portuguese gunboat and met George, and we sailed across the harbour to *Panjim*, which is only five miles away, but we were 3 hours getting there in the gunboat, which is a silly old tub which can't start under forty minutes and only goes 2 knots an hour. The bulwarks were 7 feet high and we could see nothing, and we sat in a crowd of Portuguese who smoked vile cigars and drank vermouth, and could speak no language we could understand. We were at our last gasp when we reached *Panjim*, where we drove round and round a small public square in a carriage, while the crowd threw fire crackers and squibs under

our horses' feet, howling 'Viva'. It was diabolical. The palace was only
twenty yards away, but we kept driving past in order to make the drive seem
long! In the palace, which consisted of acres of barnlike emptiness, the
Portuguese ladies met us. They were vast and brown, and I never made out
who any of them were, as the introductions were in Portuguese: but a kind
official pointed at first to one lady and then the other and said 'Dat's de
oldest' – 'Dat's de youngest' – and these thus designated were the Governor's daughters I believe. After a sort of levee and George meeting all the
officials in the Throne Room while I sat in a row with the ladies, we drove to
our residence, which was five miles away. It was *pitch* dark, and there was no
escort – only two wild creatures acting as outriders, who yelled and whooped
and ran down every carriage we met. The Natives there lighted fireworks,
which exploded like bombs under our carriage, and when I remonstrated
with the Portuguese who was with us he only said 'Dey mean it for ze best'.
The horses were too miserable to run away, so we drove over bursting squibs
and bombs and resigned ourselves to the inevitable. The house we are to stay
in is called Cabo, and used to be a nunnery when Goa was a flourishing place
in the sixteenth century. The comforts have remained mediaeval, and the
night and day we spent in inside rooms swarming with red ants, and no
sanitary arrangements of any sort, made the most ghastly experience we have
had in India. We stayed in this place until Tuesday afternoon, and as my
bedroom was over the poultry yard I got no sleep. George said most of the
party started for old Goa at 2, but as they went by the awful gunboat I elected
to go by road instead, and Major Baring went with me, and we drove 11 miles
and got to old Goa just as the gunboat did, although we left two hours after it!

The beauty of the five churches in old Goa repays us for all we have gone
through in order to see them. They are magnificent Renaissance Italian
Churches, built about 1543. One is built to St Francis Xavier,[2] who is buried
in a marvellous silver tomb in a beautiful chamber filled with pictures describing his life and miracles. The gilded wood carving in this church, which
is called *Bom Jesus*, is gorgeous; and the other four churches, which are built
around a fine open square, are one as beautiful as the other, and the church
plate and vestments magnificent. Old Goa consists only of these five
churches: the town has disappeared and is now only a jungle, and no human
being ever comes here except when there is a pilgrimage to the Xavier tomb.
Then thousands come, as local Hindus and Mohammedans as well as Cath-
olics believe in the miracle-working powers of the Saint. Every ten years he is
taken from his tomb in his mummified state and displayed to the pilgrims,
but as one devout *devoté* bit off two of his toes once, they display him with
greater care and less often now.

After seeing the churches we drove back to Panjim and again ran the
gauntlet of fireworks hurled under the carriage. Our clothes had been
brought to the Governor's house, Panjim, and here we dressed for the State

banquet. No bath of course, and no blinds to the windows and thousands looking in, so Garland pursued me round the room with a bath towel, which she held in front of me. Nine of the Staff dressed in one small hole with one wash basin, and their clothes laid out on the floor, and an enthusiastic audience gazing in upon nine furious Englishmen trying to dress for a State banquet in this black hole! About 9, after waiting and nearly fainting for an hour of intolerable heat and delay, we sat down at the banquet of 65. We were all placed according to precedence strictly, and as no one spoke any language his neighbour could understand the dinner passed off in silence, save for two bands, one in the next room and one outside in the street, which played different tunes simultaneously! The Governor made us a speech in Portuguese and George replied in English, and at 11, dead with fatigue, we said Goodbye to our Portuguese hosts and walked to the gunboat through a disorderly crowd. The local police were drunk and one charged the Governor, on whose arm I was hanging (as he insisted on arming me everywhere) and nearly knocked him over. We boarded the gunboat, and no sooner did we start than we ran aground and were stuck for an hour and in absolute despair of ever getting out to the *Clive*, which was lying two miles out to sea. After frantic efforts we got off, and only got to the *Clive*, to which we were rowed in a small boat as the gunboat could not get alongside, at 1.45 a.m.

The whole Goanese visit was too much for me, and I was ill all night, and next day George – who is dead beat too – went to Gersoppa Falls without me, as the long inland journey of 36 miles in a carrying chair through a tropical jungle was more than I could do....

1 The Marquis Luis de Soveral (1862–1922), GCMG, GCVO, Portuguese minister in London 1897–1910. A *bon vivant* and cosmopolite, de Soveral, an intimate of Edward VII, patiently endured that monarch's practical jokes (such as putting medicine in wine glasses and getting people out of bed at unearthly hours). Because of his ugliness de Soveral was known as 'The blue monkey', whereas a sobriquet for the King, 'Tum-Tum', was perhaps slightly less insensitive.
2 (1506–52), a Jesuit missionary known as the 'apostle of the Indies'. He was Ignatius Loyola's choice to succeed as head of the Society of Jesus, a post his early death prevented him from filling.

24 November 1900   VICEROY'S CAMP
                                                  ON BOARD THE *Clive*

Darling Papa & Mamma, Joe, Nancy & Daisy:
Saturday, November 17th. ... As soon as George and his following were on board we sailed for *Cochin*, and reached there Sunday afternoon at 5

o'clock.... We were met on landing by the Raja, who was a kind-looking
man in a long black coat. When he said to me 'I hope you are *doing* well' in
Johnsonian English, I of course thought that he knew – wonderful man –
that I had been ill! But not at all: this was his greeting to everyone. He
sometimes varied it with 'Are you *still* doing well', and once I believe when at
a loss for something to say he turned to the man next to him and said in his
kind voice 'Are you here!'....

What with shouting boatmen and the usual noisy Indian night we got little
sleep. George started out at 7 to see all the sights in the town on the other side
of the lagoon. I only started at 8 and joined him at the Jewish synagogue,
which is the strangest sight in the world. The Jews here claim to have come
here 70 BC, and they can show brass tablets, said to be 400 AD, showing that a
colony of Jews *were* here then. The White Jews pride themselves on never
having married amongst the Natives and they have inbred for hundreds of
years, and when the race seems likely to die out brethren and damsels are
imported from Baghdad. We only went to one synagogue, but in the Jewish
quarter there are many and black Jews and yellow Jews worship in them. The
Chief Rabbi conducted us about and showed us the sacred Scroll of the book
of Moses. He blessed us and the Maharaja (who had joined us) and we
received his blessing gratefully. The Jewesses were looking at us from a
gallery, and I suppose I am one of the few women who has ever trod the tiles
of this synagogue. The tiles, by the way, were Chinese willow pattern and
very pretty and the hangings on the walls lovely gold and silver....

Trivandrum, November 21st. I fear my language can never rise to a sufficient pitch of eloquence to describe our journey from Quilon to Trivandrum! Each of us had a boat like a Lord Mayor's barge, a cabin, a roof to sit
on, and twenty rowers. Our following is so enormous that we needed 40
boats, which made a procession a mile long. Well, at 9.30 we embarked, and
as it was early I elected to go with George and sit on his roof till bed time. So
we floated along, watching the crowds on the bank running along with
torches. After half an hour we needed an umbrella as it began to rain, and I
called to my barge behind for one. The barge came alongside and I took the
umbrella, and then for some inexplicable reason the boat disappeared into
the night, going ahead at full speed. We thought nothing of it at the time, as
it might have been a manoeuvre to allow us to get under weigh, but when the
rain began to pour, and I began to long to go to my own bed – no boat! Then
we began to shout for Major Baring to tell him my boat had disappeared. *His*
in the meantime had *stuck* and was last in the procession, and it took him 30
minutes to come. By this time my despair had become desperate, and the
confusion of the block of 40 houseboats in a solid mass awful, everyone
shouting as loud as he could, and every member of the party who had gone to
bed emerged on the roof of his boat in night clothes and a huge stick and
hammered every boat that tried to pass him. It was so grotesque that I could

have laughed till I cried but for the loss of my boat.... As soon as the river broadened into a lagoon the 40 boats began to race, and no one can believe what the noise was. All the boats were flying to get to a tunnel we had to go through. Fancy 40 boats at the entrance of one very narrow tunnel! Such a banging and bumping and inextricable muddle, and we seemed hours going through the most horrid tube, full of bats and smells, and every boatman screaming to keep off evil spirits. Gustave Doré could perhaps have depicted the scene, and likened it to the River Styx and a journey to Hell. I was never more relieved than when the sun rose after that night of horror, but when it did the stillness was wonderful. The rowers had screamed away their lungs, there was only the splash of the oars, and no boat of any kind was in sight, and for two hours I lay watching the unearthly vegetation of the river banks: enormous palms and creepers, and flowers as big as your head, mammoth lilies and orchids all hanging heavy after a night of rain. Here at last was the India of one's dreams, and it only needed pythons suspended from the branches and bison and wild elephants to complete the picture....

Love to all my darlings
Yr devoted
Mary

PART II

The letters of
Lord and Lady Curzon,
1901

Some seventy letters, many of unbridled length, were exchanged between Lord and Lady Curzon during the six months from March to September 1901 that she spent in Europe. The first few weeks of that time were passed on the Continent, in the south of France and in Paris; but by early May she reached London, at the height of the social season, and was of course immediately absorbed into the privileged and aristocratic circles. Her reasons for leaving the Viceroy for so long – their separation is a constant motif in the letters that follow – centre on the welfare of their two small daughters (the 'itty girls' in the 'little language' of the family) and on her poor health. Yet another reason for the home visit was to renew and maintain political and social links with the English ruling classes. In those days India seemed very far away indeed, communications were limited, and within the Viceregal term of five years a man could be, if not forgotten, certainly set aside. In this respect Lady Curzon was an admirable ambassadress, although some claim her American heritage rendered her blind to the subtleties of British politics.

As a candid picture of the Edwardian scene Lady Curzon's letters possess an individual quality, for her perspective is novel, her eye sharp, and her concern keen: in Curzon's replies, too, one notes his respect for her understanding of the Victorian aftermath that expired only with the First World War. Indeed, her survey of upper-class Edwardian society in its tainted bloom is in itself a social document. True, she relays trivial gossip about the Atherton divorce case, complains about poor vintages, and makes light of Mary Elcho's possessive jealousy of Arthur Balfour,* soon to be Prime Minister. Neither is the notorious Mrs Keppel* overlooked, nor the caprices of the wheezing, baccarat-playing Edward VII; in fact, Lady Curzon's letter about her Windsor visit is perhaps the most engrossing of this series. The tapestry is rich and the eye scrutinizing it unerring.

To add to the social picture there are sharply limned portraits of prominent political figures and shrewd appraisals of the bumptious young Winston Churchill* and the 'Hooligans', the mediocre St John Brodrick* who would take over the India Office in 1903 and with whom Curzon was eventually to break a lifelong friendship, and the one-time Secretary of State for India, George Hamilton,* for whom Lady Curzon had markedly little respect. Notable, too, is her friendship with Alfred Milner,* the great South African proconsul, and with Arthur Balfour whose admiration and respect for her were boundless. And she is alert to the complexities of parliamentary debate, the problems of the Boer War, and the pettiness of party strife. Yet another theme of primary importance is India, as one sees Lady Curzon constantly deploring the ignorance of India in and out of Cabinet; indeed, her emphasis upon this heightens for the reader the enormity of Curzon's problems. It is during this period that the Viceroy's quarrel with Mackworth Young (the renegade Lieutenant-Governor of the Punjab) erupted, and undoubtedly Lady Curzon's advice and support gave her husband strength and confidence in dealing with a particularly unpleasant problem. Above all, though, it is her analysis of the London social scene that is most interesting in conveying to Curzon the political situation and in underlining her puritan disapproval of upper-class *decadence. Her letters of this period, therefore, differ in tenor from those written from India.*

Lord Curzon's letters, on the other hand, whilst more heavily weighted than his wife's and lacking her exuberance, still show a sharp sense of lively phrasing: for example, in describing a staff member as 'a gravestone with a moustache hung on in front in place of an inscription' and the man's wife as 'a custard pudding' and the worthy Mrs Barnes as 'flat-bottomed as ever'. He can also write a gossipy letter, although he is less anecdotal than Lady Curzon, to whom, in more serious vein, he turns for approval and support over his Budget Speech, his stand vis-à-vis the resentful Mackworth Young, or his difficulties with the antagonistic Hensman, Times *correspondent in India. Early in his letters to Lady Curzon he writes graphically about a tiger-hunt and describes in detail the etiquette of that bizarre activity. Again, the key changes abruptly as he laments his solitude and despair without her. In fact, much of the complexity of the man is revealed in these intimate exchanges, which show the human being within the Viceroy; and his letters give credence to Jan Morris' discerning remark that 'his disdain was remembered by many, his fun by only a few'.*

Another striking feature of the 1901 correspondence is the solitude and loneliness underlying the exchanges, the isolation each feels in being apart from the other. If, indeed, the use of such nicknames as 'Kinkie', 'Pap', and 'Pappy' induces smiles or if Curzon falls into the third person – 'No Kinkie to share poached eggs with' – it is simply that such language cloaks a deep, enduring affection. It also appears that as soon as Lady Curzon left India she was making plans for her return, much as the country disagreed with her physically; again and again she alludes to sailing dates and ponders the most convenient and agreeable places for their reunion. A further indication of a marital state happier than most is the constant reference to family life, to child-bearing, and to her hopes of giving him the son he wished for. Throughout the letters of 1901 there is an unabated sense of lasting affection and heightened physical attraction between Lord and Lady Curzon.

25 March [1901]   ss *India*

Darling darling Pappy:

This is only Monday – four days since I was torn from Pappy – and it seems a month. I hope my weeks won't keep on feeling like years, as I shall be as white as Mrs Aikman who is sitting opposite to me, before I come back. Well, Angel we got to Bombay, quite breathless after our breakneck-speed journey, and the train had hardly stopped before in popped Lady Northcote, brimming with smiles and embraces, and 'Aren't they ducks' to the tired itty girls. She took possession of us, & before I knew where we were, we were flying to the Secretariat, one of those fine buildings in Bombay I am always talking about. We had an hour's talk in *Harry's*

Council room, which is adorned by an *immense* Governor's chair in which Harry must look absurd.

I discovered a *distinct* change in Lady N's attitude to Bombay, and its being the pivot of India! She admitted that poor Harry was chagrined at his failure over the Memorial.[1] Although *he* hasn't brought forth a plan, she hasn't been *quite* barren, *&* has raised 10,000 rupees the interest from which is to be given in one or two anna [a coin] donations to *women* leaving hospitals. This handsome bounty will it is supposed lighten their lives, and make them *glow* over such a fine Victorian memorial! Three hundred rupees can only produce diluted drops of gratitude, *&* I can't help wondering *which* of the thousands of women discharged from Hospitals in Bombay are to be selected....

It was very hot *&* I hurried through goodbyes *&* went off to the ship. Captain dragged me up the gangway and shewed me cabins *&* I never moved out of them until we were well out of harbour. I couldn't look at vanishing India, with my Pappy left behind. I felt a tug of war going on in my breast as to whether I should surrender to desolation or endure with the best grace possible. I feel so utterly lonely *&* friendless *&* away from all I love that I had best be serene as no one can help me but myself.

Discovery No. 1 was to find everyone on board waiting in rows to stare as soon as I appeared, so I modestly *dis*appeared. Discovery No. 2 – that our cabins were on the port side of the ship, *&* this spells discomfort in Capital letters as you get the sun all the way all day *&* no air. This was death to any comfort, so I appealed to the purser who said he couldn't think why the company had given me port side cabins. The only unoccupied starboard ones were on the deck below in front of the saloon. These I have moved into, and although I am right away in the bows I am *quite* comfy, *&* nothing can describe the kindness of Captain *&* co, and I believe he would change the route *&* go round by the Cape to be civil if asked.

The girls are very well *&* sweet *&* comforting. I wish Pappy had two to cheer him!

Love from loving
K.

1 With the death of Queen Victoria in January 1901 plans for memorials sprang up Empire wide. Curzon conceived of the Victoria Memorial Hall in Calcutta – at first view alarmingly hybrid, for it is 'Italian Renaissance in style with some Oriental features' – which he envisaged as a tribute to the Queen-Empress and to imperial grandeur. But inter-provincial and inter-capital jealousies, the possible silting-up of the nearby River Hughli, the usual stupid interventions of British politicians and even subsequent Viceregal obstacles all led to a hazardous start for Curzon's cloud-capped scheme. Indeed, not until 1921 was the Memorial Hall formally opened by the then Prince of Wales, later Edward VIII. (Bombay abstained from participation until its own scheme collapsed.) But unquestionably the whole affair

was an impressive tribute to Curzon's political and aesthetic vision, without which many Indian treasures – and a number of English country houses as well – would have deteriorated beyond restoration or simply been lost to subsequent civilizations. His own account of the Victoria Memorial Hall is pungently related in his *British Government in India*.

29 March 1901   VICEROY'S CAMP
                                                                          NEPAL

Darling Kinkie:

I will begin this now, to be continued at intervals till the mail goes. I left Calcutta, pretty well played out, on Wednesday night & travelled in your carriage (in order to test the arrangements). Next morning we came to the Ganges, crossed in a big steam-flat & changed to metre gauge on the other bank. In the middle of the day we arrived at our railway terminus & came on to camp here, 10 miles. There was a Victoria for me, elephants for the rest of the party. We arrived yesterday evening – charming but modest camp (our own tents from Agra) in an open space in midst of low jungle. The party are ourselves, Col. Pears, Col. Gordon (assisting in shoot), and Armstrong (brother of Lady MacDonald of Pekin & formerly doctor in Nepal). A Nepalese Colonel (Harak Jung) small, dapper, fussy, polite & speaking perfect English has been despatched by Nepal Govt. to run the show. Today was our first shoot. They have two hundred and twenty elephants including fifteen from Darbhanga. It has been a very tiring day. In the first place we had to ride at least eight miles on pad elephants [no howdah] to the beat. There is no shade of any sort. The country so far as one can see is an ocean of high reedy grass, through which we march in a line for hours. A tiger was reported to have been marked into a strip of this grass, but we pursued him without success to lunch. Almost directly after lunch he was put up, and trotted across the line about 120 yards in front. I fired twice but I think missed both times. Then the Nepalese plan of ringing the tiger was followed. Our formation of elephants had been

The two rings now advanced & closed in until the formation was   the tiger being presumably inside.

74

I was then moved forward on my howdah elephant inside the ring up to the far end – as per wriggly line – the main lines of elephants closing in behind.

When I got to point x out came the tiger from thick jungle & stood looking at me at 30 yards. I took a steady aim & knocked him over. He was a very big one. After a few moments he pulled himself together and struggled into some bushes further on. Here the idiotic Crespigny,[1] entirely contrary to orders & etiquette twice fired at him & fortunately missed him both times. I then went up on my elephant, and as the brute was still convulsively struggling & roaring put a second bullet into him which finished him off. He was very fat and old and a poor colour (a pale drab), but of a good size, measuring 9 feet 6 inches, much bigger than any of the Lalkua or Gwalior tigers. But he showed no pluck & was so stately in his movements that he might almost have been drugged. Marching home we shot wild boar and hog-deer in the jungle. Portman[2] is so done up that he has been asleep in bed ever since.

It is not nearly so hot as at Lalkua & quite cool at nights. But no shade of any sort. I am afraid that the long tramps on 'pads' would have quite knocked you up. Writzler is not nearly so good in camp as he was in a city, but is immensely civil & fusses about.

I send you the remarks of *Capital* on Budget Speech. Of course the *Pioneer* passes it over without comment, though the *Daily News* says it was the most remarkable speech ever delivered at the Council Table. Now I am tired out & am going to bed only sorry that Kinkie is not there to solace poor old dilapidated Pap.

March 30. Saturday night. Our second day over. We started at 9 and after one and half hours on pad elephants came to a place in the great sea of waving grass where a tiger was said to have been ringed. The elephants were in a circle all round. Col. Pears & I went in to point x & stood waiting in our howdahs. The circle was about 300 yards across. Nothing but dense grass 12– 15 feet high inside. A small party of six pad elephants then beat steadily round & round inside the circle. Not a sign, not a sound. Then the outer circum- ference of the circle gradually wedged in closer & closer to me. Meanwhile our side of the ring backed steadily so as to stand to give room to shoot without risk inside the circle. This went on for three-quarters of an hour and there did not seem an inch of the ground that had not been ransacked & trampled by the elephants over & over again. Suddenly with the familiar roar out she (a tigress) came; she flew in every direction; she charged the elephants; she darted to & fro, bullets flew about. Then she retired & skul- ked and there was another half-hour before she could be moved though she was sitting a few yards by us all. From time to time she roared & made a wild plunge & one caught a passing glimpse of the brown body lurching in the

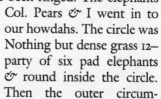

reeds. Then all was quiet again. In these rushes I got one or two shots. Finally she was forced out and plunged across the interior of the circle. Pears and I fired simultaneously & she fell mortally wounded. She had at least four bullets in her, three of which were mine. But I rather think that the mortal wound was given by Pears. Anyhow I said so and gave him the skin. I wish you could have seen the whole sight. It was magnificent: two hundred elephants ringing the little plot of jungle grass & the single beast inside laughing at us for over an hour. This afternoon we came across a huge wild buffalo & filled him with bullets, but he lay down in the dense grass & we could not find him.

The days are very long. We started at 9 a.m. & did not get back till past 6 p.m. Long hours going & coming on the pads. They would kill you. On the other hand it is not nearly as hot as Lalkua, and the tents are delightfully fresh & cool at night. Rop comes out in the most grotesque costumes, the famous baggy grey flannels yesterday with a green Norfolk jacket – white flannels today. Baring, too, is annoying. He is quite vexed at my getting the shots & proposed to me today that I should stay outside & that he & Lawrence should go in & shoot the next tiger between them & then the rest of the staff two by two. I told him I would take them one by one & give them the first shot. Of course he regards the whole shoot as having been organized for the Staff & not for me, and thinks that as I have killed my tiger the remaining ten should kill theirs before I begin again. The man drives me wild with his utter want of regard for me.

I thought that Rop would not last long, & this evening he came solemnly in & asked if I would let him go to Simla to superintend the cutting out from Neville's head of those mysterious things behind the nose (aren't they called adenoids?) which everyone develops nowadays. Lukis had reported that they were affecting the boy *intellectually*. What can this mean, said the innocent Rop? I answered 'By all means go' so he will rush away from the scurry & sweat of camp to Simla. I knew he would. He hasn't got the pluck of a sticklebat.

The *Pioneer* has never printed my big speech, only extracts from it, said not one word about the soldiers' part, & *left that out altogether from its report*. Isn't the whole thing mean?

Reuter reports that the papers at home, not only the *Daily Chronicle* (!), are loud in praise of my Budget Speech. But I very much doubt if Hensman sent a line of it to the *Times*.

Goodnight darling, your so tired

Loving
Pap

Sunday. When the poor tigress was skinned & cut up they found three little ones inside her, nearly ready to be born. Isn't it sad? Today we are all quiet in camp & I am writing. I have written for the first time since I left England to A.J. B[alfour]. Writzler has actually persuaded me to eat some mangoes & they are *delicious*. Fancy my admitting that of any Indian fruit & particularly a mango! But really Writzler's mangoes (from Bombay & well iced) are as unlike our Simla turnips as Pommeroy of '74 is unlike Shandygaff. He also brings up pomphret & other fish daily from Bombay, having a man halfway on the journey to repack them in fresh ice. This is proper organisation.

1 Claude Champion de Crespigny (1873–1910), one of Curzon's aides from December 1900 to January 1902. His relatively early death was perhaps because he was twice wounded, first in the South African wars and soon thereafter whilst serving with the West Africa Frontier Force.
2 Captain the Hon. Gerald Berkeley Portman (1875–1967) of the 10th Hussars, to become in due course the 7th Viscount Portman.

30 March [1901]   SUEZ

My darling Pappy:

We have been 24 hours off Suez waiting for the *Ophir* to come out of the Canal, she has been delayed owing to a sunk dredger, & we have been chafing at the long delay, but we have been rewarded by a splendid view of the *Ophir*. She sailed slowly out of the Canal at ten this morning, and came and anchored alongside of us. The Captain signalled, 'The Captain, officers, passengers & Lady Curzon who is one of them wish Y.R.Hs.[1] a prosperous and safe voyage.' The answer came back 'We thank you all on the *India* for yr. kind wishes. Please thank Lady Curzon for her kind wishes, & wish her for us a pleasant voyage home.' I was on the bridge with the Captain & waved & bowed as we sailed by. I could see them all distinctly. Duchess beautifully *thin* & all in white & *violet*, Duke in uniform on the bridge. Donald Mackenzie [Wallace][2] like a hoary old sheep & Bingy Wenlock very gray.

We have had a wonderfully cool voyage – not one hour of discomfort. The children are well and so am I. Sleeping only fairly on account of incessant night noises.

I had a real good talk with Job Saunders the other day. He is a most enthusiastic supporter – says India has never had such a strong Viceroy – & that this feeling is shared by everyone but the disaffected Simla ring. *He* says that Hensman's life has been a misery at the Bengal Club, as the *Pioneer* represents such a small & mean faction that the majority despise its attitude. He said there was a growing feeling of intense regret at your leaving India in 3 years, and the hope you would stay on was universal. They knew you were needed at the F.O. & couldn't *sacrifice* more than your time of 5 years to India. All this looks fulsome in ink, but as he talked after dinner it seemed only just appreciation.

Have you seen Mr Caine's idiotic remarks in the *Overland Mail* apropos of Memorial & famine; he must be an arch-ass. I am going to get you as many photos & pictures as I can of the most beautiful buildings in Europe, and those that I can't get in England I shall get in Paris if I go there to be painted. . . .

Angel do you see that after seventeen years of girls being born & perfect despair that the Duchess of Leeds has got a *boy*. I read it, & tears jumped up in my eyes at once. No one but a woman who has never borne a boy can know how that other woman's heart felt when the unbelated boy was born. I wonder if I shall ever feel it. I have often had a curious feeling that I should – when I was dying! An ache at the heart certainly keeps one's happiness from losing its sense of proportion. Another piece of news is Alice Crane's father's death. I am sorry for her, but thought him a horrid old man. Darling at Aden I found a letter from I. Lawson from Cannes & one from Blanche[3] saying they were coming to London in May.

I sent you a letter from Springy – there is one word marked which I cannot read – can you?

Darling in Lord Rosebery's* summing up of Napoleon, he exactly describes you. 'In all the offices of state he knew everything, guided everything, inspired everything. . . . His inexhaustible memory made him familiar with all the men – and all the details as well as with all the machinery of government.' Further he says 'The inherent defect of such an executive was that no less an energy or intellect could have kept it (the govt.) going for a week. So completely did it depend on the master that it was paralysed by the least severence from him.' Then – 'he had no assistance from advice, as his ministers were cyphers'. Pappy, pappy, pappy.

Precious angel. I hope you are flourishing in camp, and that Capt. Crespigny has not assassinated Rop! & that all the tigers have come to you.

Itty girls very anxious about 'Daddy left behind'.

All my love – & be kind to *my* Pappy.

Loving & very sad
Kinkie

1 The Duke and Duchess of York, later to be George V and Queen Mary; they toured the Empire – save for India – from March to November of this year.
2 Donald Mackenzie Wallace, who recorded the tour in *The Web of Empire*.
3 Probably the Viceroy's sister, Blanche Felicia (1861–1928), who was to die unmarried.

5 April 1901   ss *India*

Darling:

I shall miss this post entirely, as the outgoing mail left Marseilles yesterday, unless we pass near enough for the Captain to stop and send my letters on board. He insists on doing this, though only the object of my letter is worthy of so much trouble. The letter in itself must be deadly dull as I am 'criblèd' with 'ennui' and the voyage has seemed interminable.

We went through the Canal at night and got to Port Said at 4 a.m. and that perfectly infernal coaling began at once – how well you know the dirt, noise, and stuffiness of the ship with shut ports. I got a fine budget of news at P. Said. Your cable wh. rejoiced me, letters from Daisy White[1] (dull) & my people and Blanche, and Mungo Herbert[2] and a real Ettier[3] – joybells and all which I send to amuse you. A raft of noisy Cairo fashionables came on board, and the shrieks of over-dressed women, & the cool disdain with which they regarded the 'beyond Suez' world was killing. One vulgarian from Bayswater – I should think from her manners – looked through a diamond lorgnon at all the mass of children & Ayahs on the deck, and said in a loud voice 'Why aren't all these people in the second class!' On board ship it is the frumpy East and the gorgeous West, & these home-coming, tired, spirit-broken Anglo-Indians look in hollow-eyed wonder at these ramping noisy Cairoese.

The Carnarvons came aboard – he is a wreck and has a doctor with him – he looks as though his face has been dragged over stones behind a fast train & she must either have been shot in the face or been run over by a motor car. She is immensely fat and full of talk – our other celebrities are Mr and Mrs Rigo. She was Princesse de Chimay & ran away with a band man. She has only appeared once, & was so stared at and laughed at that she retired to her cabin & has not been seen since. Her husband went to the Captain & said that his wife would never again submit to the manners of the ship. Poor old Captain apologised & begged 'Madam' to come up again – but no – she has remained in her bed! It appears that she came to a table at breakfast and the other people at it had her removed by the head steward! I have not seen the ill-used & indignant heroine. What a come down from her French triumphs & kingly lovers.

Darling, nothing can exceed the kindness of the Captain & purser on this ship – & the P&O have quite laid themselves out, and one of the many managers has travelled all the way from Suez to see that I am comfy. I am quite overpowered by it all & shall write & thank Sir I. Sutherland.

Darling, this I hope will be my last dull epistle & I must write you a better letter next time.

Itty girls send their love to 'dear left *a*hind Daddy' as Cynthia calls you.

I hope you are not flattering disloyal Antony by paying him a visit.
Take care of precious Pappy.

Lovingly

K.

Itty girls kiss your photo eagerly every morning, it is hung over my berth *&*
they clamber up of their own accord to kiss you.

1 The Whites, 'Daisy' (*née* Emily Vanderbilt) and Harry, perhaps because they were
American, were particularly close friends of Lady Curzon and are often alluded to
during her European sojourn of 1901. At the time of this letter Harry White
(1850–1927) was 1st Secretary at the US Embassy in London; he went on to
become Ambassador to Italy (1905–7) and to France (1907–9).

2 The Hon. Sir Michael Henry Herbert (1857–1903), whose diplomatic career
culminated in his appointment as Ambassador in Washington (1902–3).

3 *Née* Ethel ('Ettie') Adine Fane (1867–1952), the wife of William Henry Grenfell
(1855–1945), MP and sportsman who eventually became 1st Baron Desborough.
This intrepid individual once stroked a rowing eight across the English Channel.
The Grenfell marriage seems to have been an oasis of fidelity in a desert of adultery,
although she was prone to platonic flirtations.

8 April 1901   HOTEL REGINA
                                                                        CIMIEZ

Angel:

Behold wondrous becrowned paper! I wrote MacMichael to send me some
with my Calcutta invitation 'chiffre' on it *&* here it is so I christen it with a
letter to Pappy. To begin with my Marseilles arrival yesterday, at *8* we
anchored off the Château d'If and we had no sooner done so than a big tug
came alongside to fetch us off, *&* who should be on board her but *Ian* ;[1] I was
never more surprised *&* pleased to see his fat smiling face. We were bundled
on to the tug with our luggage and while the *India* was in the throes of plague
inspection we were speeding to the wharf where all sorts of civil Kingses [*sic*]
P*&*O *&* Consular people met us. It was now 10 o'c *&* we had missed the only
train to Nice before 6 p.m. by 20 minutes, so there was nothing to do but
drive to the Hotel du Louvre and wait.

Ian it appears had started as soon as Parliament rose for Marseilles to meet
me, *&* had been waiting in the Hotel two days and had been called at 4.45
Saturday morning to go out to meet the *India*. George Wyndham* had come
out with him but had gone to Hyères where his people have a villa for small
Percy's health. Sibell[2] just gone back to London to help Bendor's wife with a

bazaar – it seems they are in great trouble because of the Atherton divorce which is coming on & Bendor & Lord Dudley are both *Cos* & the former was served a writ or some such legal formula on his wedding day! Fearful scandal expected & letters from both lawyers to be read in court! Now to go back to my more respectable annals. Who should I meet in the Hotel courtyard but the Tweedmouths, we had déjeuner together & such a chronique scandaleuse for half an hour. The complete supremacy of Mrs George Keppel over Kinje [Edward VII] & Sir Thomas Lipton[3] just presented with a high class Victorian order because he has made George Keppel his *American* messenger & sent him out to the States. Great amusement over the special embassies to Foreign Courts to announce the accession. Their mission entirely robbed of glory as they are sent on the *cheap* & all present giving cut down to half what it was at accession of Victoria. Kinje cutting down royal stables and no Christians – Connaughts – Beatrices etc. to have royal carriages as they have done always. They have their own shandred [light cart on springs] ones & Royal Mews provides for Kinje & Queen only. This an *immense* economy *we might* emulate it with wisdom! Now back again to my private history. Marseilles in a state of semi-siege owing to strike so I stopped in Hotel until train, Ian hovering about and brimming with news more or less old. Arthur wrapped up in motor-caring & bridge – a new fourth party in H. of Commons which Lord Salisbury calls 'The Hooligans'. Winston, Linky, Lord Percy & Ian form it, & its main object is to teach the Govt. how to govern, & to teach Winston not to talk too much. Ian says Winston's pose is to copy his father in every way – asks everyone how he walked, talked, sat, eat & drank – & does likewise – walks with shoulders stooping & hat held in front of him – all this pose laughed at rather. Ian threw a new light on St John's appointment; he said that no one ever made such a dead set for a place as he for the War Office; he badgered Lord Salisbury to distraction, & got everyone he could to do the same, & gave *no one* any peace until he got it. Ian said his struggle for it was amazing, & he *got* it. Says St John much deafer than ever. George Wyndham has become more ornate than ever and his front bench manner most theatrical – he is trying to frame another land bill and Ian is his secretary. While I was sitting in the stuffy hotel, who should appear bringing a *gigantic* French bouquet, but Mme Verdreau, smiling & enquiring for 'ce malheureux Viceroi – tout seul là bas'. Train time came at last, and at station Consul to see me off – a Mr Turner – just as train was starting my door was torn open & an Admiral of French fleet hearing I was on the train flew to pay his respects – fearful excitement – compliments – yelling & talking – & just as the train was off, he was dragged on to platform by three ADCs all screaming 'Descendez mon Amiral, Nom de Dieu descendez,' so the huge fat, polite, uniformed great man rolled out, & Ian laughing to kill himself at the episode in the corner of the carriage.

Ian was still with us as he was going to Beaulieu – the journey was *dreadful*.

Easter Saturday train jammed & we only got to Nice at midnight – & to Cimiez *dead* at 12.30 – & a miserable night in a vast caravanserai & instead of the peace of a still garden, electric trains shrieking under windows & paved streets surrounding the hotel. Such a blow, as there is an end to gardens & quiet. I loathe these gigantic hotels. You are number 843, & no one cares if you get a bath or a meal and I spend my time with my finger on a bell pleading for meat & drink! I have had letters from Alice, Violet, Helen, & every day brings a fresh batch. Alice writes that Esther Smith is to have a baby, her first sign of such a joy in seven years of matrimony.

April 10. I must close this huge budget soon – it is not unlike a bran pie & you must keep on diving in the envelope, as it is chock full of things of more or less interest, destroy them all when read.

Yesterday I went to see Anne Pozuder – she thinks she has had a small mishap & is lying up in a state of nervous frenzy in the hope of beginning again. Poor thing – she retailed to me a list of D. of Portland, D.D. Nora Bourke-Kelly Somerset, D. of Leeds who had all had babes after years of waiting and anxiety, & Esther Smith the Crowning hope of us all – so we must hope too. Anne looks ill & says she will always be an invalid; she wears a silver hat rack *inside* to support her. *Awful* idea for poor Jack!

Darling I am absolutely well, but children both look white & I shall stay here for quite ten days or a fortnight to get colour in their faces. I am sure you will agree with this. It is perfectly *deadly* here and I have my meals alone with the children. Ian moved here yesterday, but fortunately he does not bore me & leaves me alone – he had seen Lord Salisbury & said he looked terribly ill, full of enquiries about me as he had heard that Ian & G. Wyndham had gone out to meet me. I shall go over to see Lady Gwendolen[4] & will report on them in my next. Beaulieu is not far & Lord Salisbury's villa quite near Anne's. Margot [Asquith]* has had some mysterious affection of the *nose* – Godfrey Webbe cheered her by assuring it was a cancer like his! She is much better & has been at St Moritz a long time.

Darling tell me if you like all this tittletattle. I am afraid it is very Harry Whitish.

I have written St John I wld. dine the 30th, so think of us then at a friend's dinner but robbed of all its glory without beloved Pappy's presence.

Daisy White is I believe at Grasse. I feel inclined to go there as it is countrified & Cimiez is a horrid big town. Not a stone left of the old Cimiez I remember as a little child.

Bless you precious Pappy. Don't ride Luxury or the Crocodile. Your life is far too precious to run risks & Jumpy, Clio, & Sansfeo are safer.

Lovingly
K.

Itty girls send kisses to 'left ahind Daddy'.

1 Sir Ian Zachary Malcolm (1868–1944), sometime MP and from 1901 to 1903 Parliamentary Private Secretary to the then Chief Secretary for Ireland, George Wyndham. Malcolm married Jeanne Maria Langtry, the daughter of Lily Langtry.
2 (1855–1929), first the extremely wealthy widow of Earl Grosvenor and then the wife of George Wyndham. Before he met Mary Leiter the Viceroy had been enamoured of Lady Sibell Lumley, as she then was.
3 (1850–1931), wealthy merchant and owner of tea and rubber estates and an inveterate yachtsman.
4 Lady Gwendolen Cecil, the second daughter of the 3rd Marquess of Salisbury; she died in 1945 having devoted her life to her father. 'An extraordinary mixture of simplicity and wisdom' in the words of her nephew, Lord David Cecil. Lady Gwendolen remains in memory a charming exemplar of the largely extinct cult of eccentricity.

[From Lord Curzon to Lady Curzon]
Sunday, 14 April 1901   NEPAL

... I think we shall all be rather glad to get away. Tent life day after day, particularly when we spend such long hours & indeed days in camp is very sedentary & monotonous. One also gets rather tired of the same faces & voices, the more so as you know well that they have not two ideas among them. Crespigny devotes himself to bridge. Portman kills & skins every conceivable animal, & is believed to be sending them all home to his young lady. His bearer has mislaid or lost or stolen the lucky bone of the tiger that he killed, & last night the whole camp re-echoed to the furious threats from his indignant master 'If you don't find that bone by tomorrow morning I'll give you the d---dest thrashing you ever had in your life.' I offered the bone from any one of my tigers, or from all of them. But no, he was not to be consoled or pacified. Fenn appeared today in that shocking old green suit in which he looks like a puffy schoolboy who has grown out of his clothes. Now I must dress for dinner. Mail comes in tomorrow & I shall hear from darling Kinkie. ...

Fr. Knollys[1] writes that Kinge would like to come out & crown himself at Delhi, but fears he cannot spare the time; he wants the Yorks to come instead. I am not at all keen upon this. So when you see Kinge try & urge him to come. He need only be away seven weeks. Of course we must pretend to be delighted with Yorks' visit when they come. I wonder if they will want to come to our Delhi Durbar[2] on Jan 1, 1903 – or the winter after.

April 17. Back in our second camp after our three days jaunt to the frontier. I am lying in bed infested with insects. Millions are swarming all over me, over the sheet, flying pat against the lamp, biting my legs. It has been an odious day, 15 miles shaking & bumping on a pad till I cried with pain & had to get off & walk in the last part of the march. Then when we came in, a raging dust storm, everything choked with dust – had to lie in tent with all chics [small bamboo blinds] down. Hot as hell.

However we had a successful day yesterday, for I got a rhino at last. Dense jungle, very tall grass. At length I saw the great brute dimly standing in a sort of tunnel that he had forced for himself through the bottom of the grass. He turned and fled. I fired a shot that caught him in the neck & sent him over like a rabbit. Then you never saw such a commotion. He kicked & plunged & we had to pour at least a dozen shots into him before he was finished off. His whole body is covered with an armour plating of dense hide, quite impervious to bullets, & there are only one or two vulnerable spots. When he was killed the natives rushed up and golloped up his blood & carried it off in handkerchiefs & cloths. It is supposed to have some religious or medicinal value. You never saw such a sight. Another rhino charged me straight & I shot him in the head. He bolted & has not been recovered. But I think they will get him. Then we got another tiger of which I gave the shot to Fenn, so our bag in all is twelve tigers, one rhino & innumerable deer, boar, partridge & floricans [bustards].

Tomorrow we are off to Naini Tal & the great Nepal shoot is over – very tiring – disappointing as compared with the estimated bag – but yet a good shoot as compared with others. . . .

1 Surely one of the most· remarkable courtiers of any age, Francis Knollys (1837–1924) served as Private Secretary to Edward VII when he was Prince of Wales (1870–1901) and then when monarch (1901–10). He was also Gentleman Usher to Queen Victoria (1868–1901) and for those services was profusely decorated. In 1911 he became 1st Viscount Knollys.

2 Much has been written about the Delhi Coronation Durbar of January 1903, that assertion of imperial strength and Curzon's brainchild, for he obtained royal assent to convene the affair from Edward VII himself. As with the Victoria Memorial Hall, there was jealous opposition from British and from Indians as well as from some Americans, who in their anti-royalist zeal overlooked the fact that the glamorous Vicereine was a compatriot.

As impressive in their way as the Durbar itself were Curzon's preparations for it. Up, down, and across the country he went, publicizing and advocating this stupendous exhibition of power and glory. In his letters and official documents of this time he is revealed as being involved in the planning of buildings (in one case a colosseum the size of the Albert Hall), in the investigations of appropriate sites, in organizing camps of accommodation, in furthering the Indian Arts Exhibition, in planning the use of the exquisitely ornate and exotic Mogul buildings of Delhi and in supervising more mundane public pastimes and entertainments such as polo, cricket and football. No task was too trivial or too great for this indefatigable Viceroy to tackle. Nor did the consequences of such brilliantly detailed planning go unrecognized as Lord and Lady Curzon rode in regal majesty on an immense elephant along the processional route, as thousands of British and Indian troops massed and marched past, as investitures were conducted, as balls and levees

'At Govt. House [Calcutta] all the swells in India were lined up . . .' (see Lady Curzon's letter of 4 January 1899).

Simla: the Viceregal Lodge, *c.* 1900. 'This house is like a big American country house, but not so well planned . . .' (letter of 8 March 1899).

The Curzons *en route* to the Buddhist temple at Sanchi, 28 November 1899 (letter of 30 November 1899).

Sikandra: Lord and Lady Curzon at Akbar's tomb, 9 December 1899 (letter of 4–12 December 1899).

The tomb of Itimad-ud-Duala, 10 December 1899 (letter of 4–12 December 1899).

Viceregal visit to Lucknow, mid-December 1899. The group includes: (back, left to right) the Earl of Suffolk, Captain Wigram, Captain Baker-Carr, Captain Marker; (front) W. R. Lawrence, Miss Macdonell, Sir A. Macdonell, the Vicereine and Viceroy, Lady Macdonell.

Lady Curzon on a rhinoceros, Kashmir, 1900.

Lord and Lady Curzon with Cynthia and Irene on the Viceregal launch, Calcutta, January 1901.

A charming picture of the Viceroy with his daughters, *c.* 1900.

ABOVE: 'Ringing the tiger' (letter of 29 March 1901).

LEFT: The Hyderabad tiger-hunt at which the old shikari was killed, April 1902 (see Lady Curzon's Hyderabad Journal).

Hyderabad: Lord and Lady Curzon and the Nizam, with 'the usual crowd of grandees', April 1902 (see the Hyderabad Journal).

Delhi Durbar, 1903: (left to right) Lady Crewe, the Duchess of Portland, the Duke of Portland, Lady Curzon, Lord Kitchener, Lady Pearce.

Alexandra, the youngest daughter of Lord and Lady Curzon, with bodyguard, Simla, 1905.

A grievous occasion: the Curzons' final departure from India. Bombay, 18 November 1905.

abounded and as princes manifested their splendour and tribes their bizarre and colourful customs and rites. Small wonder the Durbar was spoken of as 'the Curzonation'. At the centre with Curzon the Vicereine made an unsurpassed impression. Although unwell, she rose to the Durbar with an imperial dignity that dazzled even the most worldly Europeans present.

10.30 p.m., 1 May 1901   *Same old dark den*   SIMLA
                         Same table
                         Same chair

Darling child:

I wrote last week just after arriving here. That very afternoon the usual Simla reaction seized me. I felt it coming out – backaching – utter lassitude, so I took it in time & went straight to bed at once. Four days of absolute quiet soon put me to rights and I was up again on Monday. Meanwhile on Sunday evening mail had arrived: & I can scarcely describe to you the luxury of lying in bed (Kinkie's bed, back turned away from wall) and reading precious Kinko's letters & all her doings. I think that your new monogram is quite chaste & pretty. It was really very good of fat gushing boyish Ian to come and meet you. . . .

I love all the gossip you picked up from your various friends & passed on to me. In half an hour's talk one learns more than in half a year's correspondence. Too nice of dear Mme Verdreau pouring in the news about G. Steevens[1] – surprised me very much. I cannot recollect being anything else but kind to him. But I suppose I trod on some unsuspected toe.

Now I will give Kinkie all my modest humble news. Baring is in bed with some sort of fever, & has started a most horrible spotty eruption all over his lower lip & chin. My word – he does do the Staff well. I went down to Curzon House, filled with workmen, everything being repapered & repainted (though it is only the second year). The bow windows have been thrown out. Portman of course has been given Campbell's room, and I found workmen putting up fancy bookshelves, mantelpiece etc. Suffolk & Crespigny are the two others. On the ground floor the two rooms on the left have been thrown into a single drawingroom, beautifully papered & finished – piano – pictures, so far etc. Curzon House is now one of the most delightful places you can imagine. The hideous chimneys have been taken down & pretty ones put in their place. But yesterday I happened to step down to Squire's Hall which Baring had told me was shut up. I found it alive with workmen. On the right hand side on going in, the various rooms have been thrown together to make a beautiful ballroom, nearly as big as my study here, papered with crimson paper & lit with electric light; out of this is an admirable supper room, where you could seat forty people. Beyond are new cook rooms & out houses, & beyond again a new range of stables! I gather that the

Staff have now between thirty & forty stalls between them! I spoke to Baring rather strongly about all this this morning & said that I did not think Govt. money ought to be squandered upon enabling himself & the Staff to entertain. I said that I would not sanction another penny. Don't you think it rather a shame? Under the new arrangements we can only put three ADCs into Curzon House & two into Squire's, or five in all: everything else is given up to Baring's dinners & dances & so on. That is what I dislike about the man. He does the thing behind my back and then only curls his upper lip when I speak to him. Fenn of course is stingeing [*sic*] in the house here, & doing without a pony.

They are hard at work scraping the walls of the ballroom preparatory to putting up the silk & the drawing-room is to be commenced immediately. Tell me, am I to get a pink carpet for your sitting-room or what do you wish done?

Last night I had a dinner of Councillors to say goodbye to old Trevor and Box. It was quite a small unpretentious affair. The old chap left for good today and I did not want him to depart with a bad taste in his mouth. I made a little impromptu speech, and he replied with incredible lameness. Lady Palmer[2] radiant with delight at being here once more & profuse with gratitude to me for having got him the post. Ma Law,[3] old, haggard, unpicturesque & discontented. I hardly had a word with her. Lady Rivaz plump, matronly and utterly irresponsible. Charlie's tummy visibly swelling. Mrs Barnes as simple and nice and flat-bottomed as ever (the violinist is staying with them for the season). All went very cheerily, some played billiards & others bridge afterwards & we separated at 11.

All sorts of new people are in Simla.... All sorts of beauties are reported from Mrs Sankey downwards. Fenn winks & stutters and assumes a probably fictitious familiarity. Wigger has resumed charge of the Gymkhanas which appear to be as great a success as those last year were failures. Sixty or seventy people go down. But there is reported to be an awful dearth of men, and they cannot fill the male parts in the plays. The first one is being rehearsed, & I believe consists exclusively of kissing....

A parcel came the other day. I opened it, a magnificent roll of Chinese scarlet brocade with dragons set in pattern. I don't know if this is the famous curtain of which we heard, or from whom it came. No note, card, or letter with it. It will come in splendidly for future Eastern room.

Darling, I am so entirely surrounded by Kinkie. On my left, two Devonshire House photos, also K. in black dress & Irene. Opposite, two early photos, K. with hands behind back & K. with Irene as baby on lap. Then huge Baron Meyer picture on separate table. Not a bad selection....

When I arrived poor little Fluff hardly knew me – only a few furtive licks. She skulked in corners & ran away, & would not come up & be fondled. Now she has completely recovered her equanimity. She is brought into my room (yours) every morning when I am called and jumps on to bed in a moment & practically never leaves me for rest of day. She has not quite recovered her looks or coat, but is on the way.

Darling, I am very good about taking exercise. I go out about 4.30 or 5 in the afternoon and walk (Prospect or Summer Hill), for an hour and a half. I am not going into Simla at all. I don't care about it. I shall keep myself to this end, which is quiet and pretty. I go alone (as all the Staff are mad upon Polo & Gymkhanas), followed by white Bobby.

Little Gurkhas at Gate this year – nice sharp alert little green chaps. The box-headed curate never married hair-down, tee-bach Hobday after all; and she has let it down again & resumed her rides. I am to go to the wedding of Miss Beeker to young soldier named Holloway, who wore blue bags at our dances.

Now precious I have exhausted all my petty paltry news. You cannot conceive how beautiful the outlook is. Everything is as green as after the rains, & the little round pools that look like gems on the hill tops are full of water. The crimson rhododendrons are still in full blossom and as for the snows they transcend description. The whole of the range behind the Shali are white not only on their summits but as far down as you can see. The panorama is simply magnificent, far finer than we ever saw in October. The Chor is as white & thick with snow as any of the rest of them. From the top of Prospect Hill the outlook is positively sublime. It is still very cold, & we have fires in all our rooms.

Harris is quite incompetent as Steward, can't spell, can't keep accounts, & generally has no idea what to do beyond drop his h's and be in the wrong place....

I shall be most interested to hear what you decide about Lenbach.[4] I rather believe that you will go to him after all. If you are doubtful go to both. The great thing is for K. to be done while still in prime of her beauty.

What a St Johner you did send me! The man is quite incurable – always straining to be first-class and never pulling it off....

Now I must stop & say goodnight & goodbye to darling wife. It is 11.45 & you will want me to go to forlorn & solitary couch. Next week I will write to second itty girl. Soon I hope they will be at seaside paddling about in water.

Ever lovingly
P.

1 George Warrington Steevens (1869–1900), special correspondent for the *Daily Mail*, had died a year previously at the siege of Ladysmith of enteric fever. He had represented his paper in many different parts of the world.
2 Wife of Sir Arthur Power Palmer (1840–1904); he had served during the Mutiny and was Commander-in-Chief, India 1900–2.

3 Wife of Sir Edward Fitzgerald Law (1846–1908), Financial Member of the Supreme Council 1900–5.

4 Franz von Lenbach (1836–1904) was commissioned by a Count Schack to copy famous paintings for his collection; Lenbach exhibited quite widely and ended his career a successful portrait painter. His portrait of Lady Curzon is considered one of his best works.

Mon. to Thurs., 6th to 9th May 1901   45, GROSVENOR SQUARE
[LONDON]

Precious Pappy:

The Paris budget took me up to Sunday the fifth when I met the itty girls at the Gare du Nord, *&* made the journey to Calais in their wagon lit, the French Co. of course making me pay f. 18.50 extra for the discomfort of sitting in a wagon lit in the day time. At Calais who should meet us but Frank [Curzon], full of kisses and delight at seeing us – *&* he conducted us over a perfectly smooth channel. At Dover we had the same well known filthy tea *&* then away to Charing x where Capt. Adam was waiting for us beaming and blushing.

Into Evey's[1] grand brougham and through the smoky foggy Sunday-sad streets to No. 45 where I met little Evey full of fuss and excitement waiting at the window. Of course no sleep – Sunday night – *&* Monday a.m. before breakfast St John called, but I was in bed when the friends began to pour in – Alice all love *&* hugs – and Katie almost demonstrative *&* tears in her eyes and quite choky with pleasure at seeing me. Ettie – radiant, loving and beloved as only Ettie can be – Margot very birdlike *& shabby* and *old* – terribly sad at being left out of St John's great banquet to me tonight – because of Hilda's fury at Henry opposing St John's war office. I cheered! Margot announced how bitterly she felt this cloud on the old friendship and she had sent for St John – *thrown her arms round his neck* (what a picture) and implored him not to let differences of political opinions make a change in their personal friendship. St John had walked the floor in distress but Hilda had been unforgiving. Darling Margot is the friend who seems a little unhappy – ill – poor – and indiscreet, *&* perhaps a little left behind in this race of life, but just as fine *&* loving. Lady C. bounced in *&* talked *coal* at me and engaged me to dine on the spot three different nights, *&* to two I agreed. She was bubbling with excitement, *&* to hear her talk about coal you would think that the budget had been framed to ruin *her*. As you remember all her politics are purely personal and as legislation harms or benefits their property her opinions fluctuate between censure *&* enthusiasm. In the midst of all the friends who should tumble in but Mrs Willy Gladstone about to have a baby. I was disconcerted but delighted to see her! You remember her [in] our first year in Calcutta. Next, darling, came Lord Selborne *&* sat for a solid hour and a half desiring *instruction* on 'all you are doing'. I at once dropped on to the theory that he longs to succeed you, but, George, his ignorance of India is quite *amazing* – he doesn't even know Geography, & he had read Warburton's books on the frontier and thinks he knows the whole question. He thought (I can't imagine why this is the general impression), that your frontier province – your Princes' circular[2] – your Rangoon outrage[3] policy had all been strongly opposed by your Council. The first, I told him, was strongly backed by your Council, even by the principal member. The second Sir Wm Lockhart was as strong as you were for condemning – & the third was entirely approved by the right sort of princes themselves. He said what has puzzled everyone was *how* you came to *publish* such a thing – was it in the form of an edict or a ukase. I told him that it could never have any beneficent effect unless it came out as an order in Council as a private letter to each wld. have made no impression.

I could see that what was in his mind was that it was as though the King of England had published an edict that the Dukes weren't to go to Monte Carlo & gamble and that it savoured of too great autocracy.

Well, about the Frontier[4] he said amongst the people who *knew* – your Frontier province was by far the most important achievement of your Viceroyalty but he said too, that *no* one knew anything about India, which in itself was a blessing to India, as the greater the knowledge the greater would be the meddling by the House of Commons and the great thing for you was to be let alone and unmolested in your great work.

The cessation of the long Indian Hunter letters in the *Times* is really a calamity as they did jog the ignorance of *Times* readers at least, George. India is the great unknown. The moon seems nearer to the majority, & India isn't more than a huge troublesome *name* that spells Famine and Plague. . . .

---

1 The Hon. Eveline Mary Curzon (1864–1934), who in 1893 married Sir James Percy Miller, Bt. (1864–1906), sportsman and soldier whose town house was 45 Grosvenor Square. She was one of Curzon's several sisters; the Millers had no children.

2 A Viceregal directive setting down that ruling princes proposing to visit outside India would need permission from the government of India. This Curzon promulgated to ensure that native rulers spent more time attending to their home responsibilities and less on European race-courses and polo grounds.

3 An assault in 1899 by British Army personnel upon a Burmese woman. Curzon acted stringently in this, and similar offences. Even more tragic, to look ahead to 1902, was the affair involving the 9th Queen's Royal Lancers, some of whose troopers beat to death an Indian cook. To humiliate this supercilious regiment Curzon caused leave to be cancelled for nine months and a sentry *of another regiment* to be stationed outside the individual barrack blocks. A register of the Anglo-Indian hostility incurred is evident in the marked applause for the 9th when it gave the salute at the Delhi Durbar. As Curzon dryly recorded: 'I sat alone and unmoved on my

horse.... I felt a certain gloomy pride in having dared to do the right.' Indeed, the Anglo-Indians never forgave the Viceroy his sense of justice.

4 Curzon's creation of the North-west Frontier Province, although causing a permanent rift with the Lieutenant-Governor of the Punjab, Sir Mackworth Young, was one of his outstanding administrative strokes. This is not the place to explain the complexities of the problem, but it might be noted that the political machinations, the clashes of personality and like difficulties are emblematic of many other problems facing this determinedly reforming Viceroy.

[The initial paragraphs of this letter from Lady Curzon are missing]

12 May 1901   WILTON PARK
                                                                      BEACONSFIELD[1]

... After dinner Sir Alfred Lyall* came in to see me and we talked away for a quarter of an hour until Col. Rhodes came & interrupted us. Dear old Sir Alfred, it made my heart leap to hear him talk about India with a depth of feeling, imagination & knowledge that came like a burst of radiance after all the clouds of ignorance I had been engulfed in. He said 'George Curzon has got his whole heart in his work; whether we agree with all he does or not we agree that no one ever had India's good name more truly before him, & I think he is doing wonderful work for India.' You know his rather absent far-away manner. Can't you see his old white head sunk in his narrow shoulders & the tips of his fingers together.

It is too delightful to hear about 'George Curzon' again and beloved *you* are a loss. Your brilliance & your wonderful personality make London a poor place without you. *I* miss you now in more than a wifely way. I miss you in all the well-known rooms we have so often been in together. There is no George, consequently no gaiety, chaff & laughter.

Well, in all these pages you have been wondering why I am here, so I must explain. I was being welcomed to death, & was worn out with seeing such hosts of people, so Daisy came to Evey's and persuaded me to come here for Sunday to rest & be alone, and I jumped at the chance of some quiet. I am in the same room I had when we came together, but alas! the little dressing-room next contains no Pappy....

There is the greatest indignation at the Honours list – over the men who have got undeserved rewards, & the deserving ones who have been left out. Lord Settrington, who was so praised, never heard any fighting or firing & only distinguished himself by carrying Lady Roberts' umbrella when she went out to drive! ditto Lord H. Scott, while the Duke of Marlbro[2] only succeeded in losing the only despatches he was ever given, while acting as Lord Roberts' Secretary & he was sent home because he was such a failure – he thought he was the Great Duke and felt that the Comm.-in-Chief should bring him his shaving water!! But he has a DSO. St John is much upset about the honours, and assured me that it was only his influence that had made them as good as they were.

On Friday night there was a great fight in the House with the Irish over the newspaper the *Irish People* being seized in Ireland for a vile attack on the King. Although the publication was seized in Dublin, a large number of copies had been sent to America & France, so we shall have the horrible thing reprinted all over the world. I believe it is all true – merely a realistic account of Kinge – in the divorce court, & in the Baccarat case etc. This foolish White Lodge[3] business has turned the fierce light on the throne suddenly on Kinge's seamy side – and Willie Grenfell told me that his tailor had expressed surprise while fitting on Willie's clothes that a royal residence had been given to an old *favourite* – White Lodge is called now the 'parc aux cerfs', which is as you remember the Mme de Pompadour's place where she entertained Louis XV with the most wicked follies & immoralities. Do you think it is serious? I do – that within four months of the Queen's death all this horrible scandal is public property. Arthur Ellis said to someone in February 'We are making a good start – and everything is exemplary – but you don't expect that an old leopard of 60 is going to change his spots, do you?'....

1 Country residence of the American diplomat Harry White and his wife Daisy.
2 The 9th Duke (1871–1934), who served briefly on Roberts' staff in the South African wars.
3 Built for the Hanoverian monarchs as a hunting lodge, this residence is located in Richmond Park. Many royals stayed there over the years; Princess May (later Queen Mary) spent her childhood years there and her eldest son, Edward VIII, was born at White Lodge. In the present correspondence it becomes evident that White Lodge is essentially a house of assignation.

11 p.m., 14–15 May 1901   SIMLA

Darling:

I have just returned from dining with Baring in his new mansion at Squire's Hall. No one lives there now, and it is turned into a beautiful Military Secretary's bungalow, devoted to entertainment. Everything admirably done. I took in Ma Barnes who was flat in the back and softly alluring as usual. Old Cyon glimmered thro' his glasses from the other end of the room. On my other side was the redoubtable [Mrs] Sankey who is a pretty little dark creature, half Greek, brought up in Ithaca, quite demure & rather shy, played the Guitar after dinner while Sankey, an ordinary sort of soldier, shone with conjugal pride. The Mallaby lady played excellently on the violin in a new & becoming black frock with gold passementerie. Corvie performed on the piano, the Baroness Speck, quite plump, thoroughly pleased with herself, delighted with Simla, & I really believe containing germs of a

Specklet, sat next me after dinner, laid the butter on to you, & tried to be clever. . . .

The old Chief is showing himself thoroughly stupid all round. Kitchener wants 57 of our officers for South Africa, & telegraphed to Power Palmer direct. This was entirely wrong. P.P. without ever telling me proceeded to get the men. I heard of the matter by accident, & stopped the whole show in the twinkling of an eye. Kitchener can only ask us thro' the Sec. of State, & the C.-in-C. cannot give a man without the consent of the Govt. of India. . . .

Last week the Dalys gave a dance to which our 'bloods' went. The feature of the evening was the performance of old Fenn who in Wilkinson's language 'took a heavy toss', going a fearful smasher on to his back, and hauling down Mrs Mahon on to the top of him amid thunders of applause. She retaliated by digging her knee into his stomach & taking the old chap's wind. He is more footling than ever.

Nevill Rop has had his adenoids cut out and is reported by his parents to be both more articulate & more intelligent. He still looks vacant & obese. . . .

And now I must turn to Kinkie. Everyone says that Simla is a miserable place without Kinkie. All heart gone out of it. They say this to me to cheer or please me, possibly. But I am convinced that they also think it, & your return will be greeted with a storm of applause.

My only solace is poor little Fluff, who is now quite devoted & never leaves me all day, jumps on to my bed in the morning, sits in my work room all day, comes down to lunch, & walks out with me in afternoon. She has quite recovered her looks & is less greedy than of yore.

Darling, before you think of coming back in August do regard your health. You must recover it, build it up, lay the scaffolding for itty boy – sacrifice everything to that. You might fritter it all away in a bad monsoon passage. No, I can plug along, a month more or less can be endured, & you must get out of Europe all that it can give. It does not much matter to a cabbage whether it leads a vegetable existence for five or six months, & that is my condition.

May 15, 1901. Poor Sir Arthur Strachey[1] (the brother of Barnes' first wife, and Chief Justice of Allahabad) who had been suffering from fever for some time past died in his house in Bahadoorgunge. Of course these miserable doctors never found out to the last hour that it was enteric & were treating him for something else. His poor widow is off her head & is going to be taken in by the Lawrences. He left word that he was to be cremated: and his body will have to be taken somewhere down the khud [steep hillside] to be burned. We had a little funeral service over it in the tiny church this evening. It was like most Simla funerals, utterly grim and heartless – about ten people, several of them (like myself) had never seen the deceased. Sanders and a rough deal coffin with the poor fellow inside. . . .

Goodnight precious wife. Kisses from poor solitary disconsolate

Pap

1 (1858–1901), educated at Charterhouse and Cambridge. The Strachey family name was much respected in the ICS across the years.

Wednesday [15 May 1901]   45 GROSVENOR SQUARE

Darling:

I came back from Wilton on Monday – and Papa came to tea in the afternoon looking so very well that I was quite surprised. I found your beloved letter here as I dare not trust them to country posts, and I am so glad that you are well; this is splendid. Papa talked a great deal about the two pictures at Agnew's which he abused worse than I did! I asked him to write you what he thought. He was pleased with the children – & did not ask if your hair was long – and was very dear, tender and affectionate. In the evening I dined with Julia and went to the opera to see *Roméo et Juliette*. London has changed & the house was filled with Jews I didn't know. Mr Dawkins was there & came in to see me & settle day to come & call. Rennell Rodd there too *quite* white – all full of enquiries for dear you. On Tuesday I went to call on Una Choate in the morning – and found her out & asked if I might come today, as I must see the house. I then went to lunch with Mr Lucy – because he is such a good little friend. There was the usual mixture of the known & unknown & with Mr & Mrs George Alexander,[1] Winston, Herbert Gladstone[2] & Conan Doyle[3] & Sir Wm Agnew[4] there were others I never saw before. Winston sat next to me and told me of his great speech in [the] House the night before which he seems to consider a greater success than any one else does! Everyone condemns St John's scheme – Mr Lucy said there was a great feeling of opposition on all sides to it – so St John isn't in smooth water. After lunch I went with Alice Crane to House on chance of hearing some speech worth hearing on the Army, but Dillon was up so we retreated from dear old lady's gallery, and went to see Arthur [Balfour] to enquire what course the debate was taking. He was sitting in a most radiant sun-filled new room overlooking the big entrance square and Westminster Abbey. We found him engaged in writing his book (he said) and he seemed so aloof and so beautiful – sitting writing philosophy while the Army debate raged below. He had asked me to dine at the House on Friday and I couldn't so he would set another night, & then he talked and beamed on us in real Arthurian style. Most of the talk was about Winston whose amazing conceit quite staggered him – and he condemned his speech because it was without conviction or argument, and was mere self-advertisement. We left just as

St John came in to say he was putting up Ed. Stanley to reply to Dillon – & he seemed deaf and worried.

Alice and I then went to see the White's new house in Whitehall Gardens – it is behind the banqueting hall & is being rebuilt and seemed moderate only. From here we went to New Gallery which I will spare you an account of & then home to dine alone with Evey as I hate always leaving her in all alone. She is in deep economy (*this in secret*), *such* bad food & *filthy* wine. Claret open for days until I had to ask butler for a fresh bottle, it was *so* sour! Jimmy will have none of this, I am sure, when he comes back. As Jimmy may return next Thursday, Evey has asked me to move out in time to have the house in spick & span order, so I have been looking for rooms to go to. Claridges quite wickedly dear, Coburg the same, but I found quite a new dear little hotel at 22 Grosvenor Street called Hagen's hotel so I stopped there, saw a charming suite of rooms inhabited by the Dowager Lady Annesley [?] which I could get, only 30s. a day so I may go there (Mrs Adair has asked me to come to her) – it is quite quiet, very clean & not so dear, and charming location. This *is* a relief & I shall [be] so much more free than here where I never know what I can do next for fear of offending Evey, who is always saying spiky things about the poor friends and *you* & *us*.

Now for *great* news. At 4.30 today I went by appt. to see Mrs Choate. Found outer hall *nice*, well carpeted & comfy but ovis Poli [Great Pamir horned sheep] very dirty. Inner hall *much* nicer than I expected. Mezzotints caught my eye on green background at once – and hall with white above very, very nice. I went up the long staircase & beamed on the Venetian lamps & all the well-known old landmarks & went into the big back drawing-room which didn't look half bad. Quite enough furniture & walls covered with all the pictures. *Dirt* struck me everywhere & general decay of cretonnes & curtains & ceilings & walls filthy & rugs also. . . .

The house has the air of being lived in by people who only half keep it up – Stairs not whitened and nothing *trim*. And I am sure they haven't spent sixpence on a curtain string themselves. Very shabby, their servants, and nothing *smart* & no visible signs of any style in living, so an air of dilapidation reigned over the grand simplicity of the house.

Last night I dined with the Gulleys – *delightful* – Chamberlains* – Consuelo – Roberts* – Vincents[5] – Tweedmouths[6] – Arthur took me in, and we talked straight through dinner – till his conscience smote him into putting his glasses on, looking at Lady Roberts on the other side & introducing me to her.

His chief interest in India is Afghanistan and what your plan of operation is to be in case of Amir's death – he is really keen on this as he has read an alarmist Russian book on what Russia would do, so I think if you have planned *what* you wld. do after proclaiming Habi Bullah it would be well to write him for future use in the Cabinet. I chaffed him about all the letters he wrote to us – he said 'I never write but I *love* George' – it was so simply said I could have kissed him – but didn't. . . .

I went to see Lady Lockhart yesterday, & as she was out asked her to come here today, and she has just been – black – tearful & broken hearted.

This afternoon I go to the House to hear St John on his scheme at 4.30. Then I dine with John Baring to meet Ettie, Arthur & Consuelo – and after din. go to hear Arthur speak at H. of C.

You ought to hear Arthur on officers of His Majesty's Army. He says they are the most corrupt – ignorant – jobbing lot of men he has ever known; he says 'What are you to do with a lot of men who had no sense of honour, are more disloyal to one another than the weakest of the female sex & have no brains to balance their defects.' He said 'Look at that little man over them (Lord Roberts) – I love him – *but* he cares about nothing but jobbing Dukes into the army.'

Darling, it is quite impossible to describe the frantic fuss people make of me – all because I am part of Pappy. I have 'dentist' appointments with all the aged swells like Lord Roberts, Mr Choate, Sir Wm. Harcourt,[7] Sir A. Lyall, Mr Dawkins – and G.W. Wyndham, E. Vincent, Springy, & an amazing collection of people give me no peace. I had great jokes with Edgar Vincent last night & he said 'It's quite glorious to see you & your arrival seems a greater event than the Queen's death'!!! He is too funny about Sir E. Law, whom no one seems to think sane! I haven't seen G. Hamilton though he has written to say he was coming to call. Lord Roberts is most keen about yr. *princes* scheme. Mr Chamberlain said 'In India I imagine Curzon has got enough work to satisfy *him* – we are all astounded at the amount he does.'

I know it is natural, beloved, to say kind things to wives, but in these days people are too critical to praise as they do *you* without meaning it. You often say that England doesn't know what you are doing – India is *You* now, & there isn't even a fool who doesn't feel the wonder of your work! It is very good for me to be with dear little Evey as she always brings me from the clouds of delight to the realities of my faults. She harps on the string 'How nice George's friends are to you'. I always say meekly 'Yes, I know it is all because of him', though I know too, angel, that they are a little fond of me too. This is only pouring my heart out to you. You must never repeat in your letters back, *please* – her resenting all this excitement is not strange as her house is besieged with people she doesn't know.

I must close this endless letter. I will write another line just in time for post, with more love.

Both Fancy men have just been to lunch.

All love from well itty girls.

Kinko

1 Very possibly George Alexander (1858–1919), actor-manager of the 1890s who

produced the plays of Wilde, Pinero and Henry Arthur Jones. He was particularly associated with the St James's Theatre now sadly demolished.

2 The Rt. Hon. Herbert John Gladstone (1854–1930), youngest son of W.E. Gladstone; he was a civil servant and M P for Leeds West 1880–1910.

3 Sir Arthur Conan Doyle (1859–1930), historical novelist, spiritualist and, above all, creator of Sherlock Holmes and Dr Watson.

4 Sir William Fischer Agnew (1847–1903), barrister and Recorder of Rangoon 1884–1899.

5 Edgar Vincent (1857–1941) and his wife (*née* Lady Helen Venetia Duncombe), who became Viscount and Viscountess d'Abernon. He held many government posts related to finance and to the Near East. He was also Ambassador in Berlin 1920–6.

6 He was the 2nd Baron (1849–1909) and his wife was the daughter of the 7th Duke of Marlborough. He had been Lord Privy Seal and M P for Berwick, and was later First Lord of the Admiralty. The Tweedmouths married in 1873, and she died in 1904.

7 (1827–1904), held parliamentary seats for Oxford, Derby and West Monmouthshire. A senior civil servant, Harcourt was Home Secretary 1880–5, and Chancellor of the Exchequer in 1886 and from 1892 to 1895.

18 May 1901   WESTGATE-ON-SEA

Darling Pappy:

Yesterday the babies and I came here from Victoria Station, Evey seeing us off, and I am enchanted to find the nice lodgings in a rundown sort of cottage not half bad ... but tomorrow I shall be offing to London and not be back until next week when I come from Panshanger.[1] Now I must begin where my last left off, Thurs. I think or up to late on Friday when Lord Roberts came to see me. He said he was perfectly delighted with the success of the tribal levies – greatly approved of frontier – also of your hope to improve & develop the young princelings – he said he strongly backed *your* scheme though he had not before been sanguine of accomplishing much. He spoke most warmly of Kitchener and said he had improved in two years and acquired greater leniency in dealing with men, & his only fear for India was his attitude to native troops, but this he meant to talk to him about before he went out. His coming to India is a 'secret de Polichinelle'. Arthur, St John, George Wyndham and Lord Roberts & Mr Dawkins have all talked about it, though they say 'of course no one knows yet'. I did *not* think Lord Roberts enthused about St John's reforms, which met him in print at Madeira on his return from South Africa.

Mr Dawkins came while Lord Roberts was there.... He said he thought that people's ignorance & indifference about India was growing. They recognized a great personality in *you* but he constantly heard 'Well, if a man like Lord Elgin, who had returned to what he was eminently fitted to be, a County Councillor in his Scotch town, could govern India successfully there couldn't be much required to be a success out there.' He says you have aroused interest in the intelligent but nothing will create intelligence in the ignorant. He was rather gloomy about things in general, & said he was struck by the hollowness of peoples' interests or convictions, & no one *cared* about anything, and the King only wanted to play cards with Sir Ernest Cassel[2] at private dins. at the latter's house. . . .

Saturday morning Lady Jenkins came to see me – and George Wyndham, he was greatly amused as Harris, our old friend from whom we bought Spanish curios in Regent Street, appeared with a huge Spanish silver casket to show, & a suite of jewels which had belonged to Akbar. Both were hideous but gorgeously barbaric, and it appealed to George's sense of fun to see me & see Jewish dealers dragging barbaric splendours through the door for my inspection.

The reason of Harris' call was that I had been there looking for a Pappy present, & he must have thought of you as Akbar (like St John) to suddenly produce these Akbarian 'gorgeousities'. Dear old George sat on & on, full of spirits and glowing with life, & in the middle of a harangue of his the door opened & in glided Sibell, delighted to see us both! & looking so very fat & faded but so absolutely loveable. Both babies came in to see her and then away she & George went, & I out to pursue my miserable quest for rooms. At Claridges the meanest are 78s. a day. Fortunately I shall need even [*sic*] the humblest until 17th June, as I am going on that day straight to Munich. . . . Lenbach may make me 80, but I won't be a leering Bulgarian as well; as soon as his picture is finished I go to *Ems*. There I stay four weeks, presumably from July 1 to August 1 and then to Scotland to stay till I sail back to my darling.

Friday I went to lunch with Margot and saw there Miss Jeanne Langtry[3] – *not* beautiful – haughty Charty[4] – and Neville Lyttelton.[5] Charty owned that she was a *shocking* friend in her neglect both in coming to see me & in writing – but she was old and pathetic I thought.

Margot announced to me that their finances were distressing. Henry had to sacrifice his whole political position in order to slave for money. If only the Bt. would give them £5000 instead of £2000 a year Henry [Asquith]* might have a chance – how they spent £7000 a year & had not saved a penny of the £5000 he made.

Darling, I am so glad to have had this heavenly still Sunday just to think and write and rest. The whole of my time in London is so crowded that I can do nothing quietly. . . .

Wednesday. Evey allowed me to ask Sir Wm Nicholson,[6] Miss Turner, Miss Myers & Mr Fanshawe to lunch – she then proceeded to ask Lady Savile, Capt. B.-Carr, Mrs Batleman and Lord Berkeley Paget, and this odd mixture of 'monde' amused me immensely as I heard Lord B. Paget say to Lady Savile 'Who on earth are these people?' 'Lady Curzon's Indians' said she. I had a great talk with Sir Wm Nicholson – and I must try to repeat it coherently. First he had heard from Sir Power Palmer, who thought he had been *so* badly treated, & said 'Lady Curzon thought so highly of my wife's *social* talents that I had hoped to be permanently appointed'!!!!!! Did you ever hear such a ground for being made C.-in-Chief. I then turned him on to Kitchener – he said when Lord Roberts went to South Africa he was indignant at the praise of Kitchener in the press and the general impression that though Roberts was C.-in-C. Kitchener was the man who was going to conduct operations – so as soon as Roberts arrived in South Africa he proceeded to send Kitchener off on all sorts of odd and undistinguished jobs and Lady Roberts would have nothing to say to him. Kitchener caught on to the Roberts' dislike – and proceeded to entirely efface himself, was never mentioned in the telegrams – and acted the part of a modest & retiring self-effacing uncomplaining small swell – & this continued for 9 months – until Lady Roberts suddenly discovered that Lord Kitchener was quite a different man to what she & Bobs had expected – hence sudden promotion to command at Paardeburg, eventually followed by whole Command etc. Nicholson said 'I have worked for two years with Kitchener; he is not a clever man – can't write a despatch – his knowledge of administration is *puerile* and his only quality to praise is his relentless determination to advance himself; in that he is the best worker I have ever known.' All soldiers blackguard each other, so Nicholson on Kitchener was no more [than] proof of the disloyalty of soldiers. He said Kitchener did not know the elementary rules of administration & his telegrams which had to go through Nicholson were quite astoundingly ignorant, unmethodical or clear-brained. I hope all this is a lie. I have written his exact words. Nicholson is really miserable not to have got Military Member in India & hates his War Office work. Can't endure St John, says he is a shocking bad speaker and his speech in House of Commons was a stupid statement, neither lucid or able. This is the soldier's view of old St John.

Kinge has been nearly killed on *Shamrock*, where it is believed he went with Favourite [Alice Keppel]; he went off the day after Queen's return. Neither has taken the smallest notice of me, though Charlotte Knollys[7] wired me from Sandringham saying Queen wished soon to see me. You will have read of accident on *Shamrock* – mast breaking & crashing but hurting no one on board. Perhaps Kinge was in bed below!...

Darling I hope you can make out my voluminous letters, & that all the tittle tattle doesn't bore you. My thoughts never, ever leave you and I find that my whole interest in people is what they may tell me which will interest you....

Lady Jeune[8] was at dinner last night and told me Mrs Craigie* was in a dangerously nervous state & couldn't stand any noise – clocks ticking – or eyes winking, quite upset me (allow for Kinkie exaggeration)....

Old Harry White burst like an affectionate tornado in to see me the other day. He quite overpowered me with his enthusiasm & his dense stupidity. Daisy confided to me at Wilton that he was getting tired of being only a secretary of Embassy & he would have become a Minister last winter if she hadn't been too ill to migrate to some foreign Capital. Mr Choate told me *he* thought Harry would accept another similar offer of a legation. What an upheaval this would mean. Daisy is much more spiky and knitting wildly. Yesterday she came to see me & she looked like a little steel sword blade – grey & murderous but she wasn't fierce but fond!

At Mrs Adair's Friday May 24. . . . This morning I went to the trooping of the Colours [*sic*] with Lady Roberts and it was quite like India as she & I in a landau followed the C.-in-C. & his staff down St James street.

What a vulgar old snob Lady R. is. She had asked all the Duchesses in London to her row of seats and as there was not enough room she kept saying 'You must find room (to the seat man) for this Duchess!'

The trooping was beautiful & the King rode on to the ground & got no cheers & no reception & he looked simply *elephantine*. Then I lunched with Alice Crane and she and Lord Jim & I went to meet Sir A. Milner at 2 at Waterloo.

All the Cabinet there. Hilda, Ettie, Alice and everyone you can think of. Train came in just as Lord Salisbury arrived & he & Joe, A.J.B. and Lord Roberts got in the saloon carriage. Then out got Sir A. looking worn. Crowd gave a feeble cheer. I was far away in the offing but he saw me, came across, wrung my hand & said 'I hope you have good news of George' which was thrillingly dear of him. He then proceeded to bow while crowd cheered & I quite flushed & shy was beating a retreat when Lord Salisbury came along & said 'I too must say how delighted I am to see you'. Well, while crowd cheered they got in the well-known Salisbury blue barouche, A. Milner on the right side, Lord S. next, *Joe* back to horses, and off they went. A.J.B. behind with Ettie in a brougham, St John & Hilda next in victoria, & Jim, Alice & I behind in procession. A *fair* crowd in streets who seemed waiting for Lord Roberts coming behind. *No enthusiasm.* . . .

G. Hamilton came to see me yesterday. He complained of the rise of mediocrity in the last ten years – & how in Indian Civil Service & English public life mediocrity came to the front! It was not so when he entered public life. I gasped assent but felt that he was the crowning illustration of his own theory.

He grudges much praise – speaks of *his* policy of frontier! I never knew such a hopeless dotard or such a small-minded, ferret-faced roving-eyed mediocrity. He took the line that it was such a mistake for you to talk of your programme of twelve reforms as then everyone's back rose in hostility & anticipation. He said your princeling scheme came before Cabinet today. I buttered the grim [?] idiot by saying you appreciated his capital letters. He was delighted. Fancy that fool being Sec. of State. . . .

Time is scampering & this must go beloved. All my whole heart of love.

> Loving loving
> (unspoilt unhead turned)
> Kinkie

I would give a world to kiss you.

1 One of the country seats of the 7th Earl Cowper. With his wife's death in 1913 Panshanger was inherited by 'Ettie', Lady Desborough, her niece. The house was demolished in 1952.
2 (1852–1921), Cassel was born and educated in Cologne. Financial advisor to Edward VII, Cassel fitted easily into the ruling circles for his recreations – aside from making money – were racing, hunting and shooting. It is said his GCB cost half a million pounds.
3 Daughter of Lily Langtry.
4 Charlotte Tennant (1858–1911), who in 1877 married the 4th Baron Ribblesdale. 'Haughty Charty' was said to be the loveliest of the Tennant sisters.
5 (1845–1931). Military member of the celebrated family known for its wit, piety and charm. So numerous were the Lytteltons that they were said to be able to field a full cricket eleven.
6 (1845–1918), a career soldier of distinction who served in the Afghan and South African wars and in India.
7 (1835–1930), Woman-of-the-Bedchamber to Queen Alexandra. The 'inevitable Charlotte' was in 1901 by royal warrant raised to the rank of 'the daughter of a Baron of the United Kingdom'.
8 Susan Mary Elizabeth Jeune (1845–1931), wife of Sir Francis Jeune and a prominent hostess and a contributor to the *New Review* and to the *Fortnightly Review*. She was a friend and admirer of Thomas Hardy and there are echoes of her lineage in, among other of his novels, *The Woodlanders*.

30 May [1901]   WINDSOR CASTLE

Darling:

I came down here yesterday feeling too ill to live but determined to keep up if possible. I went to Panshanger & the house was as cold as a tomb and I think I got a chill there. Anyhow I left there Tuesday morning, lunched at Mrs Adair's & 6 o'clock proceeded to Windsor from Paddington, was met by brougham & driven up to well-known door where Lord E. Clinton met me & took me up to rooms above the ones we had when here (the King was in the lower ones). He stopped sometime talking to me about the changes in the household & the customs & then retired – & left me to dress for 8.30 din. Lady Gosford came to fetch me then & I, all in black and long sleeves, went with her to the big green drawing room, where we once went with late

Queen's household after dinner. Here we waited, Ld. Gosford,[1] Miss Knollys, Lord Salisbury & Lady Gwennie, Lord Milner & the usual Stanley
Clarkes[2]& Arthur Ellis[3] until 8.45 when King & Queen came in *un*announced & *un*proceeded by anyone – she coming in first looking *lovely* in a black
vail & high gown – she went round shaking hands – he in Windsor dress –
short breeches, stockings & the garter, coming behind with a nice word for
everyone, while frantic efforts were made to kiss their hands. King then
walked into din. with Queen – rest arm in arm behind. I with Lord Kintire –
King & Queen sat side by side in the middle of the long table – & we dined in
the room with the big picture by DeSarthe of King and the Duke of Con-
naught riding. I felt very ill but played up & did my best to talk to King who
lost no time in condemning your ukase about Princes in strongest terms. I
asked if he had ever seen the Maharaja of Jeypore's letter. He said no, & was
most surprised that any Indian prince should take that line, & he wished a
copy of the letter sent him by you, so I said I would write you about it. His
informant evidently Baroda whom he cracked up to the skies. I mentioned
the mortality from famine in Baroda – also that the Great Man was not such a
pattern prince as he thought. I wish you could write him about Baroda. He
also mentioned Kuch Behar – and I said the life he led in England was
scandalous & I told him the story Mr Beaumont had told us of dining at
Princes & seeing Kuch Behar's Father & *son* dining together with their lady
loves. He was genuinely horrified at it. He said no other word of your work
& only thanks for pretty sandal cabinet. He mentioned the huge sums you
had got for memorial & expressed surprise that you should need so much.
While he was speaking of Baroda I told him that in India B. was not thought
the *most* loyal of princes and that some time ago the eye of Govt. had been
upon him but that B. was far too clever ever to do anything which could be
positively objected to, but there had been the suspicion Baroda had evidently
complained bitterly to King. Well, after dinner Queen came up & talked to
me & I didn't find her very deaf or difficult to understand, and she looked
quite heavenly. Her conversation is of infantile order – 'journey home',
'children' etc. & quite unlike old Queen, as neither King or Queen know
anything about India. I asked King if he thought he could come out to be
crowned – *he wants to* – but said he felt he couldn't – but he would not
positively say *no*. He said quite pathetically that he was all alone in his work.
His only son was in the Antipodes & his brother in Ireland, & he had no one
to do for him what he had done for late Queen, wh. is quite true. After din. he
& Queen went up to people & talked – he took Lord Salisbury – & she glided
up to A. Milner & took him off to a sofa – & I talked to Princess Victoria – &
at 11 they shook hands with us all & we went to bed. All night I had a good
old-fashioned chill & got no sleep until 4, so I didn't go down to breakfast
but saved myself for long Picnic to Virginia Water which I really enjoyed.
We started at 4: in [the first of] two gigantic charabancs were King &

Queen; opposite sat A. Milner, Princess Victoria and me, & the seat was so broad there was quite room for a fourth. King feared I minded back to horses, & wished me to come back in between *Queen and himself* but I assured him I loved going backwards; behind sat Sir Stanley Clarke & on return journey Princess Victoria sat by him which left A. Milner & me alone with the Monarchs. In the next char-a-banc were Lord Salisbury & Lady Gosford in front – Lady Gwendolen & Alick Yorke[4] next, behind the maids of honour. With two magnificent teams & four outriders we proceeded down longwalk through Windsor park to Virginia Water. The talk was chiefly rural, admiring the scenery & 'had A. Milner & I got such & such plants in our respective countries'. Queen kept making guttural sounds & I answered as best I could. Nothing could exceed their kindness. I had by this time quite recovered and was quite all right – and when we got to Virginia we had tea – at least we did, but the King had claret. I sat next to him and A. Milner the other side. After tea King invited Gwennie & me to go for a *sail* in a small sail boat. So we embarked with him & you would have laughed to see us, King in black flannel sailing the boat & an old man, Capt. Welsh, 83 years old, who had taught the King to sail when he was 7, tended the main sheet. There was no wind so we were becalmed. The Queen & Lady Gosford in a big white barge with a green silk canopy over the stern was being rowed about by A. Milner & Sir Stanley Clarke & a third boat contained the rest.

Lord Salisbury occupied a rustic seat on the bank, & he looked like a big black mountain in the distance. King never stopped smoking & frequently choked violently – he was in a beatific humour – smiling – but not talking much – though *Shamrock II* was discussed & pronounced a *complete* failure. We landed about 6.30 and Queen was full of life & little jokes & looked about sixteen – said I reminded her so of Lady Brownlow when she was young – admired my hair & was generally demonstrative.

The drive home by another road was beautiful & we got in about 7.45 and dined at 8.45. This time I went in with Lord Salisbury & he spoke very strongly against your over-working. He seemed to regard overworking as a form of selfishness. After all, England required your personality & your work, and both would eventually suffer if you did more than one brain could. He thinks no one can work the whole time, as he hears you do, & work well, that everyone needs some relaxation – recreation or change of thought. I said you had always found work both the relaxation & the recreation & that I couldn't say you did anything *but* work. Be careful, my love, & defeat the certainty that people feel you can't go on at the pace you are going.

After din. the King disappeared with that old ass-sycophant – snob Horace Farquhar,[5] & Queen & rest of us stood for one hour & forty minutes. Lord Salisbury asked to sit as he *couldn't* stand. The Queen went about from one to another – and I showed her some of the Indian photos I had with me which she had asked to see. Your shoot etc., but me on a Rhino she was *delighted* with & I never saw anyone more amused. I had brought her a piece of Benares silk & Princess Victoria a Jeypore enamel locket & both were profuse in their thanks. Queen came up quite ten times to say she thought it too dear of me to bring her such lovely presents. At 11.30 King went to play bridge and we to bed. Queen had to come back along the corridor to again thank me – so she is evidently pleased. During the whole of visit not a word of Charity-Scholarships, or India – just a charming visit & not a word of interest in India, though she did say 'Your husband is doing splendidly I hear', & said Kintire remarked they watched all you did with great interest!

The old Windsor is *gone*, the new reign hasn't the seriousness of the old – & it is still the Prince & Princess of Wales – & the old Queen seems Queen still in spirit. Next morning I departed and I am finishing this at Westgate.

The King was anxious that I should go to Frogmore before I left so he arranged that Lord E. Clinton should take me. Just as I was going Princess Victoria brought the Yorke [*sic*] children into the corridor to see me & King came out napkin in hand from his breakfast & said Goodbye to me. I promised the little Yorkes to send them a Burmese pony. I went off to Frogmore – & found the mausoleum packed [with] dying & dead flowers & huge wreaths of *artificial* violets & lilac! The monument has been raised a foot on account of the size of Queen's coffin underneath, so now you must climb up some steps to see her lying by her beloved Albert – beautiful figure – which makes her twenty-five – slim – beautiful hair softly waved under her crown & a most tender sad face turned towards him as his is towards her. A great ermine robe goes under both figures, & her hands are crossed over the sceptre, & the whole thing is very touching. Then I had a last look at Princess Alice & away to my train where I met Lawrence Drummond & he came to London with me. Lady Gosford had wired her electric motor carriage to meet me & in this I went shopping for Indian furniture & then went to see Rachel Dudley who had another miscarriage the other day & is in despair!...

1 The 4th Earl (1841–1922), who in 1901 became Vice-Chamberlain to Queen Alexandra. His wife was another attendant at the Bedchamber of the Queen.
2 A senior military officer, sometime acting Master of the King's Household.
3 (1837–1907), he was a Major-General and Senior Equerry to the King.
4 The Hon. Alexander Grantham Yorke (1847–1911), youngest son of the Earl and Countess of Hardwicke. Something of a court jester, Yorke served the Duke of Albany, Queen Victoria and Edward VII. He was a talented actor, singer and writer; his histrionic gifts appealed in particular to Queen Victoria.
5 (1844–1923), 1st Earl St Marylebone and Master of the Household of Edward VII. One of the numerous lesser lights of the Edwardian court, an opaque dubeity seems to surround many of this man's activities.

30 May to 3 June 1901   NORMANHURST
                                                                WESTGATE-ON-SEA

Darling:

After all my lamentations about late letters, this lovely lonely Sunday morning brought your precious letter by early post. You can simply not conceive my joy as I have been so depressed, firstly because I have been feeling too sick, & secondly ... without your comfort and help I feel fearfully adrift away off here in England alone. There is no one I can depend on or get any help from. Your family I *never* see, and all the thousand things that have to be done I must do unaided.

I went to Mrs Adair's from Evey's and she was most kind & let me go to & from Windsor from her house, and was so gentle & motherly to me. Then at Windsor (where it got fearfully *hot*, about 85 – after being bitterly cold) nothing could exceed the kindness of King & Queen. I always remained unostentatiously in background and was beckoned to by them to come & sit by them – & drive in their carriage – and King who was in a quiet beatific humour kept turning his dear old smile onto me. The humour of it all enchanted me. A. Milner & I driving with them & making most silly bits of conversation. Queen coyly removing mayflies from off King's billycock hat, & gurgling 'What horrible flies, do you have flies in India'! Then the water party – *can* you imagine such a party? Gwennie & me in a boat with King, no Keppel, & none of the sporting gang and oh! Lord Salisbury breathing heavily on the bank. The King is nearly as big as Lord S. & chokes so violently at times that you think he must explode. I saw no change in his manner – and his wonderful charm & kindliness are as great as ever. She is absolutely *amazing* – her slim young figure and lovely face without a line. Quite without interest in anything serious I should think. There is great feeling in the court against Horace Farquhar's appointment. Lord E. Cecil is a grand seigneur, & to be supplanted by that old braying ass is *too* bad. King said 'How is Baring getting on.' I said 'Well' & he said 'If Curzon had only taken my advice & taken him out at first he would have been spared all the blunders & gaucheries of that old school-fellow he *would* take out'!! I thought in my heart that we weren't much fonder of Baring than we had been of the much despised Sandbags. I will get his present and Adam's this week....

I asked Lady Roberts about going to India in August or early Sept.; she said her daughter had once done so and had *never* to this day recovered as she had been nearly killed by the heat. ...

Sunday, 9 June 1901   E S H E R   P L A C E[1]
                                                            S U R R E Y

Darling:

Such a lot as I have got to tell you! I must get back to the starting machine, collect my wits and gallop round the course, & try and tell you coherently about each furlong! I have crammed so much into the few hours since I posted the Friday letter.

Friday I gave up to a headache – not bad – but couldn't see St John as he very much wished me to do before the mail went to you. I was well enough in the evening to go and dine with Jennie Cornwallis-West,[2] and when I arrived who should I meet but Ma Craigie, sitting alone reading the evening paper waiting for the late host & hostess. It was a delight to see her – but oh! she has altered – face so broad that it takes your eye several seconds to get across it – especially as a heavy moustache arrests your vision and petrifies you with a fear that someday you may be blessed with a similar growth. She was robed in a white gown without shape, which hung from shoulder to ankle in a straight line and made her look like a caterpillar, her head was wreathed with white & cloth *ivy* leaves, so the whole effect was awful – but she triumphs over her clothes & is as dear as she ever was. Jennie and her youthful husband soon whirled in – & then such a funny company followed – Cowpers,[3] Marlboros, Winston, & Lady Warwick[4] who must have applied some of those slimming balms (which I believe are procurable) to portions of her body as her hips have *quite* gone – & are smaller *than mine*. She actually has *nothing* on which to sit down – and you must picture – thin legs, no hips, tiny waist – and all of a sudden such a bustiferous bust that every lb. of flesh removed from other parts has centred there & magnified that part so that you could play bridge on the table 'those fellows' make. She was all smiles & sweetness and I told her it was a joy to see her looking *so* well – upon which she said 'Don't talk about *my* looks. It is a joy to see anything in England so beautiful as you' – upon which I subsided – I can't quite get used to compliments, George – & I feel intensely the fuss people make over my looks, wh. *I* don't find altered though to hear the nonsense they talk you would think me quite 'hors coucous' in the line of beauty! George Wyndham sat by me & Duke of Marlborough on other side – so I had a delightful dinner talking to George and after talked to Pearl, as all the smart Consuelos left her alone, & I know the feeling of being out of all the little jokes etc. so she and I had a good talk till men came up – again she was left alone & Winston spoilt the evening by haranguing to the men & leaving all of us listening to Lady Maud Warrender's singing. Winston said he had heard from you, and expressed wonder at how you managed to write so many, many letters. He asked if you would stay out your time in India – said it was very unselfish work you were doing and seemed to think it was a great sacrifice of your home career. Peoples' points of view are so surprising, and A. Milner said much the same, & felt you could not sacrifice your home career by staying a whole five years in India. He said 'I feel that he has added greatly to his reputation by his Indian work though it has been bad luck for him to have people's attention centred in South Africa & not on all he is doing.' Pom[5] struck quite another note the other day, and said 'Thank God people's attention *has* been taken off India as George has been unmolested and he might have been bothered if he had been more closely followed.' Pom said he felt you had broken the backs of opposition in India and even the most strongly opposed had to admit you were doing right. Though there was much whimpering from Army, & disgruntled civilians, and of course the silly tales about our foolish formality & stiffness.

Where am I – still at dinner on Friday, so I must get on. Saturday morning Hillier came to see me & he is going to sail July 5. Then came Capt. Adam full of thanks for the pin – and anxious to come back next year to the staff, his Adjutancy of Reg. will by then be over. After him came B. Carr with his pockets bursting with P&O papers. I have settled to sail with the children from Marseilles Sept. 26th. . . .

Lady Suffolk came in on Sat. morning, a most *dear*, plain good old girl. So glad we loved her precious Suffolk, & full of gratitude for your kindness. After her came the Macleans, the same, & Miss Maclean quite recovered from typhoid. Then at 2 came St John to lunch. He wanted to know if you really were *well*, & not under nervous strain. He always carps on your feverish activity in letter writing to unnecessary people! He wanted to know if you really were strong and working *rationally* and sensibly – or half ill and near a breakdown. I assured him of the former state. Then in *great confidence* he unfolded his plan of calling upon you for your best troops in return for the spent and jaded men in South Africa. He said the men there were *done* & he felt that in asking you for soldiers that they would get a much better value than they gave to you so they would not press it if you felt it unwise – but that it might hasten the end of the war but of course they could not endanger India. India is made a commodity of – but it shews her magnificent strength that she should be squeezed in this way to fight out England's battles.

I wonder what you will do. If you will exchange a fresh, for a jaded army, or if you will think it too bad a bargain. St John was full of doubts as to how you would accept the plan. I said you would I thought go as far as you could to help Empire – but never endanger the safety of India by too greatly depleting her strength. . . .

Now for a bit o'gossip. Ettie has appropriated *Winston*, & he is now in her train – Pamela Plowden[6] quite cut out. Hugo violently and only temporarily in love with Mrs Rupert Beckett. Mary Elcho[7] follows Arthur like a faithful *slave*, and at Esher went to his side whenever he approached. Arthur smilingly appreciative of her love & devotion. Lady (Ian) Hamilton[8] was most hopelessly out of it at Esher poor woman – *she* thinks she is clever but no one else does, and Sunday evening she gave Evan & me a violent attack of 'fou rire', as she came & sat near us & talked high *art* to Evan, & the result was so comic that Edgar clutched her & romped her through the rooms shewing her pictures & saved Evan from hysterics. Gen. Hamilton is most delightful – but *she* quoted Browning to Hugo & Tolstoy to Arthur, & altogether had a magnificent failure all round. It was comic to see Helen, Alice, & Mary sit in judgment & icy condemnation on an outside Englishwoman.

Monday morning I came back to town at 9.30 as I thought I should find your letter – but alas! none came until *7.45p.m.*, though Lord Roberts whom I saw in the Esher R.R. station Monday morning told me he had already got his letter from you – about Wigram. I am so glad you wrote about him. Poor Capt. Adam was cut out of honours because he was with the Indian contingent which saved Natal – and which got no honours at all – he is not even getting the Ladysmith clasp in spite of having been through the siege and starving at Sutombi Camp for four months....

Monday night I dined with Daisy White, she had sent the virtuous Harry out to dine with Muriel, & she & I dined with Hedworth Lambton & Seymour Finch and went after to the opera. Daisy's shares are low in the friends market and she is cruelly crabbed by most as spiky, hysterical and very altered. I must say no more critical set exists in the world than the friends – & they are merciless to anyone who can't keep up in the race for pleasure. In my cynical moments I know in my heart that the great fuss they make of me is because I am a novelty – unjaded and the last edition of Georgian news! Daisy, Margot & Charty are all below par just now!...

The whole of the Lieutenant-Governor and Fanshawe episode is in the *Times*. The L.-G.'s remarks are so insolent that I cannot understand your remaining on friendly terms with him; he slanders you in public & he shows you no respect whatever & I boil with indignation at his dining next night at Govt. House. Several people have asked me about it & how a man on such terms with you should continue in office. I do hope you won't carry consideration to the extent of *sacrifice* of dignity. Mackworth Young is a contemptible coward. To behave as he does & yet remain L.-G! Fanshawe has at least been consistent & resigned....

This afternoon the Queen sent for me and I went to see her at Marlborough House and absolutely nothing could exceed her kindness – kissed me! – patted me – admired me! and wished to see me again. I brought her a black & silver piece of embroidery to shew her and she wants me to order a similar dress for her Coronation pageants – one is to be black & silver, another mauve & gold with great train. She said she would leave it all to me which I don't much like – but I shall do my very best to get her something beautiful embroidered at Delhi.

I forgot if in this letter I have told you that Evey Pelly of old Gosford days is going to Munich to Lenbach with me....

Now darling I must stop – full of apologies for such a poor letter & so unworthy of you – I see that I began by likening it to a race. I am certainly spent at the finish and am too tired to go another yard.

Lovingly, lovingly
K.

1 Country house of Sir Edgar and Lady Vincent.
2 *Née* Jennie Jerome (1854–1921), the thrice-married mother of Winston Churchill. Her first marriage, which took place in 1874, was to Lord Randolph Churchill (1850–95); her second husband was George Cornwallis-West, whom she married in 1900 and divorced in 1913. Her third marriage (contracted in 1918) was to Montague Porch. Her last two husbands were exceptionally handsome men. Jennie Jerome – an incessantly active woman – was also a playwright and magazine editor; she, like many of her generation and class, busied herself in different public causes, too.
3 The 7th Earl (1834–1905), whose wife, was the daughter of the 4th Marquess of Northampton and known to familiars as 'Katie'.
4 Frances Maynard, Countess of Warwick (1861–1938), was part of the Beresford scandal (see p. 24, n. 8) as both the latter and the King (then Prince of Wales) had enjoyed her favours. It seems harsh justice that the Prince banished her from Court in the 1890s, and perhaps even harsher that, after re-instatement, she was nudged out by Mrs Keppel. The Countess' conversion to Socialism could hardly have strengthened her hand in higher circles.
5 The Hon. Schomberg Kerr Macdonnell (1861–1915), Parliamentary Private Secretary to Lord Salisbury for twelve of the years between 1888 and 1902.
6 (1874–1971), who in 1902 married the 2nd Earl of Lytton (1876–1947).
7 (1861–1937), sister of George Wyndham. In 1883 she married Hugo Charteris (1857–1937), a tawdry creature prone to gambling and philandering. After a long wait he became 11th Earl of Wemyss and March. She entertained a hopeless passion for the emotionally reserved Arthur Balfour and was jealous of his admiration for Lady Curzon. To discuss the affairs of the Elchos – or of many others in their set – is to venture into an amatory minefield.
8 Lady Curzon alludes thus to the wife of Sir Ian Hamilton (1853–1947). A much decorated, far-serving soldier, Hamilton was from 1901 to 1902 Chief of Staff to Kitchener.

After circulating in London for some weeks Lady Curzon went first to Munich and then to Ems, returning to England at the end of July where she stayed briefly prior to going to a Scottish castle, Braemar, that she had rented for a rest period before embarking for India in late September.

Correspondence with Lord Curzon during this time continued unabated, and the Vicereine's letters from Munich where she went for her portrait to be painted by Franz von Lenbach offer a brisk account of the 'art business' of the time, for Lenbach, like others in that golden age of portraiture, seems very much the aesthetic impresario. A museum in his name is described by Lady Curzon as 'a magnificent Renaissance house which Munich has allowed him to design, build and then decorate. It was full of students and artists and as he conducted Evey and me about the crowd bowed down to him as though he were a God *– he is their Munich divinity and this house is a sort of life-work of his and in one of the magnificent rooms quite a dozen of his portraits are framed in the wall ....' Yet despite his reputation Lenbach seems to have eluded rediscovery by the dealers of our own times.*

At the end of June, her sittings for Lenbach completed, Lady Curzon left Munich for Ems, where her visit was of a very different order, for she both took the 'cure' and, as her letter of 14 July shows, underwent some sort of treatment to induce fertility. Her Ems letters are a curious blend of gossip (extracted from friends' letters) and rather poignant reflections and ruminations upon the common lot. But all show the deep affection that is the unshakeable basis of her marriage.

Lord Curzon continued to supply gossip from India, to apostrophize Lady Curzon's beauty, to throw off a pithy characterization – 'old stilted last-century Henry Adams', for instance – and to deplore the gaucherie of Simla amateur theatricals.

8 July 1901   VICEREGAL LODGE
                                                       SIMLA

Precious Kinkie:

... Our old Bhopal friend died of her cancer about three weeks ago and the daughter has been installed in her place. The Nepal Prime Minister who came down to Calcutta died this spring & was succeeded by his brother who arranged for my shoot in the Nepal Terai. This individual has now been ousted by his younger brother but strange to say there has been no bloodshedding.

Our friend Sanford is now up in Simla and is gradually breaking all the local pianos. Tonight Mrs Hawkins has a musical party, and Suffolk is to give a performance of a number of street cries, newspaper boys, race-course cads etc!...

The Youngs have asked me to either or both of two dances in August. I have declined. I really do not see how I can enter their house again – apology or no apology. He has gone too far this time, and I have no desire ever to speak to the man again.

Now my harmless gabble is over and I take and reread Kinkie's wonderful letters and comment on them.

Darling what an innings you have had with Arthur. Really cutting out poor dog-like Mary. I am so pleased to hear of the affection and interest that he has shown in you, for he is a rare and intellectual creature, and his affection is a prize. How lucky you have been in being thrown so much with him & Alfred Milner – so different from the ordinary man of the hour, such models of refinement, courtesy, high thinking & distinction.

Again how good it is to hear and read of the almost *furore* which you have excited in London. You see to Pappy Kinkie is always beautiful, always the most beautiful. It is such a platitude of existence that perhaps one ceases from giving expression to it. Hence it is delightful to know that what one is too habituated to reiterate here is shouted from the housetops in London, besides being declaimed in drawing rooms, and murmured in gardens & boudoirs. I take it too that they regard you as having 'Come on' during the past two years, while the familiar London beauties have faded somewhat & are becoming stale.

I do not think that Buckle was correct about me. Had I been at home I should not have been For. Sec. Lansdowne would still have superseded me. He is the ideal For. Sec. for these abdicating days. He is just gently backing down all the world over, and is a master of courtly surrender. He is really much better there at a time of stress than I should have been. I could not have bowed my head in the temple of every petty international Rimmon. But he does it with consummate grace.

Darling I don't see the slightest objection to your returning with B.-Carr or rather him with you. He will be useful to you in trains and on steamers, and is too tactful to bore you. There is a difference between going home with an ADC and coming out with one. In the former case you are out on a spree. In the latter you are returning to duty, and the official attendant seems all right. I should therefore certainly bring him out with you if he is desirous & willing to come.

I am quite pleased to hear of old Mar Castle.[1] I fancy it is the place that witnessed the nuptial transports of the Prince & Princess Alexis Dolgoronski[2] in which case I hope that you may not find in it a dangerous inspiration.

It is very good of old stilted last-century Henry Adams[3] to have collected the photos. No doubt they will arrive in due time & will I am sure be helpful. . . .

Your next letter will contain further news. Pappy now subsides into bed, but in it or out of it he is ever devoted & longing & even [word erased].

Pappy

1 Braemar Castle, some fifty miles west of Aberdeen.
2 As Curzon notes in a later letter, the Princess Dolgoronski was the tenant of Braemar Castle for some years at the turn of the century. She is said to have been the daughter of a wealthy Scot who perhaps owned a fishing fleet and who made the Scottish equivalent of an Anglo-American alliance : she for the title and the Prince – rarely on the scene – for the money. She entertained on a lavish scale.

3 Henry Adams (1838–1918), born in Boston, Mass. and educated at Harvard University. Adams was an editor, historian and academic perhaps best recalled as the author of *The Education of Henry Adams*, although historians might consider his *History of the United States*, which covers the first two decades of the last century, his *magnum opus*. A distinguished member of an eminent family of New England public servants, with two US Presidents among his forbears, Adams moved among the prominent in Europe and the United States. Van Wyck Brooks gives Adams discerning attention in his *New England: Indian Summer*. The 'photos' were aids for the projected memorial to Queen Victoria.

14 July 1901   EMS

Darling:

I feel that I have got into the backwater of life here. Someone once said somewhere, that life could be divided into three parts – the mainstream, the weir & the backwater. My backwater comes second, & is self imposed, & there hasn't been the exhilaration of going over a weir to deserve the horror of this isolation! Only dying health *or* a dead reputation could ever deserve a life at Ems and *thank God* my penance is half over. I have never known so foul a place – and I never leave this little brown coloured room save for a bath or a gargle of vile water. The heat is great – and Germans perspire – & whenever I go out the horror of being stared at is increased by the appearance of the starers. I hardly ever go to hear the band – in fact do anything, as I am defeated by this purgatory – & have never felt greater heat in India! I have on nothing but a dressing gown & yet I gasp. The only milestone in my day is a hot bath at 10 a.m. & my indignation over Ems in general makes the bath water fairly boil & bubble with excitement. It is *this* bath which is to work the miracle of an *almost* immaculate conception! And I hope that the patron saint of Ems will not retaliate & give me no twin sons because I hate the place so. Fortunately, there are 5 posts a day & every one brings me letters from everywhere. All the friends – & the children – keep my heart up, & on Tuesday or Wednesday I soar up and mountaineer with delight when your precious letter comes. And after it comes the reaction of loneliness – and wanting you beloved Pappy so *desperately*, and rebelling against this separation. I do love you – & what is the use of a loving woman 4000 miles away from your arms. I do feel in my heart that in one life there is a sense of comradeship almost as great as love. A man can know a woman well because her life, consequently the interests which mould her thoughts, are more or less simple. A man's life is so complex and much of it lies *outside* the woman's sphere & his mind is spiked with hundreds of magnets pointing to different possibilities that she may never know him in his entirety – but what is within her grasp has the power of making her truly happy – but take her away from it all & give her a blank six months in search of health & progeny & she must feel that she has nearly lost her anchorage. *There* now I feel better!...

Darling, Monday morning has brought your wonderful Naldera letter so I am happy – Also one from Rop which I enclose. I do not know if he magnifies the seriousness of the Young episode – but I *do* think that you allow M.Y. to win all along the line, if you allow him to insult you publicly, and then accept a private apology – surely the latter could be as public as the former. It is a shocking precedent to establish – this allowing subordinates to openly insult the Viceroy; and I think forcing his resignation would not have been worse than accepting a private apology which no one will know about – which was prompted by the Bishop whose mediation was prompted by Rop. Surely codes of honour have changed in India – and I deplore the possibility of a Lieutenant Governor insulting a Viceroy in a column of the *Times* and snapping his fingers & remaining in office. I only pray that others will not judge from your wonderful toleration that you do not resent as you might. India will become unbearable if the Civil Service inspired by Thorburn, M.Y. & Mr Fanshawe insult a Viceroy as well. It is quite awful – but perhaps in London where people all asked how such a thing was *possible*, the offense seemed worse than in India. If the apology had been as public as the insult I should not have felt so strongly. Now who of all the thousands who read the one knows of the other. Do not carry good humour to the point of *too* extreme forbearance. . . .

17 July 1901   VICEREGAL LODGE
                                                                    SIMLA

Darling sweet Kinkie:
    We have had a curious weather week. For after the monsoon seemed to have begun 8 days ago in earnest, it suddenly slackened off, we had whole days without rain & anxious telegrams began to pour in from all parts of India. Now as I write, 10.45 p.m. it has just begun to rain again, and the latest reports are more favourable. What an awful thing it would be to have another famine. I shudder at the thought of it. The week has been undistinguished by social incidents. I went to the Concert given by our band. It was much too long, 2 hours and 35 minutes, & everybody was nearly dead at the end. The band played quite beautifully but the orchestral pieces were much too long. There was a duet between Mrs Hawkins & Mrs Yorstoun – the first time that I have ever heard the former sing. The song was a poor one, Mrs H. had made Mrs Y. take the lower part whereas her voice is a high soprano, the result was a failure all round. Mrs H. produced upon me not the slightest impression.
    Baring has had one more of his big dinners, and he is now quite happy since his lady, Mrs P. Young, has come in for a fortnight from Chail and he is of course asked out to meet her at lunch and dinner on most days.
    Last night I went to the play, 2nd night, to see *Iolanthe*. None of the singers

had any voices, and in our box it was like listening to the metallic tinkle of the phonograph. Mrs Fegan was at her best, but had a small part. Incomparably the worst was Hanmer – I think positively the most atrocious performances I have ever seen in Simla. Lady Young was in the adjoining box and gave me a Medusa-like bow which would have frozen most people to stone. I have declined to go to either of her dances in August (mourning the excuse) and I am not going to dinner there either. Her husband deliberately insulted me before all India, and apology or no apology I never wish to speak to him again.

We have now finished the scheme of the new Frontier province & in sending it home to the Secretary of State for sanction, M. Young has written an acrid memorandum condemning it in the most unsparing way, and prophesying every sort of disaster. He is quite demented on the subject.

The Rana of Dholpur is dying at Pelitis villa at Mashobra. I expect that he will die tonight – acute pneumonia following upon hard drinking: one more of the disastrous consequences of English tastes, habits & sports upon an undisciplined native mind. Who would have thought a year and a half ago that Patiala and he would go within eight months of each other?

... Darling I have studied with the greatest admiration the Lenbach book: and I quite realise the Titianesque character and attributes of his work. They are much stronger however in his portraits of men – which are magnificent – than in those of women, which are apt to be sketchy & rather uncertain. A good many have rather an unfinished air and he does not seem to be strong upon hands.

However I have no doubt whatever of your wisdom in going to him, and what with his indubitable powers and his enthusiasm for yourself personally, it will be a woeful disappointment if he does not turn out a really noble picture....

I think that poor old Pappy must struggle off now to his solitary Kejouch. The rooms looks so bare with none of Kinkie's things strewn about and no Kinkie. Pappy does miss her so unutterably and life from day to day is so inexpressibly monotonous and dull. I have been out to dinner twice, theatre three times, concert once, gymkhana twice, polo once – and this in 3 long months or 90 days. I never drive out by any chance. What is the fun? & have never been round the Ladies mile. I either walk round Prospect or Summer Hills, which are absolutely deserted, or play Tennis at which I am becoming an almost respectable player. However four out of the seven months are over, so I can afford to struggle on, and then Kinkie will come back and I shall hold her in my arms once more. Love to sweet itty girls. I will write again to Cimmie before long, as I wrote Irene last. I don't quite know where to send this to, as the date of your arrival at Old Mar is uncertain. I think I had better try India Office this time.

Ever lovingly
Pappy

23 July 1901   VICEREGAL LODGE
                                                          SIMLA

Darling pet:
   ... I must just add that poor little Dholpur, as I foretold, died a few nights
ago. His Maharani who was with him when he died & was very fond of him
went straight off to her room, took poison (it is not generally known) and
died 1½ hours later. She was only twenty-five years old (he thirty-nine) & was
not the mother of the boys whom we know. The bodies were burned on
Mashobra hill the next day, & the eldest boy who is 18, though he does not
look it, succeeds. The Rana has left one million sterling of jewels in the
house. A good many of them will have to be sold. . . .

   [24 July.]   Darling. I must tell you really by far the best lie that I have ever
heard since we came to India. Geo. Hamilton wrote it to me & said it was a
favourite story of the King's: it is that old Sandbags [Col. Sandbach] left us
because I ordered him to stand behind my chair at luncheon or dinner & he
could not stomach the indignity! What next? What next? I say. How can one
contend against such colossal imagination? Geo. H. says it is all jealousy,
that your beauty & my success have given rise to the wildest inventions.
Well, well. I don't suppose it matters. But I really would almost prefer it
were said that like Lord Lytton[1] I kissed every pretty woman, or like Lord
Dufferin[2] slipped my arm round their waists & called them Dear Ladies –
than that I should be credited with being such an ineffable idiot, and now
away, away from all this nonsense to Kinkie's letters, all happiness, all peace,
all trust & all truth. Poor Pappy gets so downcast sometimes in all this
whirlwind of calumny & fiction. No one to sustain him, grind, grind, grind
with never a word of encouragement, on on on till the collar breaks and the
poor beast stumbles and dies. I suppose it is all right and it doesn't matter.
But sometimes when I think of myself spending my heart's blood here, and
no one caring one little damn, the spirit goes out of me, and I feel like giving
in. You don't know, or perhaps you do, what my isolation has been this
summer. I am crying now so that I can scarcely see the page. But it has always
been so. The willing horse is flogged till he drops & the work goes on.

   Darling, your letters are my only solace. Where should I be without them?
They don't come till Monday morning, but Monday morning in bed is the
nearest thing to Heaven. (I think however that I know a nearer). . . .

1 Edward Robert Lytton Bulwer-Lytton (1831–91), 1st Earl of Lytton and Viceroy
   of India 1875–80. During his term Queen Victoria assumed the title Empress of
   India. Under the pseudonym 'Owen Meredith' Lytton wrote some facile, deriva-
   tive verse. He could be tiresomely flirtatious.
2 Dandiacal and cultured, the 1st Marquess of Dufferin and Ava (1826–1902) was
   Viceroy 1884–8. He held many significant diplomatic posts, including the
   Governor-Generalship of Canada and the Embassies at Rome and Paris. He was

adept at allocating work, shrewd, and in the main made a favourable impression as Viceroy. The Kipling family were always welcome in the Dufferin household, and of the poet's mother the Viceroy said 'Dulness and Mrs Kipling cannot exist in the same room.' Her son's poem 'Our Viceroy Resigns' is addressed to the Marquess on his unexpected withdrawal from office.

Monday, 29 July [1901]   [LONDON]

Pappy darling:

Since I stopped writing last Sat. evening enough has happened to found a three vol. novel on – with Arthur & two Marys for dramatis personae. I must begin! Well yesterday morning I meant to start at 10 in my hired motor for Wilton – it was late in appearing so I went by train – & left word for motor to follow so that I could give it a trial at Wilton. I arrived at Wilton to find a forlorn party – Mary & Arthur out motoring – on the lawn Daisy, Harry, a stray girl, Maurice Hewlett, Edmund Gosse, Gay, Alice & Jim, Lord Cairns, Ian, Mr Griscom and Lord Kerry. I was welcomed with feverish glee – & in turn talked to all the planets but no one was in form. Well – Arthur rejoiced to see me – planted himself by me at lunch & we had great fun, & I had to tell them all about the portrait, & as there seemed to be 12 of them in Lenbach's studio he suggested that one be allowed him (he has offered to buy one!). After lunch it rained – & I wouldn't motor but got Ian to try mine & it broke down. I sat on the balcony & talked to E. Gosse[1] & M. Hewlett,[2] & Arthur golfed & Mary watched him from her window! After din. I had a word before eternal bridge with A. & settled the time for starting in his motor for London Monday. Mary getting wind of this immediately suggested coming too. In the meantime she had taken *me* to her room and said to me 'I suppose you know Arthur is very fond of you.' I said 'I don't think he is at all. I am only in the galère with all his other friends & after all Mary YOU are the only one who matters to Mr A.J.B. in the least.' 'No!' says she, 'I know when he is interested & he loves being with you.' Of course I said this was *nonsense*. Monday morning came and Arthur appeared when I was standing in the hall – he said 'What are you going to do today' & I said, 'Motoring with you to London & meeting you at dinner.' A., 'But why not lunch too at Willis' Rooms & Lady Elcho will come too', so I said '*Yes*', flew off to collect my clothing & left Arthur to invite his Mary. We started off in his motor – he Mary & I! The lunch at Willis referred to, & *time settled*. Well at 2 I went to Willis. *There* was Arthur, no Mary, so we sat on a sofa to wait for her, and A. said 'Where shall we sit for lunch', I said '*There* – for there are no mirrors, and at that table I can't see my profile from 18 points of view!' A. said simply 'I should then prefer her seat as anything more singularly perfect I have never seen!' 2.10 came & no Mary so he said 'Let's begin', & we did, & got *all through lunch & forgot Mary*, A. saying from time to time, 'I love this tête à tête', but it *was* unexpected. After coffee I said *I* am worried about Mary and shall go to Cadogan Square and see what has happened to her – so he said – very well, we will go together, so off we went to 62 Cadogan Square. Once there we asked for her, & footman went off to fetch her – while we waited in library. Suddenly Mary appeared – wild haired in a *filthy* dressing gown, & for two seconds we all stood quite still, then Arthur said 'Well why didn't you come', 'Come *where*' said Mary! 'To lunch' said A., 'You never asked me' cried Mary & hurled herself on a sofa! Arthur said 'You must be *mad*.' Then Mary said 'Don't you think I would have come if you had thought you wanted me! Would I [come ?] on home when I could be with you. I have suffered agonies to think you didn't want me & you had promised to lunch alone with me!' A. said 'I am dazed. All was arranged & time settled etc. & as you didn't come Lady Curzon & I came to see if you were ill!' I said, seeing her on the verge of tears, 'It was all a mistake – I must fly away – I will take your hansom Mr Balfour & you can get another.' Arthur was quite stern & cold with his poor trembling wild Mary, & he said 'Yes. I will go back to the House directly but let me understand clearly' – with a smile – 'that you & I meet at dinner tonight at House of Commons.' I hope for Mary's sake that she flew into his arms & repented of her aphasia – for it can only have been suspension of reason which made her think she wasn't asked!

Well at 8 I went to House of Commons. Found Arthur, George, Ian & Quiky & Consuelo & an American Miss Deacon – daughter of the famous Deacon/Abeille Mamma, & who is the latest rage in London.[3] Arthur looked chastened & had had his hair cut, & he greeted me with a wide smile & said 'I recognize the delicious *wrap* of this afternoon.' I laughed for after the tragic Comedy of 62 Cadogan Square his sudden interest in dress was comic. We went to dinner & he walked with me & he only referred to the incident by saying 'That poor lady still insists she never was asked to lunch-eon.' I made great fun of our tête à tête luncheon as A. had reiterated to the French waiter that 'une troisième' was coming – which is the old story of the tête à têtes, & I said the dubious look on the waiter's dough-like countenance had caused me transports! After dinner the romantic George walked me down the moonlit terrace but I was too cautious to remain more than 5 minutes with his flashing eyes. Ellie had joined the din. & after sitting about a table & indulging in a lame general conversation, She and I went. Everyone talks of the new beauty Miss Deacon who is striking looking and has studied Greek & looks a little like Amelie Rives did. Even the mother who has lived the life of a cocotte in Paris is asked about here. She wasn't there last night fortunately as I wouldn't have spoken to her! Ellie said no one talked of anything but the Deaconess but that A.J.B. had said at din. that it was pitiable to compare her with me & that as we two had sat there at din. her star had seemed to set.

It is disgusting, the craze for anything new. Ellie said to Seymour Finch why all this fuss about Deacons – oh! said S. only because adultery & murder were both committed in the mother's bedroom!

Alfred Lyall came to see me yesterday, and is coming to stay in Scotland with me. He says Fanshawe & Young incidentally were so extravagant and outrageous that they were universally condemned here. He said your *Great hope* should be to maintain absolute Frontier tranquility for 6 months. *Any* trouble would be disastrous.

Arthur asked me if anyone would open a letter he wrote to you, as he would write you quite a different letter about politics and people if he felt that no eyes but yours would see it – and I assured him you opened all your home letters, so he could write Cabinet secrets & anything he liked. Whatever you do when you write to him don't mention me or let him think I have exaggerated his kindness to me. His friendship is a prize, but I only tell you the incidents of it as the Marys & Ellies would tear me limb from limb if ever he cared to do more than gaze quietly at me as he does now! He is their God – & not mine! I am waiting here for Queen's command. Charlotte Knollys has written she wished to see me about ordering Coronation dress in India. . . .

1 Edmund Gosse (1849–1928), son of the eminent zoologist Philip Henry Gosse. Librarian in the British Museum and later a translator at the Board of Trade, Gosse wrote much literary criticism and biography. His critical theories are today unfashionable, but he is to be remembered for *Father and Son* (1907), a matchless study of divergence between the generations.

2 Maurice Hewlett (1861–1923), poet, novelist and essayist. If recalled at all it would be for his short pieces evocative of Wiltshire and its life.

3 The gossip in this letter about the Deacons alludes to a scandal involving Florence Baldwin Deacon whose abnormally jealous Bostonian husband, Edward Parker Deacon, in 1892 fatally wounded her lover, an over-amorous Frenchman named Emile François Abeille. Not surprisingly Edward Deacon died insane. The 'Miss Deacon' mentioned here, one of several children born to the hapless couple, was Gladys Marie (1881–1977) who, in 1921, after some years as mistress of the Duke of Marlborough became his second Duchess, thus succeeding the elegant Consuelo Vanderbilt. To enumerate the vagaries of Edwardian turpitude is a dreary pastime, but it might be noted that 'Miss Deacon' appears to have inherited her mother's talent for profligate excursion and is said to have counted Bernard Berenson among her triumphs. In an unpublished letter of Mary Curzon's written in August 1901 she remarks that Consuelo Vanderbilt has quite adopted Miss Deacon and has her living at Blenheim; and in her autobiography *The Glitter and the Gold* (1953) Consuelo Vanderbilt speaks kindly of her guest. Gladys Deacon has been the subject of a biography and she and her mother also appear, albeit fleetingly, in other memoirs of this era.

31 July 1901   VICEREGAL LODGE
                                                                         SIMLA

Darling pet:

I have been up this afternoon to see Law who has been rather seriously unwell. He has internal gripes & makes awful faces. He says it is chronic enteritis whatever that may be.... Two Arundel girls & Ma Arundel have turned up. The latter is recovering from the fatigues of the journey, but I took the girls to the theatre, tall demure dignified pious amiable young creatures, quite nice-looking & redolent of virtue.

It was a matinée. I only went in order to see Suffolk perform in a play with his lady Mrs Cleveland. The two were quite the worst performers that I have ever seen on any stage, the most hopeless amateurish sticks. I gave Suffolk a lot of hints & tips afterward for which he was most grateful and I believe that at the second performance he was much better. As an actor however he is classes below Marker which is saying a good deal. In the next play he is to be a drunkard! The theatre is very bad this year, up to date, not nearly up to the level of last year or the year before. Mrs Corfin however has just appeared & the long-nosed Holland is again upon the scene....

Our dinner dance last week was an unusually good one. There were about 150 people, 70 to dine, 80 in afterwards, & everyone out of the house by 12 midnight. These dances are so popular that many people are hoping that they will be continued in place of our big dances another year. We always have about 15 men over, & the consequence is that all the girls & most of the mothers get a turn. There is never a crowd, the floor is perfect, and every one is in bed by 12.30 so that there is a consensus of opinion that the experiment is an uncommon success.

I went to the usual Mission sermon from Bp. of Lahore last Sunday, very earnest, very able, & quite unconvincing. He dines here this week. Meanwhile Secretary of State has sent to me a proposal with consent of King, Prime Min. & Archbishop of Canterbury to make Welldon an archbishop & has asked my opinion. It puts me in a very difficult position. I can scarcely tell you the hubbub that has been caused in the Indian press by Welldon's speeches in England. He is denounced by every newspaper, English & Indian. They think he is coming back with a policy of State proselytising and the English Bills in Education. I am supposed to have sent him home in order to secure assent to this new policy, and if he comes back an Archbishop everyone will imagine that he has succeeded. He is doing me & the Govt. an immense amount of harm, and on public grounds it would be the greatest boon if he never returned to the country. I think that truth will compel me to say this to the Sec. of State.

By the way the other day I wrote a private letter to dear old Ritchie asking him to tell me as a friend what was going on in the inner councils of the India

Office. I enclose you his reply which is as clear as it is frank. It is just what I expected & indeed knew. They thwart me every day in every way. Geo. Hamilton is not man enough to stand up against them. Their latest achievement is to refuse an extension of service to Daly who is the sort of Eric Lamington × Sanderson of our Foreign Dept., on the ground that he is a soldier. Fancy Daly a soldier! I believe he was one 20 years ago for a few months. Every mail there comes out some petty criticism or censure upon some proposal of our Govt. And yet they are not courageous enough to stand up in big things, and I walk over their prostrate bodies. Godley[1] often admits to me the iniquity of the whole system. But who will be so bold as to alter it? One fine day I will expose the whole thing in Parliament in London, & then the system will be altered. As it is, in any question which involves the expenditure of one anna the Council is supreme.

The paralysis that has settled down upon the Govt. at home owing to the S. African war is appalling. Lansdowne is in a pitiable funk, and we are simply wallowing humiliated all over the world. The Russians are making hay while the sun shines on our frontier, & their officers are busy on every side. But I cannot get the India Office to put a question, make a protest, or institute an enquiry. If the country knew how we are eating dirt all round there would be an outcry against the Govt. that would run them hard. It sometimes almost makes me mad to read their arguments & despatches. . . .

I am afraid darling that Ems was a stuffy and repulsive hole. Your description was piteous. I suppose too that one cannot purchase physical fitness without physical discomfort, but thank God it is now all over and you are amid the breezes of Braemar. . . .

I am pleased that my father was affectionate & dear to you. He is a very warmhearted man at bottom, but has not communicated quite the same warmth of feeling to all his family. Did you ever see old Sophy?[2] . . .

And now goodnight and a thousand blessings & kisses to adorable Kinko who is the light of his eyes & the joy of his heart to

fatigued
worn out
but
loving &
india rubber
Pappy

Thursday morning. I have just got your sudden & startling wire about poor Hilda and am telegraphing to St John. I wonder what it all is. So glad your wire ends with *Vigor.*

---

1 Sir Arthur Godley (1847–1932), later 1st Baron Kilbracken. Private Secretary to

Gladstone and from 1883 to 1909 Under-Secretary of State for India, he was an able public servant.

2 Sophia Caroline Curzon (1857–1929), another of Lord Curzon's sisters; in 1882 she married a parson.

31 July 1901   [LONDON]

Darling – The first I knew of Hilda's illness[1] was yesterday. She went to Esher for Sunday with a sore throat – and on Monday she wrote me the throat was worse. Tuesday night St John and Muriel were sent for & went down with two doctors; all of Tuesday night she nearly died. Yesterday there was little hope and that morning St John wired me the terrible news. Last night at dinner I heard from Arthur who took me in how dangerous it was so I left dinner early & cabled to you to prepare you for the worst & to enable you to cable enquiries – and as soon as I heard the worst I cabled you again.

Poor poor Hilda – the tragedy is more awful because her life had been lived in striving & when all had come which could make her happy it is snatched away, and they had staked so much on the unreal and the social success & seem to have ignored the really deep side of life which was being all in all to each other. So there is the agony of feeling that both somehow could have been happier than they were in the struggles after success. And now it is all over and St John faces life broken and alone. Everyone seemed broken last night. Arthur quite dead beat and the gloom of approaching sorrow hanging over us all. . . . Hilda's illness & death are still a complete mystery – she died at Esher and it was so sudden that G. Wyndham who came here this morning did not know she was dead. I enclose my last wires from St John. I shall stay for her funeral because he is your dearest friend and his dearness to me since I have been back has been beyond words. I will write more details as I hear them. Now I know *nothing* beyond the grim fact that she was ill on Monday with a sore throat, and *dead* Thursday morning.

Poor bubbling discontented Hilda – only by last mail I wrote about her joy over the engagement of Muriel[2] & I would give worlds now not to have said what I did about her worldly ambitions for her Muriel – you will only read the letter when she has been dead a fortnight. Darling I can never in the world put all in this letter that I should like, so I must wait till my next. I have had a talk with Lord Cromer* which can keep – but one with Welldon which must go to you at once. He came here this morning & said *this* : 'I have come to ask you to advise me. You and George are my greatest friends in the World & as George is so far away I must ask you to advise me. I have my doubts about returning to India. I do not feel that I am fitted for the work. I cannot bridle my speech & my aims sufficiently for a post which is so hampered by difficulties as is the Bish. of Cal. My friendship for George is a thing so deep that I cannot work *counter* to him, & to the line the Govt. imposes upon him as Viceroy & I dread the trouble I would cause him if I carried out much that I think right. Frankly I do not consider I am the man for India. I resent the suspicion with which work is watched in India & the desire there seems to be to put a man in the wrong who is trying to do right, by quoting a passage in a speech or sermon which can harm him. I resent this attitude of suspicion by the official world. George in a greater way suffers from this too – but I have come to a point when I must decide my future life and I come – You must forgive me for asking so much of you who are after all only a friend because I value your counsel & shall be guided by it in my decision.'

I told him perfectly frankly that with all his great gifts etc. etc. I felt India was not really the field for him and after a long, long talk he left me – I think decided not to return or at least only for a time if at all.

He said he had not the tact or the willingness to remain silent when he felt strongly on a subject & this he knew was a danger in India where the Govt. could not encourage missions. I told him that he would be the greatest loss to us if he did not return but in my heart I knew it would be a good thing to have a Bishop who was a comforting element in society instead of one who provoked conflict and dislike as he does.

Darling – I feel as though I had begun this letter 10 years ago and I am almost ashamed to send the chapter which I have written about the Mary Elcho comedy on Monday. We have met so often since and she is always the same sweet patient creature whom Arthur adores. Last night we sat either side of him at dinner & we were all too tired and too distressed over St John to talk or think.

I believe it is just the life of London which has killed Hilda. She has worked herself literally to death and was it seems on the verge of a nervous collapse so that she had no force or strength to resist the poison. She went to Esher with St John and Muriel Saturday & was only tired. She played bridge until late & Sunday felt unwell but only retired to her bed after that. Monday St John & Muriel returned to London leaving her in Helen Vincent's care & she thought her ill enough to get in a nurse & a doctor. *Tuesday morning* she was worse and at 4 p.m. Helen wired to St John to come down & bring Felix Semon.[3] St John had a big dinner at the house Tuesday & said he wasn't anxious but would go down at 9 and take the Dr. so he went in the midst of the dinner. While the guests were still at the party sitting on the terrace of the house a telephone [call] came from St John summoning Muriel at once – and she went off with Evan. It seems that before any of the Brodricks arrived Helen had had a battle with death with Hilda & from 4 p.m. until St John came she felt she must die – as soon as Semon came he performed tracheotomy & this gave her relief. All Tuesday night and Wednesday she lingered though Semon gave her no hope. Wed. at 9 she became unconscious and died at 7.30 this morning. Of course two things must come into all our heads, 1st that she should not have been left with such a throat at Esher & that the specialist should have come long before as she had battled with death 5 hours before he arrived, while that hideous dinner was going on in the house, & poor St John not worried, though Helen had wired that Drs. & nurses *must come* – but time was not thought pressing & she slipped through all their hands choked to death from Quinzy or blood poisoning – no one knows really what!...

1 Hilda Brodrick's death jolted her contemporaries very hard. She was a sister of Lord Elcho and, as Lady Hilda Charteris, married Brodrick in 1880.
2 Muriel Brodrick, who later married into the Tweedmouth family.
3 (1845–1921), a well-known throat specialist.

6 August 1901   4 ST JAMES SQUARE[1]

Darling – This is a strange and unexpected place to write you from, but Katie and I came up to Hilda's memorial service at St Margaret's, and instead of going back to rest with her I am waiting here for my Scotch train to go North tonight to Braemar in. We all were too sad and depressed to enjoy our Sunday and a cold East wind Sunday completely defeated our spirits. Ellie was ill in her bed and only carried downstairs yesterday p.m. Arthur wizened, worried and exhausted, and Henry Asquith obese and hopeful about his political future, and Margot revelling in a garrulous selfish grief which got on every ones' nerves. Her attitude was to feel remorse for having quarrelled politically with Hilda and never made it up but her remorse was unnecessary as she had been ever ready to make peace with Hilda after the Colville speech episode – so Margot's hysterical remorse was only a trial to each one of us in turn. Margot's nervous state has developed a tendency of always hurting and wounding, and she made a succession of crashers during the party which were astounding. . . .

London is a grave – and it seems too unnatural to be sitting at Lord Cowper's writing table writing to you – but ever since Hilda's death I have felt in a dream, & surprised at nothing & I should not even wonder if the Van Dyck opposite got out of his frame & broke the deafening stillness by starting to talk. There is a bank holiday dismalness out of doors, and a ghostly stillness of a shut up house in the room. I have had no greater day of abject loneliness since I left you. At 8 I shall start from King's Cross and get to Mamma & the babies for luncheon tomorrow, thank God.

Darling, one startling development in the character of one of your friends I think I have never written you about. It is Henry Asquith's amorous interest in various people, his reckless consumption of champagne, & his loss of that old strong granite sense of *right* & his abomination of the disreputable. When talking to Katie yesterday I said I felt it strange that Henry's influence on Margot had not resulted in her being more temperate & balanced. Katie said 'How could you expect Henry Asquith to give her qualities of which he is destitute!' She then told me in deep secrecy, as she naturally did not care to talk of it, of Henry's having fallen in love with Pamela Plowden & gone to her room at night! That he was quite uncontrollable in the emotional side of his nature, & had been caught kissing someone passionately, the name Katie would not tell me! – He had then had a flirtation with Mouche Duncombe, & had seen a great deal of her, so much so that Katie condemned him for his absurdity. Can you conceive of anything more grotesque than Henry in the role of a lover of girls! I must say that the men who are allied by love or marriage to the Tennants deteriorate! Harry Cust[2] & Lucy, Charty & her two Tommies – *both* in love with Sibyl Westmoreland – & Margot & Henry! I must say that in trying to acquire the conversation of the class he has been transplanted into, that he has acquired quite shocking coarseness. Last night at dinner as he was describing to me the last phase of the Cust-Violet episode, he began by saying that Harry had 'resumed relations' with V., but that she was his 'door mat' as well as his mistress! That Violet now contended that the whole story of Nina being about to have a child before she married Harry Cust was a fabrication, & an intrigue & plot to marry Harry – & that she had not been in the family way etc. etc. This is really too strong, and Violet has lost all sense of decency in her mania about that old horrible trouble.

Well to turn to more healthy topics I must write you about Lord Cromer – I had a talk with him at John Revelstoke's – and was wonderfully interested as he started straight off about India, said he *disliked* it intensely, & that he would never consent to go there, because he knew he could never work under the conditions there. The isolation, never coming home to the more active interests of the broader life of England etc., the *horror* he had of the social side of India – etc. I was amazed at the *feeling* he showed & couldn't understand him. Two nights later I met him again at the House dining with Alice & after din. he said come over here & sit down & talk & he settled himself in a chair by me on the terrace, hauled his hat over his eyes, smoked, & told me the *whole* story of the Ilbert bill[3] – he was a Member of Council at the time & had agreed to it, & made no defence of the awful mistake they had all made, but what he *condemned* most deeply was the *disloyalty* of English officials in India to their chief. He said that Lord Ripon might have gone back at one time from his support of the bill, but that the outrageous behaviour of the English in India made it impossible – he said Calcutta was like a mad town – Ashley Eden deserted his Chief when he had been responsible for introducing the bill – he talked on & on and I thrilled with interest & saw at last what made him so hate official India. He said the sense of honour amongst subordinates to the Chief was different in India to England or Egypt. Every single *word* he said was true – and how often we have said the same about the disloyalty. You now see why he never would go back, and I see why he feels so strongly against India. He talked for over an hour so it was a *real* pleasure – he asked me about the Cadet Corps scheme and I explained it coherently as A. Lyall had told me about it the day before – he said bluntly, 'Thank you. You have explained it quite clearly. I should have been strongly opposed to any scheme which allowed a native to hold a *Regimental Commission* which could place him in a position of command over English officers'....

1 Town house of the 7th Earl Cowper.
2 Henry John Cockayne Cust (1861–1917), educated at Eton and Cambridge, MP for Stamford 1890–5 and for Bermondsey 1901–6. For a few years Cust edited, with success, the *Pall Mall Gazette*. He was said to be of great charm but self-indulgent and 'deficient in will power'. He was apparently a relentless pursuer of women, some sort of sexual fireship in fact. Sadly but not surprisingly his wife, *née* Nina Welby-Gregory, who loved him deeply and to whom he was married for many years, was neglected by him. The 'Violet' mentioned was the then Duchess of Rutland.
3 A controversial Bill of the 1880s introduced by one Courtenay Ilbert during the Viceroyalty of Lord Ripon. Ultimately defeated, it advocated putting Indians in the Civil Service on comparable footing with Europeans in the dispensation of justice. This would have meant that Indian magistrates could try Europeans. The outcry by businessmen, planters and other whites – to say nothing of the memsahibs – was more than clamorous. Ironically, the matter of the Ilbert Bill revealed much good about the Raj. Central to this complex legislation was loyalty to one's chief – a focal civil service problem then as now.

7 August 1901   BRAEMAR CASTLE
                                                            BRAEMAR, N.B.

Darling precious Pappy:

I arrived here last night and thought of you all the way to Balmoral as you had described the drive so wonderfully when you went there in September to see Queen before we went to India. I thought Balmoral sat too low down in the hollow of the Dee to be really fine and the drive beyond to Braemar went through a far finer country and is far more beautiful. Invercauld stood out on a fine bend of the river and the Dee took a sudden wonderful turn and right away before me a lovely view opened out *&* in the middle of a few tall pines stood quite the most fantastic amazing erection I ever ever have seen. I laughed from sheer astonishment *&* pleasure *&* knew it was my Castle, standing out in the open – like a slender white exclamation mark against the pines beyond. Windowless – turreted – charming – as though King Lear might have built it up in a moment of melancholy. The road swept past it to a gate on the far side. All the time I stared quite fascinated, then up swept the drive to a low castellated wall with pink roses leaning against the dear old sides. A huge iron gate wide open and Mamma (wearing a newly bought and horribly curling fringe) waiting inside it. Between the wall *&* the castle is a little space of ten feet of granite and then came another immense massive door of iron bars and a corkscrew stair twisting up in front of you as you step through the door. The house is exactly like a hyacinth if you think of the stem as the stairs, and unexpected rooms growing off at the sides as the flowers on the hyacinth stalk – 6 steps up came a big smoking room – 6 more a charming red papered dining room – another few and a large low charmingly furnished sitting room – then a succession of bed rooms with such low doors that you must crouch in and out, until up at the top of the hyacinth – my girls in such pretty bright nurseries – both in bed (it was midday) and looking too pretty.

The main artery of the house is the stone stair carpeted with bright apple green – and along the stone wall is a red silk rope on to which you cling as you go from room to room. There are no halls or passages. All the rooms from top to bottom peep on to the broad stone stairs. The whole house is furnished with exquisite taste and it reminds me of the Priory[1] – and I have never been in so completely fascinating a building. I climb about from room to room never in the least knowing which I am in and laughing the whole time. The stair is Piccadilly & up and down clinging to the broad red rope with the girls thinking it the greatest lark, Mamma going very slowly saying 'Each of these steps is a different height – one is seven inches & the other three!' Miss Garland throbbing with Scotch pride in so marvellous a castle – new butler cat-footed and surprised at nothing, a magnificent gray haired housemaid immensely pleased at my glee over the house, & then my idiotic footman rushing up with a dozen letters come by the first post I am here – knocking his empty pate on the low stone door jamb & narrowly escaping sudden death!

The most wonderful thing of all is that every room is *light*. The windows are wide enough to shoot a bow and arrow through, but daylight must love to pour in through the narrow windows and there isn't a dark corner anywhere. It is a beloved spot....

How soon the time will pass now my precious Pappy & you will get your loving bedraggled old Kinkie back to your arms.

Love from Mamma and the girls.

K.

1 A house in Reigate, Surrey, rented by the Curzons early in their married lives.

9 August 1901   BRAEMAR CASTLE
                                                                BRAEMAR, N.B.

Angel. Here is a letter from Baron Speck wh. Papa sent to me and I pass it on to amuse you. He is certainly enthusiastic isn't he! And all he says about Pappy is quite true. I hope he has informed William III of all you are doing.

Poor Empress Frederick's death is very sad, as her life seemed so over-crowded with tragedy and suffering. Charlotte Knollys told me that her suffering was ghastly, that the cancer was all *over* her externally & she was swathed in cotton wool – her screams were so awful that the sentries outside the Castle had implored to be moved further off.

To branch to better things Charlotte Knollys told me that the Munshi bogie which had frightened all the household at Windsor for many years had proved a ridiculous farce, as the poor man had not only given up *all* his letters but even the photos signed by Queen, and had returned to India like a whipped hound. All the Indian servants have gone back so that now there is no Oriental picture & queerness at Court. Lord Cromer told me (he *said* confidentially) that when Lord Rosebery offered him India he urged him to make up his mind quickly as it was of grave importance that the appointment should be made *before the Munshi* returned from India to England (he was on his way) as he might object & prevent any appointment! How funny this sounds now. Lord C. went on to say that all the Queen's Eastern ideas were the Munshi's and were invariably wrong – he had no opinion of her judgment which surprised me. He told a good story of a visit to Balmoral when they played pencil games after dinner & you were told to write down what famous names you could beginning with N. In looking over Princess Beatrice's list he saw Napoleon – Nelson – NA & he said who *is* the 3rd & she replied the french Marshall of course, NA (meaning Ney): have you never heard of him!

As we went the other night on our way to bed we described people with two adjectives or nouns & quite the best was Lord Cowper's, 'A pagaent and a stomach', who was the King! 'Dyed hair and anecdotes of George III' was Arthur's description of Sir Wm Harcourt & I guessed it! These two were so malicious that we stopped the game. . . .

22 August 1901 [BRAEMAR]

Darling, I did not half answer your letter of 31st as I only got back from Aberdeen on Tuesday night, and had to post off my fat letters to you Wednesday as the posts from this place are so casual and I don't know that this can catch the post at all.

What you tell me of Welldon is most interesting. The very day you were writing to me what a mercy it would be if he never returned to India, *I* was seeing him in London and telling him as I wrote you that perhaps India wasn't the place for him! I never finished the conversation as George Wyndham called in the midst of the Bishop's confessions, but between his name coming up & his appearance Welldon said 'I must see what can be done as I feel with you that [I] would do better not to return. I know I should cause George trouble, & I am reluctant in any way to interfere with his work.' What amazes me is the Archbishopric and he must have known of it when I saw him but how or why he got it I simply cannot imagine as *no one*, King, G. Hamilton, Lord Salisbury or Arthur thinks him a success in India. Lady Jeune told me the impression was universal – so *why on earth* make him this. I think with his blundering tactlessness he would do you infinite harm in this new capacity, as no one would know exactly what he was – as a common or garden Bishop he was innocuous but as a Viceroy of the Church he has a sort of undefined *&* unlimited power. Of course you have had to write G. Hamilton the truth about him, and I know you have hated doing so. He was strangely revolting to behold when I saw him in London, his head under his hair was in a most frightful state – eczema *&* dandruff and it made me sick to look at him!

Darling I was rather sad that India was left to the last day of Parliament and then opened up to an empty house. It is partly George Hamilton, who is thought the weakest minister on the front bench, and partly the apathy *&* indifference to India, but one thing I do think remarkable and that is the confidence which both sides feel in your rule – there is never any *party feeling* about you and the radicals are as enthusiastic about you as the Unionists, and one thing has very much struck me since I have been back and that is the thankfulness in everyone's brain that during all the wretched S. African war *you* have been in India. Arthur voiced this very strongly *&* so did Lord Salisbury. Darling I think you should really be very jubilant over the real appreciation of your work. You have had no one to blow the trumpet of your achievements as I should like to hear it done, but the sheer force *&* magnitude of your work has made itself felt in every class. I haven't had half time to tell you *all* the nice things I have heard. I went to see Lyall the old Scotch house agent in London and I am not sure if I told you that he greeted me with 'I'm delighted to see ye, *&* I must just tell you it's grand work Lord Curzon is doin' out there *&* if I may be allowed to add ye have done your part verra gracefully!' The station master at Cole Green asked for you *&* remarked respectfully that you were making a great Viceroy. The feeling is universal – so beam with joy my love *&* never feel like the unappreciated willing horse who works till the collar breaks. You arouse jealousy naturally but you are successful. . . .

Darling I am so hopelessly indiscreet *&* outspoken in my letters that I hope you tear them up. I keep yours locked up. Letters get about in the most mysterious ways and Kinge has been much upset by all sorts of letters of old Queen's being sold at Christies which could only have been stolen through servants as they were written to foreign potentates and all sorts of people who would never sell them. My calumnies about Kinge would land me in the tower. . . .

My general health is quite quite fit – the trouble is only local so no one can say I am ill, and if only we had children enough there would be no cause to be laid up!

Lovingly
K.

Darling pet:
 ... The Laws gave one of their extraordinary banquets last week. Fenn was
a guest. Mr *&* Mrs Fanshaw sat next each other! Two officers from Jutogh
were similarly placed! and finally Lady Law and two ladies (a mother *&*
daughter) sat in a row. This was the dinner table arrangement. Did you ever
hear of such a woman? He [Law] is going to take leave after his next Budget
& Finlay will probably act. I wonder if she will ever allow him to come back.
It doesn't much matter one way or the other....

You will have seen that I made Geo. H[amilton] apologise publicly for his
wholly undeserved censure on our Govt. He has also sent profuse apologies
in private. The fact is that he promised Seymour King the papers in House of
Commons without revealing the contents *&* an idiot in the office sent them
off to the printers without submitting them to Godley or to him! But all the
apologies I get seem to me in the main in private! However it don't matter.
These things are forgotten.

Darling I was perfectly amazed at your report about H. Asquith, bed-sides,
a loose tongue, *&* champagne. The latter was developing a little before we
left, but the two others are new to me. Margot always used to enlarge upon
his amorous propensities but I presumed they were confined to the marital
couch: and certainly mid-night visits to virginal chambers were the last thing
of which I dreamed. You cannot transplant the middle classes. Chamberlain
was first decoyed by Duchesses, until he became a snob and a Tory. Similarly
Henry has been tempted into other *&* covert fields. Fortunately his total lack
of physical charm must act as a barrier if not to his own passions at any rate to
their gratification. As for H[arry] C[ust] I do not believe in his having
resumed relations with V[iolet], because I do not myself believe that they
have ever been interrupted. That man has gone far to ruin every woman with
whom he has ever been brought into contact and it is he who has elevated the
inherent duplicity in V. to a fine art.

Your conversations with Lord Cromer so admirably depicted, greatly interested me. He is a strong capable resolute unemotional man. When I was at
the F.O. we had only two diplomats worthy of the name. Pauncefoot for
temper *&* skill, Cromer for knowing his mind, biding his time *&* getting
what he wanted. The rest were pigmies where they were not idiots.

I am very very much struck by the weakening of Arthur's hold upon the
public mind. In every quarterly, monthly, *&* weekly magazine or paper I see
cries for *a man*, and in none of them is he ever mentioned as a possible
candidate for the category. Again it is very distressing to see his House of
Commons leadership openly derided *&* continued, although he seems to me
to bear it with admirable fortitude *&* good temper. The story about him *&*

the funeral was rather disappointing too. The fact is he is not interested in other people's private lives except at the casual points where he is brought into contact with them. He would never do for a husband. . . .

Darling your description of your castle was even more fascinating if that were possible than the picture of it. I never saw a more delightful looking place though as it seems rather destitute of grounds. What is the cottage-like house under the trees on the other side of the river? How happy you must be in such a quaint spot amid that champagne air. The only sorrow is that this is the first Scotch chateau that we have not enjoyed together. How did old Ma Dolgoronski get hold of the house. I presume that she rents it from Farquharson or Fife or is it from Kinge? . . .

11 September [1901]   BRAEMAR CASTLE
                                                        BRAEMAR, N.B.

Darling – Sir Alfred Lyall came yesterday afternoon and we had a nice yap till dressing time – *&* he quite fell under the spell of the portrait-sketch. . . . He enquired eagerly after you *&* was rejoiced to hear good news. We were talking about soldiers *&* about the lies about us in India – he said these were entirely invented by soldiers – he said soldiers quite outdistanced women in their inventive powers and he said that all gossip *&* lies in India emanated from soldiers and *always* had done so. He said the lies about us were so amazing that no one credited them in the least. They might be believed if they were in the range of even wild probability but most of them were not. He is strong for Princes cadet corps but thinks you should not dwell too much on *Princely* houses in carrying it out as you would get a better class of young man from [illegible] *&* good families other than Princes – and that the plan should not be for great chiefs' sons alone. Speaking of Chiefs he mentioned King having sent for the papers relating to the scheme last May or whenever it was being considered as someone had alarmed him about it – he said Dighton Probyn was undoubtedly the King's Indian adviser. Regarding 'Chiefs Ukase' he knew of King's feeling against it *&* said his only feeling about it was that it should have been *Gazetted*. However that is a chose faite. He is full of delight at the treaty with the Sheik of Kuwait[1] and says it is a grand move – due to your instigation – and known to *no one* yet – but that there will be a row when it is known as Germany will be wild at England's protecting the terminus to her railroad. A. Lyall tells me that the book which so alarmed A.J.B[alfour] about Russia and Afghanistan was a book in possession of Foreign Office which he had seen also. He thinks Russia too involved in Manchuria to be at present a real bogie in Afghanistan. . . .

I have not said a word about Welldon though he has talked about him a great deal *&* says he must return to India as he can get nothing in England –

he is so disliked here, & so feared for his power of blundering hopelessly in delicate situations, & in the church here they won't risk tactless Experiments. . . .

Mrs Favourite Keppel is bringing forth another questionable offspring! Either Lord Stavordale's or H. Sturt's!! Lord Stavordale is going to be married off to Birdie Stewart as Mrs Keppel made a promise to Lady Ilchester to *allow* him to marry at end of this summer! Jenny said people were seriously disgusted at goings on of King – his pursuit of the Keppel and daily visit there in his green brougham & his boon companions Ernest Cassel etc. She said King was miserable in the company of any but his few bridge friends as he feels himself so hopelessly out of it with intelligence or intellect – on the whole he had begun *badly*! I thought I scented personal pique in much of her tirade, as since she married she has dropped out of her old position. . . .

All for today Beloved Pappy, soon to hold loving K. in his arms.

1 Presumably the secret agreement of February 1899 concluded between the Viceroy and Sheikh Mubarak in which Kuwait's concerns were placed under British protection.

12 September 1901   BRAEMAR CASTLE
                                                                  BRAEMAR, N.B.

Darling precious Pappy:

Sir Alfred has departed this morning and I have greatly enjoyed long yaps with him and we have been quite inseparable. Yesterday he went out with children & me & we talked about Fouché[1] and how far he was instrumental in the downfall of Napoleon. There is a new book on Fouché which he thinks will interest you very much and I shall get it in case spare hours ever come, you could glance at it. Last night he and Bron and I discussed at dinner who we would choose as the three greatest living popular writers. Sara Bernhart[2] was asked this question by [illegible] & greatly impressed him by replying Maurice Hewlett – Kipling, & *Wells*! She must have cribbed the three from some enthusiast, but the two first showed considerable insight for a French woman. We didn't get very far as I began with Meredith,[3] Kipling & S. Philips[4] [*sic*] & A. Lyall agreed to all but Philips and Bron went strongly anti-Meredith, and then began the usual wrangle 'If Stevenson[5] were living wouldn't he be greater than them all?' Of course the Stevenson school put him ahead of Scott & Meredith, & Bron voiced this & Sir A. & I stuck up for Scott and I for Meredith. . . .

Darling your memorial in India is enough to make King very angry, for the gold mine of the wealth of Princes has been tapped for the Indian Memorial & his London one languishes at £143,000. Of course if there had been no Calcutta one the Princes of India could have brought the London subscriptions up to the required sum – and there is without doubt a feeling of resentment against; your moves have checkmated theirs. It is beginning to be a disgrace that all interest has gone from the Queen's London Memorial. How right you were to strike while the iron was hot and not let the enthusiasm fizzle out. It will be more & more difficult to raise money here as Coronation Year will divert interest from the Memorial & after it is over time will have levelled peoples' interest in the matter to indifference almost. Even this year no one seemed to care in the least what was done. Repeatedly people have said to me 'What in the world does George want with such an Amount. Surely India doesn't need such a sum as that to commemorate Queen!'

We have begun packing so journey back is fairly begun and a month from today I should be at Simla – Oh! how glad I am the six months have nearly come to an end. I shall never leave you again and if you stay longer in India you will come home for a few months & freshen up before the last two years of work. All love.

Your loving K.

1 Generously termed 'statesman', Joseph Fouché (1763–1820) was a powerful police chief under Napoleon. His agents were unpleasantly ubiquitous and his methods despicable.
2 (1845–1923), the notorious French actress known as 'the divine Sarah'.
3 George Meredith (1828–1909), one of the most poetically gifted of the Victorian novelists and now generally unread.
4 Stephen Phillips (1868–1915), a poetaster who flickered briefly as a writer of tragedy.
5 Robert Louis Stevenson (1850–1894), Scottish novelist, essayist and short-story writer.

[From Lord Curzon to Lady Curzon]
18 September 1901   VICEREGAL LODGE
                                                     SIMLA

 ... Darling, it is quite true. You are the most humble most unspoiled creature in the world. I have never detected in you a ray of vanity, and it is your sublime unconsciousness of all that is most remarkable in you that is one of your unconquerable charms. As for being allied to poor old Pappy, it is a bit of a penance to any one for it involves considerable self sacrifice and some subordination. Still he tries to do his duty and he is devoted to Kinkie which are perhaps the two sole redeeming merits in an otherwise grim personality. The Psalmist once wrote 'Desire of me & I shall give thee *the heathen for thine inheritance, & the uttermost parts of the earth for thy possession*. Thou shalt bruise them with a rod of iron & break them in pieces like a potter's vessel.'

He was a bit of a prophet. Now good night to sweet angelic Kinkie drawing near on the sandals of the ocean & on the wings of love.

Ever loving
P.

19 September 1901   BRAEMAR CASTLE
                                                       BRAEMAR, N.B.

Darling Pappy:

I hope you sent an Indian telly to America of grief on account of poor McKinley.[1] I have read Tellies from all corners of earth – Dublin – Ceylon – Wellington & Shanghai – but no mention has been made of India. I hope all the same that one went....

I entirely agree with your last letter about Arthur and there is undoubtedly great discontent in the party over his slackness and his bad leadership. Lord Percy told me at Wrest that his personal popularity was as great as ever but his Manchester speech had permanently weakened his position in the party & he could never command the same confidence as before he made that astounding speech. His charm will always give him a following – but no one thinks him a strong man to lead & to be followed in a moment of national danger.

As you see the papers are full of Lord Salisbury's resignation. I believe the rumour to be quite without foundation, he can't resign until the war is over as the belief the country has in him is unique, and the moment he went there would be chaos and all the party dissatisfaction which is kept in check by his powerful personality would break out, & no one knows what it would lead to.

Poor old George Wyndham is pining away to be put in the Cabinet as he can never do anything so long as this ridiculous pigmy Lord Cadogan hangs on. *He* won't go until the new King has been to Ireland – he got nothing from the Queen's visit & lives in hopes of a *Dukedom*. The Dudleys chances are behind the Marlboroughs for Ireland. The Dudleys & Essexes have a moor together & people like Evie who live on the outer fringe of the fast set hint all sorts of horrors about Rachel & Adele. I can't believe them – peoples' minds are so corrupt now that the most innocent friendships are misunderstood, I believe.

John Hay[2] is quite certain to resign now as he & Roosevelt[3] are not friends at all. Lodge[4] and Roosevelt were always jingo fire-eaters, & Hay far too conciliatory & diplomatic for their taste – & in the old days in Washington they were not friends. Mr Root[5] will I believe take Hay's place, and Mamma says he is the ablest man in the Cabinet, thoroughly American – quite untempered by European experience such as Hay's. Hanna's[6] sun has set – he has been the corrupting influence behind McKinley's throne & the first swish of the new broom will send him out of the administration.

Lodge is travelling in Russia with H. Adams & I heard from H.A. from Moscow. Lodge will not leave the Senate for any Cabinet post so his influence will only be indirect. Roosevelt is far too impulsive a creature to be looked upon with anything but fear at first – but nothing tempers madness so much as great power & responsibility. How many Teddian tirades I remember when he raved in Bunker Hill fashion against England & ground his teeth with rage & longing to have a 'go at the damned British'. Once dining at the Lodges he & Lodge & Wolcott⁷ discussed what posts they would accept in administration in preference to the Senate. Lodge said *none* – Wolcott said he would go to London if he had the chance. Teddy flew at him like a panther – clapped his mouth shut, & hissed through grinding yellowed fangs 'You say that in my hearing! You would go from preference to the Enemy of your Country! I'm *ashamed* of you.'

If Springy goes through Canal with me we can have such revelages about 'Teddy'. Springy & Speck knew him like brothers. Just one more Roosevelt story. Long ago in Washington I went in his house & found his little boy of eight crumpled up in a chair in the drawing room. I said 'What's the matter with you Ted you look so white' – 'Oh! it's only fighting' said Ted. 'Dad makes me fight him whenever he has time & we've just been fighting in the yard & Dad's the strongest & I'm sick. I don't like fights!' Teddy père on his knees in the dirt pummelling his son of eight round the back yard! What a picture.

Darling I have inflicted pages on you this week – but it is my last letter, & writing has been such a relief & my only consolation, as it has brought me near Pappy almost every day.

I send enclosed from Arthur. . . . The 'am writing' is a wonder for Arthur and I shall have to frame the letter along with a note he wrote me in June. I wonder if he has ever written to you. I suppose he is vext with me for chucking Whittinghame, but I didn't really want to go & be scourged by that odious Red Campbell fiend – & I did tell A. in joke, I wouldn't have my last Sun. in England defeated by Lady Frances,⁸ & he said 'I'll send her away', but I said of course I was in jest! But I do detest her, & am not sorry [not] to go within range of the fiery tongue of flaming hair. She is a brute.

Really goodbye now.

Loving K.

1 President William McKinley (1843–1901) had died on 14 September from an assassin's bullet fired on 2 September.

2 John Milton Hay (1838–1905), American Ambassador to the Court of St James 1897–8; US Secretary of State 1898–1905.

3 Theodore ('Teddy') Roosevelt (1858–1919), twenty-sixth President of the United States from 1901 – when he succeeded McKinley – until 1909.

4 Henry Cabot Lodge (1850–1924), American statesman and author.

5 Elihu Root (1845–1937), American lawyer who from August 1899 to February 1904 was Secretary of War in the Cabinets of Presidents McKinley and Roosevelt respectively. Root subsequently became Secretary of State under Roosevelt.

6 Marcus Alonzo Hanna (1837–1904), a mid-western tycoon with interests in mining, banking and construction who supported McKinley and who in due course became a Senator from Ohio. He was even spoken of as a possible Presidential candidate.

7 Presumably Edward Oliver Wolcott (1848–1905), Senator from Colorado 1889–1901. The Wolcotts were a prominent American family who distinguished themselves in law, medicine and politics over several generations.

8 A formidable advocate of women's suffrage, the energetic Lady Frances Balfour, daughter of the 8th Duke of Argyll, had married Balfour's youngest brother, Eustace, in 1879. She is said to have introduced a lively zeal into a cool household.

PART III

*Lady Curzon's
Hyderabad Journal
of 1902:
her Persian Gulf Journal
of 1903:
letters to her mother,
1905–6*

The journals, diaries and letters of Mary Curzon's last years (1902–1906) furnish the basis of the pages that follow, commencing with two journals – the Hyderabad and the Persian Gulf – followed by correspondence with her mother.

Mary Curzon returned to India in late October 1901 and began once more to record her life there, so it is not surprising that her writings of this time should sound familiar themes: her pride in her family, her awareness of high position and her intended visit to Washington. Little of this may seem of primary importance, but her varied activities and interests collectively show the pattern of her existence. Much, too, of this correspondence echoes the freshness, animation and vivacity of her earliest Indian days. Similarly, the two journals are marked by qualities reminiscent of the India she first came to in 1899.

The Hyderabad Journal of March–April 1902 delineates one of Curzon's numerous progresses, but from an angle quite different from that of his own weekly letters to the Secretary of State for India. Lady Curzon's journal is a straight piece of reporting that again reveals her acute eye for detail. The description of their arrival, the colour, noise and lights of the Nizam's palace, and the linguistic gaffes at the Resident's banquet combine into an arresting and graphic social picture. This is followed by a series of tiger 'beats', none of which is more than a prelude to the appalling accident at the second camp: Lady Curzon's plain, direct account impressively underlines the tragedy of that occasion. But the journal is rounded off in a lighter vein with an amusing description of a 'huge lady' in green and an old man of atrocious table manners. Indeed, the entire record is so deftly assembled as to suggest a professional writer at work.

Much of what is said about the Hyderabad Journal applies to the Persian Gulf Journal of November–December 1903, which is preceded by a letter of 25 November written to Mrs Leiter nine days after the journal proper was commenced. By now Lady Curzon is expecting her third child, her daughter Alexandra (Sandra), who was born in March 1904; and, as one of the letters states, the Vicereine leads 'the most extravagant lazy life' enjoying both good spirits and good health aboard the Viceregal Hardinge.

The Persian Gulf Journal is a bustling, energetic piece of writing full of movement and life, much of it amusing as the tortures of sea-sickness are juxtaposed with the pomp of Empire. It is a racy journal dealing freely with personalities – Sheikhs, Residents and Sultans – in a light-humoured way that renders those potentates figures of fun and harmless ridicule. It is almost wholly free from the intricacies of political machination and relies largely for its effect upon the caprices of the human animal. The journal registers, then, as a blithe and cheerful commentary upon the pompous and self-important.

The Hyderabad Journal

We arrived at Hyderabad from Calcutta on Saturday morning, March 29th, and were met by the Nizam, the heir – a fat boy of fifteen – the British Resident, the Ministers of the Hyderabad Government, and the General of the British troops stationed at Secunderabad, Sir George Prettyman. After handshaking and introductions and inspecting the Guard of Honour, we proceeded to our carriage, which was an immense canary yellow chariot, with a yellow damask canopy supported on silver poles, and drawn by four white horses covered with gold and silver harness and trappings, ridden by yellow postillions and led by innumerable runners and grooms. In this barge George and I proceeded through the decorated and densely crowded streets. Behind us came the Nizam in a second royal yellow shandrydan, the Staff, Ministers, and Generals following in vehicles of decreasing splendour, till the tail of the procession shewed a dilapidated fiacre in yellow. The streets to the Residency were lined with the Nizam's troops in every variety of costume, from the gorgeous Golconda lancers in yellow and silver to the Arab regiments in Turkish turbans and flowing drapery. At the Residence where we are staying we took leave of the Nizam and his son, and sat under punkahs and had breakfast. It is only ninety-two, and not so hot as we expected.

At 11.30 George received the Nizam in Durbar. He came attended by all his nobles, with his full escort of Golconda lancers, and made a very fine show. He is a very small, shy little man, who seldom speaks. He is without any of the gorgeous ornaments usually inseparable from Oriental majesty, and only wears a black frock coat and a small yellow turban, and the blue ribbon of the Star of India across his narrow chest.

After George received the Nizam in Durbar he saw the Ministers in private audience; and in the afternoon he returned the Nizam's visit, going with the full escort of Fourth Hussars and his own Staff – Mr Lawrence, Captain Baker-Carr, Captain Wigram, and Captain Yarde-Buller.[1]

In the evening Colonel Barr, the British Resident, gave a banquet for us. I went in to dinner with the Nizam, and the fat fifteen year old son, the Sahibzada [son of a sahib], took in Evey Pelley. His only coherent remark to her was 'You play polo Miss Polly?' The Nizam sat imperturbable and silent at my side, while I went through the alphabet with subjects, in my attempts to talk to him: A – Arab horses; B – Colonel Barr; C – Calcutta and Curries; D – Diamonds; E – Elephants; F – Foreign Princes who infest India at present; G – Golconda, the old diamond mines which are in Hyderabad; H – Habibulla, the Ameer of Afghanistan. You would have thought that this magnificent variety would have lasted through dinner, but each topic died at its birth and only produced a gentle 'Yes' or 'Exactly' from His Highness. George witnessed my efforts with amusement, and eventually leaned over the narrow table and asked him about the Delhi Durbar next January, but even this inspiring subject produced only a flutter of the eyelid. After dinner George held a levee and I went to bed, but was too hot to sleep even after three sleepless nights in the train.

Sunday we had a quiet day until 4.30, when George had a private interview with the Nizam, to discuss with him the Berar Question,[2] which has been a vexed problem between the British Government and Hyderabad for sixty years, and is now in a fair way to being settled, which will be a great triumph for George.

At 6.30 we went to Church to a pretentious service, during which the parson prayed for the Nizam, and the punkahs shrieked so loud that they drowned the sermon and fanned the oil lamps into smoking chimneys. There was a small dinner at the Residency in the evening.

Monday morning I went over a hospital and a school, and saw my class of Victoria midwives which is being trained by the Nizam.

The heat is intense between 11 and 5, about 104 on our covered balcony and 95 under a punkah, so we do little but read and write till the sun goes down. This (Monday) afternoon we drove in state through the town to a palace of the Nizam's about 5 miles away. The Nizam & Co. met us and showed us over a really magnificent marble-halled, Maple-furnished palace, which stood on a barren rocky hill and looked over Hyderabad town. We drove back just in time to dress for the Nizam's banquet. Again we went forth in the yellow chariot with the escort of Fourth Hussars, and drove through brilliantly illuminated streets packed with people who seem to have taken up their positions by the roadway indefinitely to watch every carriage procession that comes out of the Residency. We drove under triumphal arches, on which gigantic portraits of George and me were painted and illuminated from behind, so we shone forth in red nosed radiance. In all the pictures I wore my big tiara, and as I had it on in the carriage there was no mistaking my identity. Bands played all along the streets and bugles tootled, and at the foot of the palace steps we were met by the Nizam & Co. and taken in to an immense courtyard with a huge tank in the centre. The four sides of the palace were a mass of lights, which were reflected in the water. Down the side was a broad walk lined by Arabs with drawn swords, and we walked down this to the middle of the palace, where, at the top of an immense flight of steps were 250 people waiting for us and their dinner. Here there was a wait of five minutes in a hall full of statuary, and then dinner was announced, and George with the Resident's wife leading, and the Nizam and I following, we walked through several rooms of the palace, and emerged on to a terrace and into a second courtyard identical with the first, save that instead of a huge lake in the centre an enormous tent stood, and under it tables for 250 people. The four sides of the square were a mass of lights fixed on to the palace walls, and the effect was dazzling and the heat stifling as there were no punkahs, and until I could get some ice and soda I thought I should suffocate. Dinner was short and beautifully served, and ended with little pies being served from which flew little live birds as you cut open the lid. They flew wildly about and lit on my tiara, and one rested comfortably on George's head, but soon they all flew away in the night, and we settled down to the more serious business of listening to the Nizam propose our health and make a speech, which George answered by proposing the Nizam's. The Nizam's Ministers were in a state of wild suspense before George's speech, as the wildest reports had gone abroad about what he would say: so their relief was boundless when he made no soul-stirring announcement. After dinner we climbed to the roof of the palace to watch fireworks, which were considerably damped by a shower of rain, which was refreshing to clothes and diamonds. The rain hurried us off the roof, and we retired through the bedimmed courtyards and started off in our yellow chariot. The din of bands and bugles was so deafening that the Arab horses of the escort of the Fourth Hussars discharged their riders right and left, and our progress was enlivened by riderless chargers bolting past the carriage and a general roar of excitement from the crowd. We were lucky to get home without broken heads. . . .

Our third day began with a long ride, and then a walk and a climb into the usual machan, which is a small railed platform about four feet long and two feet six inches wide. On this we sit, and I don't take up more than eight square inches, and rifles and cartridge bags are stowed away and George kneels or stands while I crouch and watch. An old shikari [native hunter] stands on the ladder, and usually two or three orderlies perch in neighbouring trees. We had just got in the machan, George was loading, Captain Wigram and Major Afzal-ud-daula and a group of servants were standing on the ground, when without warning and with a wild roar out bounded a tiger forty yards away. No group of men ever made such time as the group under the tree. Some climbed the ladder, others trees, and Captain Wigram and Major Afzal-ud-daula ran for their lives and clambered up the elephants by the tails! George, quite unprepared, pulled frantically at his rifle, which was at 'safety' and not cocked, and by the time he got it to go off the tiger was a hundred yards away, bellowing and bounding and scattering humanity and getting clean away. The tiger could not have been fifty yards away while we were under our machan, and it would have been a great spectacle if he had met us as we walked through the jungle. We were miserable at our loss of the tiger, but such wild tales were told of hairbreadth escapes that we could only laugh thankfully at the successful stampede of the beautiful Staff pursued by tiger.

We rode (temperature 100) to our afternoon beat, and lost no time in being ready for tiger this time, so of course we had a long wait, but a funny one, as a big bear came bounding out of the jungle, and the first person he met was Captain Yarde-Buller on an elephant. The bear gave him one look and then dashed at a tree in which Captain Wigram sat on a branch. He 'booed' at the bear who sat down with surprise, and then rushed to another tree in which Lord Suffolk sat. This was a third shock, so off he bounded only to meet *us* in our machan, and his surprise was so complete that he sat spellbound! We were posted in a long line waiting for the tiger, so could see the bear's adventures, and were shaking with laughter. He bounded up a bank where he met Evey Pelley on an elephant, and this shock was too much, and he turned a back summersault, and then fled grunting back into the jungle. In a tiger beat no one shoots anything else, but we were all sad not to have got the nice black rug.

As soon as our mirth subsided out came a flock of monkeys, chattering, bounding, and making a great fuss; and in five minutes out came an enormous tiger, which George had three shots at and we thought him dead, when to our stupefaction he got up and walked off, but was so wounded that he only got a hundred yards, and was finished by other guns. . . .

Wednesday (April 9th) news came of a tiger 8 miles away down the line, so we all set out in trolleys. This was trying and slow, and the heat and glare off the rails and the iron railroad sleepers was like the breath from an open furnace door. We climbed on to elephants, as this country is too bare and treeless for machans. I think the movement of an elephant is much worse than any other, and our bones were racked as we jerked along. George was in front in the howdah, I behind, and the old shikari, who is our constant companion in our joys and shooting sorrows, crouched at the back. We stopped in a horrid hot spot, in front of a kopje [small hill] of huge, hot black rocks, where the tiger was supposed to be hiding in a cave, and we waited and waited and despaired. The seven howdah elephants are very sore footed after so many days' shooting and their constant changing and shuffling of feet is noisy, and the restless movement most uncomfortable for those in the howdah.

As the beat got near a big angry tiger dashed out, but was too hidden in the rocks to aim at; so he only bounded about roaring, and then returned to his cave. Then a furious tomtoming and shouting by beaters began, and fuses were thrown among the rocks to dislodge him; and we advanced on our elephants to get a nearer shot, the shikari thinking the tiger was sulking. Still nothing happened, and several shikaris boldly descended from the elephants to direct the beat, and the line of guns closed up. Captain Wigram, horrified to see men on the ground while a tiger was known to be within a few yards, shouted to the men to get back in the trees and to their elephants, but, alas! too late, as with a roar the tiger dashed out in hot pursuit of a flying shikari. Captain Wigram fired as it came on, but the beast was too near the man to aim, and with a wild leap the tiger bounded on the man, and as he and the man went down I saw the great jaws close on the back of the man's head. I said to George, 'The tiger has killed a man', but he had not seen it and said 'I think you are mistaken'. In the meantime four seconds were passing while both man and beast were in sickening silence behind a rock. Then back came the tiger, slowly *trotting*; again Captain Wigram shot, and although the shot killed, the tiger got back to his cave. Then I said to George, 'Now we must go on', so I turned to our shikari to ask him to tell the mahout to go ahead to the left; but I saw a blank space where the old man had been, so I said, 'Why, our old shikari has got down. What can he have been dreaming of as we are alone?' With great difficulty we got the mahout to move the elephant to where I thought the wounded man was. By this time everything was roar and confusion, elephants coming up on all sides and no one knowing what had happened. Slowly we lurched forward round the rocks, and there lay a man stone dead, and I said to George, 'It is our own dear old shikari, and I saw him killed'. I had not dreamt who it was, as in the second leap of the tiger I only saw a man in the shikari's brown uniform and little knew our shikari had left the howdah. A shout came from the rocks that the tiger was dead, so Dr Armstrong and Captain Wigram bounded down, and I threw them ice which I had in the howdah, but the man was dead, and his head half gone from the awful maul of the tiger. The shock of the accident was awful, and only Captain Wigram and I had seen the whole thing happen. The poor old man was put on an elephant's ladder, covered with the folds of his turban, and borne back solemnly through the scorching forest. He was a most fearless old veteran and had once before been mauled by a tiger, and had proudly showed us the scars on his head. He was the Nizam's old shikari, and so the gloom was very deep that this fine old hunter should lose his life by an act of folly.

We stopped the shoot, though another tiger was marked down, and trollied back to camp. George was in favour of stopping the shoot & returning to Hyderabad, but Major Afzal-ud-daula insisted that this was unnecessary, that if it was done people would say the Viceroy had wounded a tiger which killed a man, instead of which he had had nothing whatever to do with the accident.

Next day proved a blank day, and I went to Hyderabad, as Mrs Barr had arranged a Purdah party for me before the return of the male members of the party, and I was glad to go as the accident had sickened me for wild animals. George stayed in camp another two days, but one was blank and the other resulted in only seeing and not shooting a tiger.

Hyderabad was restful and hot, and the Purdah party very amusing. All men were banished from the Residency for an hour and a half, & a screened entrance arranged where veiled ladies got out of their carriages after the horses had been taken out and the coachmen had retired. Ayahs conducted them upstairs, where Mrs Barr, Evey and I received them. The wives of the Nizam's officials came, and most of them wore cloth of gold tight trousers and long saris twined about their fat forms, bare arms covered with bracelets, and anklets tinkling and necklets jangling. None of the ladies had seen each other before, as the purdah is so strict here that they never go out and had only come to see me, and then were as interested in staring at each other as at me. Mrs Barr interpreted for me, while I made feeble conversation and Evey played for them, and we fed them on tea and then they went away giggling and pleased. One huge lady amused us. She wore green plush trousers, and above her waist was a broad expense of nakedness, then a short transparent green lace coat, and over all a transparent gauze sari. So very little was left to the imagination. . . .

On Monday morning at 7 we went to see the yearly Lungar procession which takes place on the fifth day of the moon and is the chief event of the Mohurrum (a Mahommedan religious season) in Hyderabad. George and I went to the Prime Minister's palace (which was a square mile of ground) in full state with an escort of Fourth Hussars. It was fearfully hot though we started at 7.30. At the Palace we were met by the Nizam and the usual crowd of grandees, and we went to a balcony overlooking a courtyard through which the procession passed, coming in at a gate facing us and passing out on the right, so the scene was very extraordinary, as we saw the procession approach from afar, pass us, and then disappear. There never was anything more quaint than this show, which is a procession of nobles and their re-tainers, hordes of wild Arabs dancing and screaming, elephants covered with Nawabs, palanquins, silver carriages, horses of every colour and shape, dyed and undyed, leaping past in Persian fashion; the irregular army of the Nizam, which is the most motley troop in the world, in every kind of dress, from a Lohengrin helmet and a toga to 18th century tunics and sailor hats. We watched this fantastic stream go by for two hours, laughing, gasping, and sighing; – and were relieved when the regular army came past led by Major Afzal-ud-daula and bringing us back to the present after two hours of Arabian Nights fantasy and squalor. At the end of the procession came the Nizam's stud, and this was fine, though many of the fine horses were dyed or had gold eyebrows on their astonished faces! After them came a fine show of gold and silver howdahs and palanquins, and then we shook ourselves and thanked Heaven the barbaric spectacle was over, and went to breakfast on the Minister's balcony. One hundred and forty people sat down, as all the English residents in Hyderabad and Secunderabad had been asked. We began with Mulligatawny soup, had fourteen courses, and ended with ice cream.

The Nizam ate it all – I mean his share – but George and I wanted tea and bacon and eggs! A horrid old man, a follower of the Nizam's, sat opposite me: he ate chicken curry and threw all bones under the table. When I came to get up I found they had most of them landed on my white muslin dress, so my wrath rose at his table manners! After being photographed in a group we drove home in scorching heat, and took leave of Nizam and Co. as we go north this afternoon.

1 The Hon. John Reginald Lopes Yarde-Buller (1873–1930), to be 3rd Baron Churston. Served in the South African wars.
2 As Lady Curzon makes clear, the Berar question had long, deep roots. That Curzon solved this vexing problem and placated a hostile Nizam was another of his major diplomatic triumphs. Ronaldshay has a pertinent chapter on 'The Question of Berar' in his *Life of Lord Curzon*.

[25 November 1903]   [ABOARD THE *Hardinge*]

Darling precious Mother:

I have written Papa a long typed account of our journey and to you I must write an account of myself. I lead the most extravagant lazy life. I have my tea & bath in my Cabin at 8. My Cabin is 24 feet long by 10 wide and hung with most lovely pink brocade – & pink furniture – writing table, long mirror, beautiful bed & a pink satin sofa – electric fans – tea kettles and punkahs – etc. I have my breakfast on deck in a lovely cool breeze. I have fresh fish – minced turkey omlet – Coffee – fruit. After breakfast I sit in my long chair in the breeze and read, and watch all the party go ashore to see the sights. They go off *every day*, and I have *not once* left the ship. At 11.30 I have a glass of fresh milk (we have cows for me on board) and French Vichy and some plasmon biscuits. At 1.30 I have a good lunch of fish, fowls, red beefsteak, vegetables, rice pudding and stewed fruit, and I eat *well*. After lunch I sit or walk about the deck until tea time when I have tea – or Cocoa – and again I sit in the Sea air and have a walk before I dress for dinner at 7.30 & I put on a tea gown for dinner & after dinner Mouche [Duncombe] and I sit on deck again in the lovely air until 9.30 or ten when I go to bed and sleep all night. If I wake I ring for my nurse who brings me hot chicken tea.

I was very hot for two days & now it is Cool, & getting colder so I have to wear serge & a fur coat after dinner. It must be very good for me to take this sea journey & I am *very well indeed*. I do not go off of the ship because of the difficulty of climbing in and out of the launch – & I don't run any risk I can tell you & miss all the fun of the journey. . . .

The Persian Gulf Journal

Nov. 16 [1903]. We left Karachi Monday afternoon November 16th, in the *Hardinge*. George arrived in his special train at 3 o'clock from Bahawalpur, where he had been installing the young Nawab, and I arrived half an hour later in my special. George had been for ten days touring in the Punjab, and had been to Patiala, Jind, Nabha, and Bahawalpur, four Native states. At Patiala the Chief is only ten. The beautiful camp, which had been weeks preparing to receive the Viceroy, and the splendid hangings and carpets, valued it is said at £150,000, were all destroyed, and a camp had to be hastily borrowed from the Raja of Kapurthala and put up to receive George. He described the decorations of the camp as most quaint. A broad avenue led to his tents, and the mustard and cress plots of green before the tents were adorned with immense glass bowls of gold fish and gigantic coloured glass chandeliers sitting on the ground. The father of the present Maharaja of Patiala died last year after a short life of debauchery, and this boy, who is the son of a fine Jat woman, has a horror of his father's taste for racing and drinking, polo and debts; so it is to be hoped that he will grow up a greater credit to British training than his father did. The late Maharaja of Patiala married for one wife the sister of his trainer, and she was known as Florence Maharani. When at the Maharaja's death, some of his jewels were sold, I saw watches, tiaras, and great vulgar ornaments blazoned with 'F.M.' – meaning Florence Maharani – surmounted by an Imperial Crown, all of fabulous value, waiting in vain for a purchaser.

At Jind, where George went next, the Raja has married the adopted daughter of a balloonist, so the matrimonial adventures of these two Sikhs are considerable.

While George was going through official receptions and banquets, I stayed at Lahore with Lady Rivaz, and Mouche Duncombe joined me. We enjoyed the stay immensely in a big delightful house, and the Lahore climate was absolutely perfect, cool by day and fresh at night.

We found general excitement at the dock at Karachi: ships dressed, a fleet in the harbour, consisting of our escort of four ships, crowds of people about, and the *Hardinge*, on which we were to embark, drawn up alongside the wharf. As soon as the special trains were unloaded we sailed out of harbour, to the booming of guns in the forts and manning of ships. Our squadron was drawn up two on either side, and our ship was slightly in advance. We kept this formation until dark, when the Admiral signalled proposing our falling to the rear, which we were not loath to do, as not being nautical I was convinced that the war ships would run into us from the rear. We fell back and followed the four grey monsters all night and the next day and the next night; and when Muscat was sighted, we glided between the quartet and sailed into harbour at Muscat, our great white ship leading, and the four iron grey ones following behind.

Muscat harbour is wonderfully picturesque: a cove walled by gigantic jagged yellow-brown rocks, which are topped by 16th Century Spanish forts. These proceeded to pour forth salutes, which crashed and echoed against the harbour walls. The town, which faces the entrance of the harbour, was decorated with flags, suspended from the forts behind the Sultan's palace in great festoons, which looked most quaint. We anchored in the centre of the harbour, while the squadron ranged itself across the mouth; and instantly boats, barges, launches, and cutters began flying to and fro, as Colonel Kemball, the British representative in the Gulf had come to meet George on one ship, and Sir A. Hardinge, English Minister in Teheran, on another, and Major Cox, the Resident at Muscat, appeared in a pinnace. So we were kept busy watching arrivals, while the big deck aft was prepared for the official reception of the Sultan. It was hung with our gorgeous golden hangings, which we had brought with us to decorate the ship, as well as the great gold and silver chairs. Everyone seemed panting with excitement, the guns roared and banged, and the Staff flew about in uniform, and presently His Excellency the Admiral came off his flag-ship and made an official call, and was received by George on the gold hung deck. Next came Sir A. Hardinge, and at 12 the Sultan of Muscat was received in full state and sat on the silver throne. He came out in a launch with about a dozen retainers, and he is a fine-looking man with much grace of manner. Coffee and Sherbet were served to him, and Mouche and I peeped through the fringes of the golden hangings from an unseen corner at the rear. After the Sultan's call, George received the French and American Consuls, and at 1.30 he and the Admiral and most of the Staff went ashore to lunch at the British Residency. Mouche and I stopped on the ship, as it was fearfully hot, and we had occupation enough looking over the sides of the ship. After lunch at the Residency, George went to return the visit of the Sultan, walking, as it is only a step, through carpeted, decorated little alleys lined by the Sultan's soldiers. After the visit he was shewn the palace, which is undistinguished and partly composed of the old Spanish fort. 350 years ago Spain was supreme in these parts, but there is only the trace left now of the forts on the high hills, which are obsolete and picturesque, and fire salutes for British Viceroys in British men-of-war.

The Sultan of Muscat is subsidized by us, and his little kingdom is the scene of diplomatic struggles between France and England over the vexed question of a coaling station. Three years ago, after much fluttering in Foreign Office dovecots, Lord Salisbury granted France a coaling shed, and this has now given France and presumably Russia, the coveted privilege of coaling at the mouth of the Persian Gulf. We may repent it bitterly some day, if the long expected combat with Russia comes.

I stopped all day on the ship, but all the rest bustled to the shore, and the boats were very busy. In the evening, the Admiral, the Captains of the Fleet, the British Resident and his wife, Colonel Kemball and his wife, and Sir A. Hardinge all came to dinner, and we were 64 at two long tables on the deck. It was very hot indeed, and I can't say it was pleasant. After dinner all the officers of the fleet came to a party. The shore and the ships were illuminated and looked very brilliant. We had a stifling night, and sensible people slept on deck. It seemed that we had no sooner gone to bed before a gun went off, which fairly knocked us out of bed as it crashed and echoed round the rocks. It was only 5 o'clock, and we thought it most unnecessary; it was probably a signal for the Admiral to turn over in bed.

Thursday, November 19th. The decks of the *Argonaut*, our big Cruiser, had been hung with the golden hangings for the Durbar for the Sultan of Muscat and the Chiefs of Oman, as the big guns aft and the general appearance of might and fight were supposed to have a soothing effect on any Russian or French sympathies Muscatis might have. The heat was so great that I did not go to the *Argonaut*, but watched the Sheikhs and the British arrivals arriving in full dress from the peaceful decks of the *Hardinge*. All the staff had to wear full dress, and their sufferings in their tunics were pitiful. George wore his fullest dress, and fairly suffocated at the prospect of investing the Sultan with the GCIE and robing himself as Grand Master to conduct the ceremony. The Admiral's guns announced his arrival on the *Argonaut*. Then Sir A. Hardinge went off; and as soon as the Sultan was seen to board the ship guns poured from everything that could shoot. George next set off in his launch, and the fusillade was appalling. I was left alone on the ship, as every creature had gone to the *Argonaut*, except Captain Armstrong who has a bad leg and can't even move from a couch, which is very trying while such rushing about is general. They were all back in an hour, and reported the Durbar as most impressive. The deck of the *Argonaut* looked very fine with the golden trappings, and the guns duly impressed the Sultan and the Sheikhs. The Sultan made a speech in which he referred to me as a pearl, and George replied gently laying down the important fact that Great Britain meant to retain her paramount position in these parts in order to protect her trade and her many Indian subjects trading in the Gulf and in Muscat. He then invested the

Sultan, and sherbet was served in true Persian style to the hot Sheikhs and the roasted Staff. Mouche went to look on, looking most beautiful, and I hope I got the credit of her being thought the Lady Sahib.

After the Durbar the Sultan came to pay a private visit to George, and in the afternoon, to more guns, we sailed off, greatly pleased with our visit. All had gone off very well. We sat on the deck watching the rocky coast until darkness shut it out, and then we watched our fleet leading us like four phantom light-ships.

I have never enumerated our party. It consists of George and me, Lady Mouche, Mr Dane, Foreign Secretary, Mr Lorimer, who has come to write an official account of the trip, Mr Chirol, the Special Correspondent of the *Times*, Colonel Lukis, the doctor, Colonel Baring, Major Adam, Captains Wigram, Baker-Carr, and Keighley,[1] and Major Poynter, besides the ship's crew of officers, and a Naval ADC in the shape of Captain Drury Low, who is Commander of the flagship *Hyacinth* and a cousin of George's, and Captain Armstrong, our doctor, whom we brought to recover at sea from an operation he had [had] performed at Simla.

The morning after we left Muscat we reached Musandam and we cruised all day amongst islands and fjords of the most barren description. The land is uninhabited save for a few fishermen, and its main interest is a strategic one, as the bays and inlets afford anchorage for a fleet, and as the land is No Man's Russia or France could take advantage of harbourage in the event of war. In 1867 England controlled the region by putting up a flag and a telegraph station, but the heat was so awful, and the isolation so great, that the poor signallers died and it was abandoned. In the afternoon the Viceroy and the Admiral went ashore to examine a particular spot for a cable station, and the *Hardinge* anchored in the most beautiful rock-bound inlet. At sunset we sailed out of the network of islands and pursued our way towards Sharjah. The fleet had been waiting for us outside, and we again formed a procession.

A sea got up in the night and was running quite high when we got to Sharjah, where George was to hold a Durbar for the Arabian Sheikhs. These had been collected together by Colonel Kemball and were all aboard a small ship and reported to be very seasick: a good many of our party were very feeble, and as it looked impossible to get boats off to the *Argonaut*, it was settled to postpone the Durbar until afternoon in the hope that the sea would calm and the Sheikhs revive. A certain number of brave men got into boats and launches and went over to the *Argonaut*, but no one was enthusiastic about the prospect of getting into full dress and holding a seasick Durbar. Watching the gymnastics of people boarding boats and getting very wet kept us fairly cheerful, and when 3.30 o'clock came and the sea had not calmed, Mouche and I had a most amusing time watching the distress of the Staff in red tunics at the bottom of the companion ladder waiting for the magic moment in which to spring into a dancing launch. It took forty minutes to get one boat off, and pitiful screams rose as waves dashed over Captain Keighley and Captain's Wigram's uniformed legs, and feathered hats flew off as they leaped in the air in the hope of landing in the launch. Launch loads of green-faced soldiers danced on the waves, and presently two barge loads of Sheikhs were seen appearing and I got a good photo of them as they went by. George was the last to start, and his full dress and gold collar of the Star of India contrasted oddly with his efforts to board the wobbling launch. Fortunately there were no *contretemps*, and only one Sheikh's retainer fell into the sea; and the *Argonaut* was fairly steady, and George made a speech to the Sheikhs (one of whom was sick over the side), and then came the return to the *Hardinge* and Mouche's and my intense amusement at the acrobatic feats of boarding the ship from the launch. We had a rough two hours after we weighed anchor, and we none of us felt too robust. The Sharjah Durbar will remain unique for sick Sheikhs, high sea, and a pea-green staff.

We anchored off Bandar Abbas at 7, and Sir A. Hardinge, who had come from Muscat in his own boat, joined us on the *Hardinge* as we are now in Persia. While it was still very early the Persian Governor sent off to enquire after George's health, but his emissary lost his way among so many ships and had to be recovered after making unsuccessful attempts to board all the battle-ships. We feared a diplomatic incident, as the Persian grandee grew more and more incensed as he in turn left the sides of the four ships, returned to the shore with hurt feelings, and George's health was never enquired after. The Governor was to come off to be received officially at 11, so we sent a guide to conduct him and there was no *contretemps*, and he welcomed George to the Shah's dominions and poured forth the usual flow of compliments, which George accepted with reservation when he announced that every heart in Khorasan and Laristan (the two provinces most under Russian influence) was beating high with pleasure at his honoured visit. The sea was smooth, so all was conducted with dignity and decorum.

Bandar Abbas has for so long inspired columns in the press on Russian and British diplomacy in the Gulf, and so much has been written about the place, that it was almost a grief to behold a small mud town skirting the shore, with a desert of sand and low hills at its back. But the political importance of a place is not decided by its dimensions or its beauty, and Bandar Abbas, with its mud huts and confined limits, will continue to form part of the Persian Question.[2] Opposite the town is the island of Hormoz, which was once a flourishing Portuguese town of 40,000 people. Now it is deserted, and we sailed round a scarlet range of sandstone hills, which have cornucopia-like crests of lime, and make a most phenomenal effect of blood mountains crested with snow. All the party went ashore to see the deserted fort and town, excepting Captain Armstrong and me, and we watched an orange sunset make wonderful colour effects on the strange hills of Hormoz.

Monday, November 23rd. Early this morning George and the rest went ashore to see the town of Qeshm. The surf was tremendous, and the landing of the party on the heads of Natives irresistibly comic, as huge breakers entirely swamped them, and they were drenched from heel to head, and returned to the ship simply bedraggled. Sir A. Hardinge had lost his hat, the trousers of most were torn and shrunk, and Perks, the fox terrier, was as sick as a dog could be. None of them had had any breakfast, or they would all have been as sick as Perks.

Tuesday, November 24th 1903. Between Qeshm and Lingeh George went to see Bassadore, a former telegraph station, and then he made an attempt to see some salt mines, but in spite of two attempts on shore, the salt caves were undiscovered. We set sail for Lingeh, and arrived there in the afternoon. It is a very picturesque place, and looks most prosperous, as the houses are of brick instead of mud, and there are trees, and each house has a wind tower to catch the breezes. The Governor's house is built on the water, and the surf, which was very high, seemed to be dashing in the first floor windows. All the party went ashore, except George and myself. I could watch Mouche and the Staff walking along the sea-front, followed by an enormous crowd of Arabs. The Persian Governor of the Gulf had come from Bandar Abbas in his little ship *Persepolis*, and he came to dine with us in the evening. He was a pale unshaved Persian in a black fez and a full pleated black cloth coat. He was told to take me in to dinner, and never having had to do such a thing before he had no idea how to proceed, and instead of giving me his arm he clutched my right hand with his right hand and made a sort of *chassé croisé*, which was complicated by an iron post, as he got one side of it and I the other, but after some considerable dodging about we reached the table, which was on the other side of the deck. Sir Arthur Hardinge sat on the other side of the Persian, and entirely relieved me of conversation, as he talked a steady stream of Persian to him. On George's left sat the Governor's brother, who was white with fright for fear he should do something wrong. He watched how we ate soup and fish, and then gingerly followed suit: but he got something in his mouth which he didn't like and promptly ejected it, and then proceeded to wipe his tongue, which he ran out for the purpose. Sir Arthur Hardinge told us the highest compliment a Persian could pay you was to stay for many hours as your guest when you invited him to dinner, and at his house in Teheran he and Lady Hardinge had frequently to entertain the Grand Vizier until 3 a.m. when he honoured them by dining with them. We did not run this risk, and after sitting stiffly on the deck in a cold wind for half an hour we said goodnight, and His Excellency the Lord of the Oceans departed after a parting shower of beautiful compliments.

Those who went ashore in the afternoon reported a Guard of Persian soldiers at the Governor's house, all in most bedraggled rags, and this reminds me of a story Sir Arthur Hardinge told me. He said when Lord Downe went to Teheran the other day to invest the Shah with the Garter he was quartered in a Palace of the Shah's, and at his door was stationed a sentry wearing one trouser leg, who presented arms, whenever he beheld the gallant Lord Downe, with the broken leg of a table! The Persian army is unpaid, unarmed, and undressed. All the loans made by Russia to Persia go into the private purse of the Shah, who buys 1000 French clocks at a time, or 200 motor cars. A share of the gold goes to the Persian Governors, and the Army has not been paid in the memory of man. The Russian Government provides and pays some Cossack regiments, and these are the only armed or dressed soldiers.

Thursday, November 26th. Wednesday we sailed for Bahrein, the great pearl island, which yearly produces half a million in revenue from pearl fishing. The island is under British protection, but ruled by a Sheikh who is in the hands of a few Indian moneylenders, and these control the wealth of his priceless island, as he leases out the fisheries. The Sheikh came on to the *Hardinge* to see George, and was received in Durbar. He is a pure Arab, and looks just like a Bible prophet. George returned his visit on shore, but as we are anchored 5 miles out and the tide was low, his launch stuck on a reef. The landing in the surf was very funny, as the party had to transfer themselves from the launch to donkeys' backs and ride through the waves. A good many fell off, and as donkeys fell short Captain Wigram and Captain Drury Low rode the same. So much time was lost in landing that they saw very little of Bahrein, and were two and a half hours getting back to the ship; so I was very anxious and was trying to find the launch with the aid of a searchlight when the Admiral arrived to dine. There was no one on the ship but crippled Captain Armstrong and myself. We were much relieved when the launch appeared with a very tired dejected party.

Friday the Sheikh came off to have a private interview with George. He looked obstinate and stubborn, and knew he was going to be scolded for the miserable financial condition of his island. While George was lecturing the Sheikh I was surrounded by pearl merchants, looking at the most heavenly pearls, for which my mouth watered, but which are quite prohibitive in price. As soon as the Sheikh went away we sailed out of the pearl waters for Kuwait....

We got to Kuwait about 11, and the weather changed from cool to cold, so we put on everything warm we could find and waited for the arrival of Mubarak, the Sheikh of Kuwait. He was fetched by Colonel Kemball in our launch, and was received by George on the deck after. He brought his eldest son, who looked considerably older than his father, whose beard had just been dyed from white to blue black.

So much ink has been expended on descriptions of Kuwait and the political importance of the place that I won't write reams about the Baghdad Railway having its outlet here, or the great question of England establishing a protectorate over the place. At present the Sheikh is fighting the Amir of Nejd and has just won a victory, so he is particularly cheerful. At the Durbar George talked to him about Kuwait politics, and at the end of the interview presents were presented to the Sheikh – several rifles, a gold watch with a gigantic chain, and a sword of honour in a scarlet velvet case. This greatly excited him, and he bounded to his feet and said he desired to be considered a fighting subject of England and tried instantly to put on the sword. The sword had no belt, so he cried loudly for one, but none was forthcoming so George suggested his postponing wearing the sword until tomorrow, to which the Sheikh reluctantly agreed. But he was quite an altered being, and sat literally beaming with delight, hugging his tawdry sword like a huge child.

Sunday, November 29th. This morning George went to return the visit of the Sheikh, and went in the launch to a place on the shores of the desert two miles distant from the town, where the Sheikh met him with the only carriage in Kuwait, and an immense escort of Arabs, riding every kind of animal from donkeys to camels, and carrying every kind of blunderbuss. Wild horses without bridles were provided for Sir Arthur Hardinge, Mr Dane, and the Staff. They mounted the quadrupeds and George, with equal bravery, mounted into the shandrydan. Thousands of Arabs swarmed round them shooting off rifles: Bedouins, seated on camels, discharged guns in the air; and the glorious confusion defies description. Quantities of women had turned out, and the entire population of Kuwait joined in the general pandemonium. Sir Arthur Hardinge, on a flea-bitten gray with a rope round its nose, caracoled along, and was almost instantly shot off, as an Arab fired off his musket in his face, and George saw the gaitered legs of the Minister disappear into the rabble. Mr Dane, in full dress, was hauling in vain with a rope at the nose of his pony, while an immense camel, ridden by a shooting Bedouin in chain armour, was biting off the top of his head. The Naval ADC, Captain Drury Low, who is not a finished horseman, was clinging to the neck of a horse with a purple velvet saddle; and a pack of ADCs, who could find no mounts in the general confusion, were running hotly in the rear, literally deafened by the *feu de joie* going on around them. George said that never in his many comic experiences had he seen anything approaching this ballyrag, which was prolonged for 2 miles through desert and bazaar until the Sheikh's house was reached, by some miracle without an accident; but no sooner had George left the carriage than the horses set to and kicked the vehicle to matchwood!

George had coffee in the Sheikh's mud residence, and all the sons of the house were produced and introduced, and they ranged from 7 years of age to 50! The house of Mubarak is famed for its progeny and longevity, and only five generations have ruled at Kuwait for 250 years. One Sheikh died at 120, and was remarried at 80.

The launch had come to the landing in front of the Sheikh's house, so the circus procession was not resumed, and the party had only to walk to the boats and take leave of the Kuwait populace, who swarmed in thousands.

They returned quite enchanted with their adventures, and we laughed all the rest of the day at each one's account of his particular escapade on horse, or camel, or foot. . . .

In the afternoon the Sheikh came off for a private interview with George, and he brought two little sons of 8 and 10 with him, a number of Arab retainers, as well as a gazelle. This he presented to us. I tried to feed the boys with sweets, but they did not take to chocolates and cherries; but one of their attendants, fearing their lukewarm reception of British sweets might be interpreted as rudeness, forced open the boys' mouths and pushed the sweets in. This was so amusing and cruel that I stopped him. I then sent for sherbet for them. They tried this and made the most awful faces and cried out for water, and this was brought and they were comforted. From our ship the Sheikh and the boys went to see the Admiral on his flagship, and altogether had a thrilling afternoon.

After dinner George and Sir Arthur Hardinge, Mr Dane, and Colonel Baring went off in the little ship *Sphinx* to explore the upper reaches of the Khor Abdulla, the waterway above Kuwait, and we join them with the fleet on Tuesday at the mouth of the Euphrates River, and then we go on to Bushire.

1 Vernon Aubrey Scott Keighley (1874–1939), of the 18th Lancers. He had the distinction of commanding the Viceroy's bodyguard at the Coronation Durbar.
2 Curzon was *the* authority on the 'Persian Question', which concerned England's commanding position in the area and her determination to ward off the encroachments of other powers. Ronaldshay gives this imperial struggle an illuminating chapter in his *Life of Lord Curzon*.

In January 1904 Mary Curzon returned to England for the birth in March of her daughter, Alexandra, and save for that event and the marriages of her two sisters in November and December, it was a year of physical and mental suffering for her. In June her father, Levi Leiter, died and her hopes of returning to America were dashed by Curzon's accepting, in the event unwisely and unhappily, an extension of his Viceroyalty to complete the plans and reforms he had ceaselessly struggled for. Taking leave, he joined his wife and children in the spring, and in August, upon his appointment as Lord Warden of the Cinque Ports, the family repaired to the decrepit Walmer Castle (in Kent) whose primitive drainage perhaps contributed to Lady Curzon's subsequent illness. It is likely, too, that she had a miscarriage at this time: in addition, she was dogged with minor upsets and discomforts throughout the summer. Then, in September, a few days before their return to India, she fell gravely ill, apparently with peritonitis and phlebitis, and had to be operated upon. For a month she lay between life and death, sometimes comatose, and ominously phrased bulletins described her condition as 'critical', or 'very grave' or deteriorating. Curzon, who remained at her bedside, kept a minute record of what she said and it is a measure of her quality that even in her seeming death throes Mary Curzon sought the welfare of others, meditated upon the happiness of her marriage and ensured the well-being of her children. The document is unique in its sad intensity and its poignant reflections upon the human lot.[1] Yet she made a miraculous recovery and Curzon took Highcliffe Castle in Hampshire for her re- cuperation, but so strong was his sense of mission, so great his confidence that no one else could develop what he had initiated, that he returned to India in November determined to carry on without her. It is, then, a tribute to her affection, loyalty and sense of duty – as the letter of 21 February 1905 indicates – that she decided to leave Highcliffe and join her husband in India.

The first letters from India to the newly widowed Mrs Leiter were full of family affection and of Lady Curzon's delight at her welcome back – a service of thanks- giving celebrated her return – and at the Viceroy's happiness ('quite touching'); she remarked to her mother 'I feel young again', and was confident of regaining health and strength. Curzon himself wrote to his mother-in-law optimistically of Lady Curzon's progress and reminded her that their time in India was limited, for Mrs Leiter always believed, and rightly, that the country was harmful for her daughter.

But for all Mary Curzon's determination to regain health and restore family happiness and for all Curzon's grandiose and worthy plans, other factors interfered, and with disastrous consequences. Even setting aside the worry and fear occasioned by the earthquake (April 1905 letters), there was disagreement between Curzon and Kitchener, the public's idol and Army Commander-in-Chief, India, which was slowly coming to its vicious climax. Historians argue over this conflict – of 'dual control' over military matters between two proud, determined men (the Lord of the Realm and the Lord of War) – a conflict that began with Kitchener's demand that the role of the Military Member of the Viceroy's Council should be redefined as subordinate to the Commander-in-Chief of the Army. Curzon, rightly suspicious of the military mind, was unsympathetic to this, but after argument and political manoeuvring a compromise was reached. However, largely due to endemic bun- gling in Whitehall, an appointment was made in a manner unsatisfactory to the Viceroy, who thereupon resigned. But of course the affair was far more complicated than a simple outline suggests, for Kitchener, the god of the people, the legendary hero, behaved unscrupulously whilst St John Brodrick, Secretary of State for India and supposedly one of Curzon's closest friends, played at the least a questionable role in the controversy. Words flew, claims and counterclaims were made, patience snapped, and the whole matter was obscured in a miasma of political fog and personal recrimination. As the sympathetic wife Lady Curzon was deeply concerned and it does not surprise us that she wrote with uncharacteristic severity of Kitchener. And even if her letters do not trace in detail the decline of relations between Kitchener on the one hand and the Viceroy and herself on the other, they are among the most compelling of her writings for they possess a drama and an immediacy that cannot effectively be conveyed through paraphrase.

Because of her husband's illness late in 1905 Lady Curzon experienced much worry. The incessant wrangling with Kitchener, the accreted strain of seven years as Viceroy, the indignant reaction attending the recent partition of Bengal, all weakened Curzon's physical and mental state. Also, responsibilities for the arrangements of the impending Indian tour of the Prince and Princess of Wales fell to him, responsibilities he carried out with his customary zeal and authority. However, the protocol regarding their reception caused problems for such was the Viceroy's nervous state that some considered he might break under the strain, but after much argument it was decided he should receive the royal couple at Bombay. It takes little imagination to see how Lady Curzon must have suffered at this time.

Thus there is sadness underlying the correspondence, not only because the Curzons left India under distressing circumstances but also due to Mary Curzon's increasing illness. Her letters in these final months show little self-pity and she bears up admirably in adversity. But the discomforts of her declining health – shortness of breath, difficulty in climbing stairs – particularly in a younger woman, suggest serious physical problems. It is likely, too, that residuum from her severe illness of 1904 re-asserted itself; and these setbacks, coupled with mental anguish at her husband's untenable position – it should be remembered that when the Viceroy returned to England no political figure of consequence had the decency to meet him at the railway station – discomposed her to the point where deterioration accelerated in the spring of 1906. And on 18 July of that year Mary Curzon, aged thirty-six, died at her home in London, 1 Carlton House Terrace, her husband at her bedside.

1 See Nigel Nicolson's *Mary Curzon*, pp. 176–80.

21 February [1905] SS *Arabia*
PORT SAID

Darling Mother:

The journey has done me enormous good and the freedom from care has been such a blessing to me and I have sat all day in peace on deck and tried not to think of all the months of suffering I have borne since last I sailed over these seas before Sandra was born. It has been a terrible year and the only bright spots are pretty little Sandra and darling Nancy & Daisy's marriages. I shall never rest, darling, until I get you near us and Daisy, Nancy, and I will keep our beloved mother from being lonely and sad. I know so well, beloved, how desolate you are and if only I had been near I would have left you the dear little girls to love & cheer you.

Sandra has improved so on the journey & has regained her weight & the cow has provided us all with splendid milk. We have had a perfect journey – not a ripple – and lovely sunshine and Sir Ernest Cassel has sent me down a fine supply of fresh food from Cairo so I shall be well supplied in the Red Sea.

George's happiness is quite touching now that I am coming back & he is coming to meet me in Bombay. The reason he has had to stay is that there may be trouble in Afghanistan (this is private). There is also a row with Lord Kitchener and the Military Department. Lord K. wants to demolish the Military Department and make the Chief an autocrat over the Army – and altho' this might answer in his time the system would utterly collapse with his successor, & the whole system of government cannot be altered solely for an individual. It is a big question and I will write you more of it when I get to India, darling.

Your lovely dressing-gown has been cleaned and is as good as new and has wrapped me warmly up all winter. Oh! how glad I am to be away from that cold Highcliffe – I wonder how I lived through the winter as my bedroom was *46* & the chimney smoked so I couldn't have a fire if there was a wind – & before we left we had a siege of dead rats *under the floor*!

I was thankful when I got all the little girls safely on to the ship. All the nice doctors came down to see me off – and they were *unanimous* in wishing me to go, as I had not the strength to grapple with any more care and I can be as quiet as I like in Simla. And then it is my *duty* and no one, darling, knows better what that means to a woman than your precious self. . . .

9 March [1905]   GOVERNMENT HOUSE
                                                            CALCUTTA

Dear darling Mother:

We have landed safely and the children are at Dehra Dun with the Doctor and I am here. I had a great welcome in Bombay, where it was very cool, and a remarkable one here. The Lt.-Governor of Bengal & Lord K[itchener] and the Calcutta Corporation met me at the station & the Chairman of the Corporation presented me with a diamond spray. There was a great crowd, triumphal arches, the streets packed. The Volunteer Corps asked to escort me from the station and they formed the escort. At Government House there must have been 800 to 1000 people on the steps who cheered to the echo as I drove up. The Council met me & the whole of Calcutta & 200 ladies presented me with an address of welcome. It has been most touching and now the Bishop of Calcutta has announced a service of public thanksgiving for my return. There has been a wave of enthusiasm over India & I can never forget the affection & regard everyone has shown for me.[1]

It is very cold here and yesterday, 8th of March, I drove out in my *chinchilla cloak*. George's care of me is simply touching & I am so relieved to be back to help & comfort him. I shall run no risk and the first hot day will send me off to Dehra Dun. Simla is still under snow & I dare not go there while it is melting as Sandra and I would both feel it I fear.

I do not think anyone has ever received such a spontaneous welcome to India – and I am deeply touched by it all.

I went to lunch with Lord K. – and he shewed me all his new Chinese porcelain – he told me to tell you that he had kept a case free for your yellow and rose crackley bottles which he thought you proposed to give him! I told him he was a beggar & that the bottles were meant for me; he assured me you meant him to have them. I made his mouth water by describing your china so he will no doubt write & ask you for it! We laughed greatly over his greed. There is a fine row on between him & the Military Department & I don't know what the outcome of it all will be.

Darling, I know you will think I have done right to come back to George – life is too short for separations.

Love from George.

Your devoted
Mary

1 Excerpts from other letters written at this time attest to the warmth of her welcome and to her pleasure at returning: 'People treat me as though I were a miracle returned from the dead, & the affection is affecting. No one ever had such a welcome to India....' Again, 'My heart is very tender towards India – and I shall do my best to get well here.'

6 April [1905]   VICEROY'S CAMP
                                                          [SIMLA]

My darling Mother:

We have had a most fearful earthquake[1] here & Viceregal Lodge has been badly damaged, walls split and chimneys and gables down. I had a most miraculous escape as a huge stone chimney weighing *20 tons* crashed through the roof & fell on to the floor of the room immediately over my *bed*. The crash was like the crack of doom as the stone balcony outside my room came down also. I shot out of bed like a rocket and dashed into the hall just as another chimney came through the skylight. I flew for safety to my sitting-room and as I got there three of the staff running like hares to save me called not to go in that room as the walls were caving in. Again I turned & flew through the racking swaying hall to the nurseries, gathered up the precious children & ran out on the lawn. I started my flight in nightgown & bare feet and Baker, my maid, had put various articles on me as I went along. We had to abandon the big house & go into the bungalow that had suffered least, & we are now packed into a tiny house which we can get out of at the first sound of danger. Shocks have gone on for two days and [the] night before last there were *fifteen* shocks & we sat up the whole night & I watched over the precious children as they slept like little mice. They are the best children that ever lived. They mind no moving and discomfort and little Sandra smiles sweetly in the general pandemonium. She is the most darling baby & looks very like Irene. I have a charming governess for the children; she is an English lady and they are happy with her.

This house will be many months rebuilding so we cannot entertain much and I shall have plenty of peace. I have a little summer house in the garden where I sit on much of the day and it is quite like an open air Cure.

We cannot go out to the Retreat this year as Mashobra has been terribly shaken and the poor little house has nearly collapsed, but we shall go to Naldera and live in a camp as soon as it gets warmer. Now it is cold.

Darling, I hope and pray that you are well. I send you our dearest love & a kiss to you from

Yr loving
Mary

1 As late as 17 April letters to *The Times* remarked that details on this disaster were 'imperfect', although it was reported in that newspaper from Calcutta as early as 5 April.

13 April [1905]   VICEROY'S CAMP
                                                                    SIMLA

Mother beloved:

I imagine that the news of the earthquake has now got into the American papers – & that you do not know what a wonderful escape I had as I have had no cable from you. I cabled you I was safe so that you should not worry. Darling, do send me an occasional cable just telling me where & how you are; it comforts me and brings me near you.[1] This last mail brought no letters from any of my dear ones so I was very, very sad.

George came yesterday so I am happy. We have given 10,000 rupees, about $3000, as a thank offering for my Providential escape. 15,000 people have been killed by the earthquake; whole villages have been entirely swept away and the desolation is frightful. Dharmsala & Kangra which are ruined are near Simla & we might have fared much worse as we were in the midst of the earthquake wave. For a week we have had shocks & we have been living in one of the bungalows for safety....

The walls of my bedroom have parted, the ceiling sunk in, the balconies & gables are down, & the main part of the house will take three months to rebuild! We shall have to move into the low wing where the staff live as soon as that is put right.

I have had a terrible fright and now feel no sense of security in the shaken house – but as I might have been killed I must thank God for another mercy in again saving my life.

George was on tour when all this happened – and wished at once to come here to us – but there is literally not a place for him as our largest bungalow is down & we are all on the sofas and beds & floor of Curzon House, a staff bungalow. Just as soon as we can get a room patched up for him he will come up.

Darling, when this reaches you I hope that all will be as serene as a summer's day – but my mind is so full of earthquakes now that I can think of nothing else. I shall be so glad when we can go into Camp at Naldera at the end of May. I can be there in peace and quiet on the anniversary of our beloved ones death. We shall all spend this day of our sorrow together in thought, darling, though the world divides us.

Darling, I hope I may lose no more babies until I am safe in England. I have had all I can bear for a long time. . . .

1 At the head of this letter in Mrs Leiter's hand is a note reading: 'I was too ill to be told of the earthquake & knew nothing of it until May 1905. Mother.'

18 April [1905]   VICEROY'S CAMP
                                                                              [SIMLA]

Darling:

We are all well and settled into our new rooms in the undamaged wing of the house. Here I have the joy of the sweet children next to me and they can all come in and slip into my bed, & then I get a general smothering with little Sandra creeping over me like a little kitten – she jabbers & does all the sweet baby things you love so well. I devoutly hope that I shall have no more babies until I am strong. My feelings about the boy are much less keen than they were, as if I have one he will not be well enough & can hardly live at Kedleston! . . .

I cannot tell you how we miss Hillier – he was the most invaluable person in the house, and without him there is fearful confusion. We cannot get anything done & life is not as smooth as it was in Hillier's time when the wheels went round so smoothly.

George has been in bed a week with his bad back. He gives himself no rest and works twice as hard in bed as out of it. . . .

24 May [1905]   VICEROY'S CAMP
                                                                              MASHOBRA

Mother mine beloved:

I am staying out all alone at Mashobra with the children and we are very happy and peaceful. The children have their lessons out of doors and Sandra crawls about the ground in an absurd helmet to keep off the sun. . . . I am longing for the time to come to leave India and settle down in England so that the children can have all the joy of a country life without fear of sunstrokes.

We had a garden party last week, and as George's foot was bad I had to do all the receiving and after shaking hands with 500 people I nearly cried with fatigue. I sometimes feel overwhelmed at having to do all the social part weak as I am and unless George is better I shall decline to go on with our parties. I

am a willing horse but I cannot be driven too hard. George has barely been
out of bed for six weeks! Unless he gets better we must stop entertaining &
do nothing. We are going to Camp at Naldera soon and that will be a rest. I
hope my darling is well & happy with sweet Nan & Daisy.

Kisses from all
Mary

27 July [1905]   VICEROY'S CAMP
[SIMLA]

Mother beloved:

We have had a week of darkness as George has been ill & Irene has been ill
with a temperature of 103.8 and I have had the most cruel cough – and added
to these bodily ills St John Brodrick has embarked upon a policy of such
insult & outrage that he went too far & had finally to climb down, and send
little short of an apology from the Cabinet for this outrageous treatment
George has received. There has never been such feeling in India as there is
now against St John – & the populace longs for his blood – and no one is
more indignant than Lord Kitchener. St John was so anxious to give Lord K.
all he wanted & more that he formulated a wild scheme that is unworkable &
which can only break down. The Civilians are wild & the soldiers furious as
Lord K. has been censured by Indian opinion for bringing about such a state
of things. Altogether it is a fine row – & no two opinions are held about the
unstatesmanlike actions of St John. I do long to leave India – & be out of
reach of his bludgeon which we feel *daily* in an insulting telegram, order, or
letter. He had the same experience at the War Office as he is having at the
India Office & he is a public *disgrace*.

There has never been any personal disagreement between Lord K. and
George & they are on absolutely friendly terms, but I hope we may never
have to speak to St John again as long as we live. . . .

[August 1905?]   VICEREGAL LODGE
SIMLA

Darling:

The resignation will be over before you get this & I shall be able to tell you
when we are coming home. Our life here under St John Brodrick has been a
perfect hell – & you would not treat a dog as he has treated George. The
reason of the final resignation is that the Govt. at home have practically gone
back on the modifications to the army reform scheme which they accepted in
order to prevent George from resigning when Parliament was sitting. Now

they have gone back to their original scheme of a dangerous Army despotism with no control over the Comm.-in-Chief, so that he may dash on unchecked into the most fatal mistakes which have so far been prevented by the wise counsels of old Indian officers. There is the greatest unrest amongst the native Indian Army because they fear the revolutionary character of many of the Chief's wildcat schemes, but the Government at home know and care nothing for this and it is heartrending to think of the trouble in store for India if K. is to go unchecked. He will be at war with the tribes on the frontier in no time I fear.

I hope that you will wait for us as we shall be back so soon. I must try and place the children at Cap Martin or some warm place, & I will come to see you wherever you are.

George is ill in bed from anxiety & prolonged diarrhoea and the children are all isolated in different parts of the house on account of measles – & I have more than I can bear. I do not know what will happen about the P. of Wales visit & it is calamitous that George has been forced to resign just at this moment, as they will be hard put to find anyone to come who can carry out the Prince's tour which George has arranged in every little detail. I do not know how soon they can send out his successor. It is a sad end up to our Indian life, and the party has done George a great wrong to throw him over as they have. It has been a whole campaign of calumny & lying and unfair play & they never showed their hand until the day Parliament rose – then they sent the most outrageous peremptory telegram and George resigned. I wish that he had done so before so that we could have got away before the bitter cold of the winter. . . .

24 August [1905]   VICEROY'S CAMP
                                                                        [SIMLA]

Private
Beloved Mother:

George's resignation has come – and now the Home Govt. are bent upon kicking him out with as little delay as possible but we cannot leave India in this great heat, which is terribly trying, until October. We do not know how soon Lord Minto[1] is coming out but the Home Govt. is so anxious to get us out that Brodrick has proposed our going at once and Lord Ampthill[2] acting as Viceroy until Lord Minto comes. George's seven years of work are as though they had never been and all he has earned from Home Govt. are insult and ingratitude. There has been an immense intrigue going on of which we have just learned. Last year when we were at home & George was attending the meetings of the Defence Committee and pushing his views about Indian defence before the Cabinet & the Defence Committee Lord Kitchener sent a man from India named Mullaly[3] who is a bitter enemy of George's and who writes all Lord Kitchener's notes & despatches. This man worked relentlessly under Kitchener's orders against all the proposals made by George. He supplied the London press with a mass of lies, he laid the wires for the campaign for Lord Kitchener, and he on his return conducted the whole of the clandestine campaign from here. Even the Reuter Telegraph Co. were got at & agreed only to wire Lord Kitchener's side of the case *from England to India* and the same from here. More than this, Lord K. supplied the London papers and the Home Govt. with his own exposition of his case – and a whole year had been spent in laying his plans. It is a masterpiece of unscrupulous intrigue. The great mistake George made was in ever coming back to India, but as you know nothing would prevent him. The strain of all this has been terrible and my solitude has been cruel. I feel sometimes that I shall go out of my mind if I have to bear much more stress and worry. The whole of my life seems sacrificed to this thankless public life for which there is no thanks.

I do not know when we shall go or what we shall do when we leave here. We cannot go to London and we have no other home, & our fate will lie in hotels. I will ask Daisy perhaps to help me out with the children, but I shall have to keep them in a warm climate at first as the cold will be very severe when we first get home.

Darling, I am sure that you grieve at all this – surely we are passing through a year of stress & trouble & I hope some day the clouds will lift.

Goodbye, my darling. Love to all.

Your devoted
Mary

1 The 4th Earl of Minto (1845–1914), Governor-General of Canada 1898–1904, Viceroy of India 1905–10. 'Isn't that the gentleman who only jumps hedges?' Curzon is said to have asked when told of his successor.
2 Arthur Oliver Villiers Russell (1869–1935), 2nd Baron Ampthill. Governor of Madras 1899–1906, but from May to December 1904 he was acting Viceroy in the period between Curzon's first and second terms of office. Ampthill was a prominent Freemason and a distinguished soldier.
3 Colonel H. Mullaly, Kitchener's spokesman in the 'right' quarters. Ampthill wrote of this man that he was 'a schemer and wire-puller of none too scrupulous a description'.

[From Lord Curzon to Mrs Leiter]
14 September [1905]   VICEREGAL LODGE
                                                                          SIMLA

My dearest Mother:
I knew you would be the happiest woman in the world at my going. And indeed I could not stand it any longer – with such indignity have I been treated. People seem to have discerned this very swiftly at home, and here in India there is only one feeling.

It would gratify you to read the magnificent tributes that are pouring in upon us from all parts of the country.

I shall be glad also to get Mary away because she never thinks that India suits her, although I truly believe that she is far better now than she would have been had she spent the last six months in England. Barring the headaches she is splendidly well.

At last, at last after all these years we shall have a rest.

Your affectionate
George

2 October [1905]   VICEREGAL LODGE
SIMLA

Mother beloved:

Our plans are changed again as the King wishes George to remain to meet the Prince of Wales. Brodrick has been dead against this and some delay has been caused. We now shall meet the Prince & Princess at Bombay,[1] and meet Lord Minto whose arrival has been put off and he has to come on a small ship – the *Egypt* – & then we sail away on Nov. 18th in great state on the new Cruiser the *Dufferin* and this takes us to Suez, where we join the *Mongolia* & go to Marseilles and go direct to London.

You can have no idea of the intensity of feeling about George. The new scheme has been hung up, and after his barefaced lies Lord Kitchener can't show his face here and is perspiring in the plains afraid to come here while Simla is giving us farewell parties & laying itself out. Raymond Marker has been Lord K's agent in London – he gets the cypher telegrams for the Pearson Press and does all the dirty work. You can tell anyone this. Marker will deny it but I know the actual telegrams which were sent him, & if you see him you can tell him that his friends thought him above such things. Lord K's intrigues and lies are all coming out and in India he is *abhorred*, and the Army hate him. He saw Barrow[2] before George did & urged him to become the new member and then denied it. He wrote his own proposals and then said he never saw them. Privately I tell you that he has never been the same since that accident – he is *purple* & his hands & feet shake like palsy! England thinks him a hero. I know him to be a liar. No Viceroy has ever left India with such demonstrations as G. Everyone is stirred to their depths to lose the great man and keep the ignoble one. Such is life.

Darling I will come to America just as soon as I can. I must consult Barlow about my lungs. I cough a great deal in the mornings, but I know the air of my own country & my own home will be splendid for me. I have great difficulty going upstairs as I cannot breathe well yet, but you have a lift.

Yr devoted

Mary

1 As Curzon had, with customary meticulousness, planned the tour of the royal couple, it was only fitting he should receive them. But this was effected only after much political malevolence on the part of Brodrick and others was allayed.
2 Sir Edmund George Barrow (1852–1934), Secretary to the Government of India, Military Department (1901–3) and later Military Secretary, India Office, 1914–17. Barrow was Curzon's choice as Military Member.

18 October [1905]

VICEREGAL LODGE

SIMLA

Darling Mother:

I quite missed the last mail as I went out shooting with George and fell down & hurt my back, & on the day I should have been writing to you I had to lie on my face with poultices of linseed & laudanum on my poor back, which is better now but very painful & I have got a belladonna plaster. My cough & breathing are very troublesome, and I get upstairs with infinite difficulty. I shall see Barlow about my wheezing as soon as I get home, as the perpetual breathlessness is a terrible nuisance.

We land at Marseilles Dec. 2nd and settle the children at Cap Martin with George's sister Sophy I hope & we get to London Dec. 4th and only stay as long as business requires....

India is ablaze with appreciation & regret. The Civil & Military Services gave George a magnificent parting banquet. The Residents of Simla combined to give us a beautiful ball. The townspeople illuminated the town and tried to drag our carriage through the streets. Every class of society has presented addresses & there has been a perpetual oration of sympathy & regret.

Lord Kitchener had to clear out as he is absolutely abhorred by everyone, & he is wandering about in the heat of the plains. He has to come back for our public departure and so our driving away will be dramatic enough with Lord K. on the scene. His scheme has not even been started & no one knows when it will be. His prestige is shattered in India & he has lied so that he is a pricked bubble & no one respects him & in the army he is detested because of his intrigues & his methods. For a weak little old man like Minto to come here at this time is calamitous, he knows nothing of the country or the questions and poor India will be at the mercy of Brodrick....

I am so thankful that we are leaving. I simply long to get away & be at rest.

Bless you darling

Yr loving

Mary

24 October 1905   VICEROY'S CAMP
                                                    [DEHRA DUN?]

My dearest Mother:

You have written me such affectionate and discerning letters since my resignation that I must pursue you to America with a reply. How shrewdly you have detected the animus of Brodrick who has been unstinting in his malevolence. There may be a few disclosures when I get home.

We arrive in England on December 4 to see how the land lies and to make our plans.

You will be pleased to see Mary looking quite a different person from the last time when you saw her, stouter but in splendid looks. What she wants is exercise. Till she can take that she will not be thoroughly strong.

I do hope that after all our adversity we are going to steer into calm waters.

You would have been touched at our departure from Simla yesterday. Many of the people were in tears.

How delightful it will be when we all meet again.

Your affec.
George

25 October [1905]   JAMMU

Darling Mother:

We left Simla last Monday at 11 o'clock and had a most touching and dramatic departure. Lord Kitchener had been away ever since George resigned as the feeling against him was so intense that he could not stay in Simla. Well everyone in Simla came to say Goodbye, and we solemnly walked out onto the lawn where hundreds of people were standing. First came the Guard of Honour, and next it stood that unscrupulous warrior Lord K. in uniform surrounded by the whole of his staff. George shook his hand in silence. I said one word 'Goodbye' and passed on, & never spoke to him again. His face was twitching and he undoubtedly felt the icy nature of the situation, & the breaking of our friendship forever; he knows too that he has gained nothing by all this and lost not only our regard but his prestige in India & the respect of the whole of India, for his lying and intrigues are now known.

A great many people were weeping and it was a trying ordeal. When we had made the round we turned and faced everyone and I bowed to right and left, George stood with hat off, the band played 'God save the King', then we got into the postilion carriage escorted by the body guard and the whole crowd cheered and cheered. Lord Kitchener had never moved – he raised his white helmet & stood like a sphinx and our procession moved away and we left Simla and its troubles behind us forever. It was a most dramatic exit, the man who has worked for seven long years for the good of India taking his hat off to the man who has intrigued & laboured to be rid of him, has become more loathed in three years than any man has ever been in India, hated by the army, detested by the troops. For years I have succeeded in keeping him [Kitchener] from some of the most awful mistakes – and kept him on friendly terms – now I feel no hesitation in telling what I know of his lies – and [letting] the King as well as everyone in England know what he is – & we shall ruin him if it is in our power as he is bringing the Indian Army to the verge of mutiny by his evil stupidity & total lack of knowledge.

Yesterday we went to Dehra Dun and saw the Cadet Corps – & had lunch with Major and Mrs Watson – it was too sweet to hear about all my darlings and I had a most happy talk with her. Now we have come to Jammu for two days and then we go to Lahore. The King has been very firm about George staying to meet the Prince and the Mintos have been ordered to delay their departure. They had told everyone that they had to hurry out to India as the King wished them to meet the Prince of Wales. The King sent for Lord Minto to Balmoral – (Lady Minto did not go) he was told not to arrive until after George had met the Prince. Brodrick's rage was awful – but the King had his way and Brodrick is writhing – his scheme which was to be introduced by Oct. 1st has not been touched and there will be just as stiff a fight as ever when Lord Minto tries to bring it in, and I should think the end of it all would be that Lord K. will have to resign – & how India will rejoice if he does.

I have just had one of the Queen's dear telegrams saying she knows how sad we are to be leaving & that she hopes I am well. She is a wonderfully thoughtful woman.

I feel the heat very much – but the sudden change has quite dried up my cough. I left the children well and they are coming to join us at Agra on our way to Bombay.

I hope you are well, darling. Your last letter made me so happy, and we will have a happy time together in Scotland darling.

Yr devoted
Mary

10 November [1905] VICEROY'S CAMP
[BOMBAY]

Darling:

George has been quite ill & has only just been able to come and meet the Prince & Princess, which he did in full state. We both went on board the

Renown & were received & came ashore with the Prince & Princess in a launch. I had on my most beautiful gray embroidered gown, hat, parasol, gloves all to match & my pearls, and to *my horror* I found the Princess in a little common white muslin – like Sandra's! with a narrow blue sash & a little blue ribbon round her neck. This for her great public entry to India – to finish off she had a most common sun umbrella and a tiny little blue pin. Well, we all marched through the great pavillon with guards of honour & the whole official show & the Prince (in white linen clothes) walked first with George who was in full uniform. I behind with the Princess – I think people were taken aback by their appearance for there was no cheering at all when they walked up on the platform & received the address. Then we stood thus:

Mary   George   Prince   Princess   Lavington

and a thousand photographers were levelled at us. Bands played but there was no shouting or enthusiasm.

At dinner the Prince gave George a magnificent present of an *immense* vase – & gave me a diamond badge which is lovely. We parted from them after dinner & went off to our train. All having gone off well. We rest at Agra for a few days & then leave India forever.

Goodbye for today darling.

Mary

14 December 1905   CARLTON HOTEL
LONDON

Sweet darling:

Bless you for your darling letter – it has made me very happy – and I wish that I were coming in this letter to bring you my Christmas Kiss & put my arms round your neck and see your dear face and be comforted by your courage and advice. I would have come to you now but I am absolutely undone by the cold and my lungs have given out & I cough terribly. Barlow thinks it asthma & a catarrhal affection of the tubes of the lungs. I have infinite trouble with breathing & the spasms of coughing are perfectly horrible. I stay indoors all day & inhale & try to keep from getting worse – & we go to the South [of France] next week I hope.

Darling Daisy has been up several times to see me and is well – she & Suffolk are coming to dine tonight.

We have had a very exciting week, welcomed by everyone but the ex-Cabinet whose hostility & venom pursues George. We have exposed some of their lies & people are on George's side I think. Minto is a mere puppet & he looks like a tiny gray mouse. I can't think he will shine in India.

Goodnight my beloved Darling. I send you my dear tender love & am

Your loving, loving
Mary

I sent you a birthday telly yesterday.

[From Lady Curzon to her mother]
31 December [1905]   CAP MARTIN HOTEL
                                                            PRÈS MENTON, A.M.

... We then had to drive to Cap Martin. We were completely exhausted & I fell unconscious on my bed & simply couldn't move. This morning we were somewhat rested & all the children so happy to see us but I am too done up to move and am writing from my bed.

In one of your letters you ask about the political situation. I think it likely that this new Cabinet will not go on without altering Brodrick's scheme in India but George has the unbroken ranks of the hostility of the old Government against him & Balfour & Brodrick are bitter enemies, and will do all they can against him. Not a member of the old Government came to meet him & the only member of it he saw was A. Lyttelton who is a strong Balfourite. All the outsiders like Chamberlain – Rosebery – & Milner were charming, & the whole Liberal Govt. we saw often but the old friends of a lifetime were mute – politics are a hard task aren't they, & the lies of Brodrick astounding. George did much useful work in London in exposing the methods & lies of his enemies and K. seems much discredited though people have known for years that he is an intriguer & a liar so no one is surprised at him & standards of honour do not seem to apply to him. I wish they would go so far as to recall him & censure him – but that is too much to hope for. ...

9 January 1906   HOTEL CALIFORNIE
                                                            CANNES

My darling Mother:

We have come to Cannes as the cold was so great at that unsheltered hotel at Cap Martin, and I think my cough is better and I do not raise so much in the morning. I have had to see the doctor here about my heart as I nearly suffocate from breathlessness at the least exertion such as dressing or going upstairs. He says the heart went through a terrible strain at the time of my illness & has never recovered. He says I am good for many years of life with care but I cannot undergo strain & *going upstairs I cannot do*, as the fearful pace the heart goes at is the danger signal to be careful. It may grow stronger as the effects of my illness vanish; now I still have the cough, the white leg and the heart! What a heritage from Walmer.

If I walk upstairs when I get to the top everything is black, I cannot get my breath, & it is some minutes before I can move. It is such a nuisance. The children are well, and often talk of going to see you. Let me know how you are darling. My last letter from you is dated Dec. 18, none since. I had hoped to hear if you had met Mr Crane.

Your devoted
Mary

[From Lord Curzon to Mrs Leiter]

19 July 1906   1, CARLTON HOUSE TERRACE

My dearest Mother:

Our darling passed away at 5.40 yesterday afternoon. I had been with her the whole day for after a bad night it was clear to me her strength was weakening and that the end could not be long delayed. We practically kept her alive through the day by oxygen, champagne & finally strychnine but it was the collapse of breathing power that brought on the last fierce struggle, and then when this was over her life faded out in peace. My arms were round her and the only two other persons present were Caley and excellent Nurse Read. They did all that was required, the room was shut up, and no one not even I have been in since. She had, like me, a horror of anyone seeing the dead. Tonight she is put into the shell with one beautiful flower from me and my photograph in her hand, and tomorrow the coffin will be closed. There has gone from me the truest, most devoted, most unselfish, most beautiful & brilliant wife that a man ever had and I am left with three little motherless children and a broken life.

Nothing however can take from me the memory of eleven happy and lovely years, and somewhere her spirit is watching over me and doing me what good she can.

I have telegraphed you about Kedleston & hope my plans will be suitable. Frank will bring down her body on Sunday evening & the funeral will be at 12 on Monday. Bishop Welldon will perform it and only our two families will be there. I hope that you will all come & that the strain may not be too great. The best train is 2.30 to Derby on Saturday.

Daisy who has been a loving darling throughout has taken away the children to Charlton but will come to Kedleston with Suffolk on Saturday.

Perhaps it is better that Mary should have been taken than live the life of a chronic invalid. Anyhow all pain and toil & tribulation are over. Somewhere my precious darling is happy and blessed. I owe to her all the happiness of my life.

Your ever affec.
George

Appendix

ASQUITH, Herbert Henry (1852–1928), 1st Earl of Oxford and Asquith; educated City of London School and Oxford. Called to the Bar 1876; QC 1890; Liberal MP for East Fife 1886–1918. Harshly assailed as a Liberal imperialist during the Boer War, Asquith occupied several important governmental posts, including Home Secretary (1892–5) and Chancellor of the Exchequer (1905–8). He was Prime Minister 1908–16, an unusually long span in political annals. Lady Curzon's account of him in her outspoken letter of 6 August, 1901 brings Asquith to life, albeit in a rather seamy light.

ASQUITH, Margot Tennant (1864–1945); one of the five unconventional daughters of Sir Charles Tennant, 'a rich and influential ironmaster'. One obituarist writes of her uninhibited childhood, her love of admiration and her ambition to excel. Over the years she acquired a glittering reputation, although her real prominence came as Asquith's second wife and as mistress of No. 10 Downing Street. Her profound interest in politics, her innate liveliness, animation and curiosity made her an accomplished hostess as well as a resolute supporter of her husband, to whom she knew when to defer. Because of her commanding position she influenced social taste, fashions and modes even if, as was said, she herself remained 'unteachable' and often chillingly forthright. By the end of the First World War Lady Asquith was out of tune with the times. Her autobiographical writings are chatty, diffuse, colloquial and, in their earlier pages, were considered wanting in reticence.

BALFOUR, Arthur James (1848–1930), 1st Earl of Balfour; educated Eton and Cambridge. As Conservative MP for Hertford and later for East Manchester and Private Secretary to his uncle, Lord Salisbury, Balfour received a good start in political life. Initially he gave the impression of being no more than 'an elegant trifler', a dilettante, and it was not until the mid 1880s, when Salisbury gave him Cabinet status, that the House recognized his skill in debate and his ability to slough off criticism. In due course Balfour became First Lord of the Treasury (1891–2 and 1895–1902) and in the latter year Prime Minister; but three years later his Party was split and, rather than dissolve Parliament, Balfour resigned. Yet during his time at No. 10 he effected reforms in the Army; and he also brought about other improvements through the Licensing Act, the Education Bill and the Irish Land Purchase Act. Balfour was later Leader of the Opposition and he served in coalition governments during the First World War. He died a bachelor.

A curious opaqueness seems to envelop Balfour, known in that world of pet-names and nicknames as 'King Arthur' and 'The Adored Gazelle'. To the noted French student of Victorian England, Elie Halévy, he was 'a great and wise Conservative', yet he was derisively known as the Prime Minister who never read a newspaper. And one historian remarked that he 'was firmly convinced of the foolishness of moving at all, except in the manner known as marking time'. He was seen as an imperturbable man, indifferent to the dignities of high places and, in a sense, removed from many of the social realities of life. Yet Mary Curzon speaks warmly of him and there is no doubt he found her immensely attractive.

BRODRICK, St John (1856–1942), 9th Viscount Midleton and 1st Earl of Midleton; educated Eton and Oxford, where he was President of the Union and, like Curzon, received a second-class degree. A Conservative MP, Brodrick occupied various Government posts, among them Financial Secretary to the War Office, Secretary of State for War (1900–3) – where he instituted various Army reforms – and Secretary of State for India (1903–5). After his parliamentary defeat in 1906 Brodrick continued to sustain political interests, especially in Irish affairs. His career is an upper-class archetype: some assisted success coupled with marked mediocrity.

Brodrick is important in this context as – initially – a close friend of the Curzons who, when at the centre of the quarrel with Kitchener, strained that relationship most unreasonably. So keenly did Brodrick feel the break with Curzon that in attempted explanation of his viewpoint he wrote a pamphlet censuring the Viceroy's policies in Tibet and Afghanistan and rebuking him for 'persistent indifference towards the Government's wishes'. Brodrick's autobiography – a bloodless book – is self-defensive and, once more, harsh to Curzon and to Lady Curzon who, he claims, 'had no experience in the "give and take" of English politics'. Two years after his first wife's death (noted in Lady Curzon's letters of July–August 1901 to her husband) Brodrick remarried and the two sons of that marriage were killed at Salerno in 1943.

CHAMBERLAIN, Joseph (1836–1914); educated University College School. Relatively early in life Chamberlain made a fortune in commerce in Birmingham and retired in 1874 to address himself to the social and political welfare of that city, of which he was at one time mayor. In 1876 he entered Parliament for Birmingham and quickly became an invigorating power in the Liberal Party. Gladstone appointed him President of the Board of Trade, but both that great statesman and the Queen eyed Chamberlain's form of republicanism with suspicion. He resigned from Gladstone's Government, and from 1886 to 1895 led the Liberal Unionists. Under Lord Salisbury he served as Secretary of State for the Colonies, a post that involved him in the notorious Jameson Raid and in the Boer War of 1899–1902; he also visited South Africa during the Balfour premiership to negotiate financial and other settlements arising from that tragic conflict. Chamberlain later resigned from the Balfour Cabinet over tariff reform and he continued for a few short years thereafter to be a voice in political affairs, but serious illness subsequently incapacitated him.

Chamberlain married three times: his first wife died giving birth to their son Austen in 1863; he next married his wife's cousin, who died in 1875 – one child of that union was Neville Chamberlain. He met his third wife, née Mary Endicott and descended from an old New England family, in 1887 in Washington whilst engaged in the unromantic task of negotiating an Anglo-American fishing treaty: it was a marriage of deep mutual affection. Chamberlain was a man of considerable vitality, of wide-ranging interests and of such contradictory political views as to remain an enigma even into our own time.

CHURCHILL, Winston Leonard Spencer (1874–1965), KG 1953; educated Harrow and Sandhurst; commissioned in the 4th Queen's Own Hussars. The Churchill of Lady Curzon's day was a brash, up-and-coming young man, making his way as a journalist in Cuba and elsewhere and serving with his regiment in India, Egypt and Africa. He was with Kitchener at Omdurman and made a famous escape from captivity during the Boer War. Also, at this time of his life he published extensively on current history and in 1900 produced his one novel, *Savrola*. In the same year he became Unionist MP for Oldham; in due course he joined the dissenting young Tories headed by Hugh Cecil and known as the 'Hooligans' or 'Hughligans'. It was the Churchill of these years who remarked to his American mother, Lady Randolph Churchill (*née* Jennie Jerome): 'In a pushing age we must shove with the rest.' Something of that quality is revealed in Mary Curzon's account of his conduct during the summer of 1901. The rest is history.

CRAIGIE, Pearl Mary Teresa (1867–1906); born of American parents who settled in London in her infancy. She adopted the pen-name 'John Oliver Hobbes' and after a short-lived marriage was received into the Catholic Church. Although her early work is trifling, Pearl Craigie went on to write *Some Emotions and a Moral* and *The Sinner's Comedy* which, if they failed to rechart the direction of the novel, were at least commercially successful. From then on, in fact, she had little difficulty in placing her work; she was her own literary agent and wrote of that discouraging endeavour, 'I find it so difficult to be at once a Christian, an author, and a woman of business.'

Although the spiritual life informs some of Mrs Craigie's novels she also wrote plays that were performed by such notable thespians as Ellen Terry and Forbes-Robertson but hardly with outstanding success. Her friendship with the Curzons took her to India, at their invitation, for the Delhi Durbar, of which she wrote an informative (if rococo) account. She lectured in the States and continued to write, but her nervous condition, the death of her good friend Mary Curzon and an increasing debility hastened her own end, which came just a few weeks after the Vicereine's.

CROMER, Lord: Evelyn Baring (1841–1917), 1st Earl of Cromer; of naval and financial background (he was connected with the banking house of Baring), a man born to master and control. In the 1870s Cromer was Private Secretary to his cousin, Lord Northbrook, Viceroy of India 1872–6. In 1883 Baring was appointed British Agent and Consul-General in Egypt and for many years he played a salient political and economic part in the affairs of that chaotic country; in fact, he systematically re-viewed, re-organized and reformed, with financial and other help, the administration of Egypt. In 1907 he received for his services a 'golden handshake' of £50,000 from the British Government. He was heavily decorated as his career progressed.

Cromer was reportedly abrupt in manner, autocratic, and had authority in his looks. Of him was written: 'The virtues of Patience are known,/But I think that, when put to the touch,/The people of Egypt will own, with a groan,/There's an Evil in Baring too much.' The sobriquet 'Over Baring' (dating from his Indian days) was probably apt.

HAMILTON, Lord: George Francis (1845–1927), third son of 1st Duke of Abercorn, GCIE 1903; educated Harrow; honorary degrees from Glasgow and Oxford; Conservative MP for Middlesex 1868–84; First Lord of the Admiralty 1885–6, 1886–92; Under-Secretary of State for India 1874–80; Secretary of State for India 1895–1903.

Hamilton, as Secretary of State for India, had much to do with Lord Curzon during the most fruitful time of his Viceroyalty. Between them the two men were responsible for several improvements in India, including the development of Curzon's Imperial Cadet Corps, which is mentioned in his letters to his wife in the spring and summer of 1901. As personal friends sharing common objectives the two men worked well together, but in the spring of 1902 Curzon felt the India Office was thwarting him and great strain was placed upon their relations, both personal and governmental. During this period Hamilton sought Lady Curzon as mediator, but to little avail, and the following year, under unpleasant political circumstances, Hamilton resigned his office.

KEPPEL, Alice Frederica (1869–1947), daughter of Admiral Sir William Edmonstone. In 1891 she married Lieutenant-Colonel the Hon. George Keppel by whom she had two daughters. From 1898, when she first met the Prince of Wales (later Edward VII), until his death she was a great favourite of the King and therefore a considerable power in society and elsewhere. Although opinion of Mrs Keppel seems in general to have been favourable, it has been remarked that 'the adventurer in her was ever at the masthead'. However, numerous accounts suggest she was a charming woman, humorous, good-natured and certainly vivacious – qualities she miraculously exercised without rousing undue resentment. Above all, her tact was consummate, and her singular understanding of the King enabled her easily to allay his fits of boredom. Only at Hatfield, Arundel and Welbeck was she not a welcome member of the royal entourage.

KITCHENER, Horatio Herbert (1850–1916), Field Marshal, 1st Earl Kitchener of Khartoum and of Broome; educated Royal Military Academy, Woolwich; commissioned 2nd Lieutenant, Royal Engineers in 1871. A man of uniquely varied abilities, Kitchener served in many parts of the Empire, distinguishing himself in one campaign after another. It is with Khartoum that his name is most closely associated, for in the autumn of 1898 he routed the forces of the Khalifa and thus avenged the killing of General Gordon. With this remarkable victory – the Dervishes lost some eleven thousand men, the British less than 50 – the Kitchener legend, already nurtured on dangerous and romantic missions, came to full fruition. For his services at Khartoum, which included the desecration of the tomb of the Mahdi, a grateful Government rewarded Kitchener with a barony, a GCB and £30,000. He later became Commander-in-Chief in South Africa, and India of course, and was granted further titles, decorations and financial emoluments. Invested with prestige and glamour, Kitchener moved from one pinnacle to another, a living legend; he ended his career as Secretary of State for War during the First World War. The Cabinet of that time is said to have been 'frankly intimidated' by him. In June 1916, a time of terrible strain for the Allied cause, Kitchener was drowned in HMS *Hampshire* en route to Russia on a military/diplomatic mission.

Kitchener's character was baffling and complex. On the one hand he was a fastidious and knowledgeable collector of porcelain and antique furniture, fluent in

French and, if so inclined, a capable diplomat; on the other hand, he could manifest an abruptness and an insensitivity, a brutality, a menacing presence that terrified. He seemed indifferent to hatred or affection, impervious to popularity, and ruthless in pursuit of his objectives.

Both Curzon and Kitchener were of fatally similar temperaments, driving to their goals with ceaseless energy and taking too much upon themselves. Yet both had a gentler side (even if Kitchener's was far more difficult to reach than Curzon's) and both were iron-willed men who publicly subjected their emotions to stringent self-control. But in his clash with Curzon Kitchener emerges with very little credit indeed, as his conduct – backstairs manoeuvring, especially in his correspondence with the powerful Lady Cranborne – is far from admirable.

LAWRENCE, Walter Roper ('Rop'), (1857–1940), KCIE 1903, Bt. 1906, GCVO 1918; educated Cheltenham College and Oxford; passed into ICS in 1877. Lawrence served as Settlement Commissioner in Kashmir 1888–95, an experience recorded in his *The Valley of Kashmir*. Returning to England, he was briefly chief agent to the Duke of Bedford but became Curzon's Private Secretary in India in 1898, a post he held until 1903. He then went back to England to pursue various business interests but was recalled to be Chief of Staff to the Prince and Princess of Wales for their Indian tour of 1905–6, a tour fully planned by Curzon. Lawrence later became a member of the Council of India and an elder statesman frequently consulted about Indian affairs. He also wrote for *The Times* and one of his contributions was Curzon's obituary.

Lawrence was one of the few civil servants to become close to the Viceroy – or as close as it was possible to come. His account of his Indian life, *The India We Served* (1928), is revealing of Curzon as man and administrator, of his impatience and incisiveness, of his fascination with India, and of his 'contempt of meanness'. Lawrence also dwells appreciatively on Curzon's many visits to many parts of the continent, his reverence for his royal mandate, and his constant efforts to improve all aspects of Indian life. Lawrence, with reason, plainly saw Curzon as the last of the great imperial Viceroys.

LYALL, Alfred Comyn (1835–1911); KCB 1881; educated Eton and East India Company's College at Haileybury, which he left in 1855 to begin a career of over thirty years abroad. Lyall, who experienced the Mutiny and the Second Afghan War, ascended the rungs of the ICS ladder, serving as acting, deputy and full commissioner in various districts and provinces. In 1874 he became Agent to the Governor-General of Rajputana where he carried out distinguished diplomatic work. Subsequently he conducted the affairs of the Indian Foreign Office and in 1882 became Lieutenant-Governor of the North-west Provinces. In 1887 he bade farewell to India but continued service to that country as a member in England of the Council of India.

Like many unsung, relatively unimportant Victorians, Lyall was, in his own way, a polymath. Beyond his governmental service he wrote for the *Fortnightly, Quarterly Review* and *Edinburgh Review*; his range was wide and included writings on French colonial policy, religious subjects, and many aspects of Indian government and administration. Like Curzon he possessed an unusually sensitive and profound knowledge of India, its history and civilization. Lyall also wrote poetry and a more than passable study of Tennyson as well as a volume on Warren Hastings in the *Men of*

Action series. Perhaps his most ambitious work is *The Rise and Expansion of the British Dominion in India*, a book widely praised as 'a reasoned and definite idea' of the British achievement in that country. Lyall supported Curzon in the struggle with Kitchener.

MILNER, Alfred (1854–1925), created Viscount 1902; educated Tübingen, London and Oxford Universities. Called to the bar 1881. Milner entered public life by way of journalism and the civil service. He became a major political figure upon his appointment in 1897 as High Commissioner for South Africa and Governor of Cape Colony. His failure to reconcile the opposing views of the Boers and the British contributed to the Boer War. A Liberal imperialist, Milner was an adherent to the concept of Empire and in 1902, at the conclusion of the conflict, he sought to improve conditions throughout South Africa by developing programmes for irrigation, resettlement, education, agriculture and mining. He also brought in some young Oxonians – his kindergarten, as they were known – to assist in these ventures. But in spite of Milner's grandiose plans and the hopes embodied in the Union of South Africa of 1910 his policies eventually foundered. He continued until his death to occupy important posts in the home Government. Milner was essentially a man with a mission, a disciple of imperial unity, a passionate advocate of British hegemony, but one not sympathetic toward or understanding of the vagaries of the democratic process.

Lady Curzon's reflections on Milner are of singular interest as they coincide with his triumphant return to London in May 1901 a few days before he was decorated and raised to the peerage.

RIVAZ, Charles Montgomery (1845–1926), KCSI 1901; educated Blackheath Proprietary School. From an ICS family, Rivaz entered that Service himself in 1864. Following six years of district work, he became Commissioner of Lahore (1887–92), then Financial Commissioner of the Punjab and from 1902 to 1907 Lieutenant-Governor of the latter province. Rivaz was no initiator of reforms, but he was skilful at executing them, and with the assistance of Curzon and Denzil Ibbetson he dealt more than competently with land improvements in the Punjab.

Rivaz was not deeply involved with Indian nationalism, but the welfare of the people was always important to him. He did excellent work during the Kangra earthquake of 1905. In fact, as a first-rate public servant Rivaz exemplified the ICS at its best. He is noted as 'scornful of all pretence and yet contemptuously tolerant of much that would offend others'. Unlike many of his contemporaries, he washed his hands of Indian affairs upon retirement.

ROBERTS, Frederick Sleigh (1832–1914), Field Marshal, 1st Earl Roberts of Kandahar, Pretoria and Waterford; educated Eton and Sandhurst; commissioned in the Bengal Artillery in 1851. Most of Roberts' career was spent in India, as his autobiography *Forty-one Years in India* attests; such was his reputation that within twenty-one months of publication the book went into its thirtieth edition. As a serving soldier Roberts' responsibilities were numerous over the years. He supervised the arrangements for the Delhi Durbar of 1877 when Queen Victoria was proclaimed Empress of India, and for his services in the Afghan campaigns of 1878 and 1880 he was well rewarded; he was subsequently appointed Commander-in-Chief of the

Madras Army, and upon rising to be Commander-in-Chief, India, a post he held for seven years, he made many improvements in the forces and in frontier communications. He left India for good in 1893 but went on to play a central role in the Boer War after which, in succession to Viscount Wolseley in 1901, he was made Commander-in-Chief of the British Army, holding the post until February 1905. He received the thanks of Parliament, was heaped with further decorations and accolades and – a really tangible recognition of his services – an award of £100,000. 'Bobs', a neat, trim figure, was a man of simple, kindly personality; he was greatly loved by his soldiers, and as early as the Afghan campaign had also caught the public fancy.

ROSEBERY, Lord: Archibald Philip Primrose (1847–1929), 5th Earl of Rosebery; educated Eton and Oxford. One of his tutors wrote of him that he 'desired the palm without the dust'. Rosebery occupied a post in the Home Office, became Secretary of State for Foreign Affairs and acquired a certain popularity for his deft handling of a coal strike in the winter of 1893. With the resignation of Gladstone in 1894 Rosebery was selected by Queen Victoria to be Prime Minister, but he lasted only a short time for the Government fell fifteen months later, in June 1895. Early in this century Lord Rosebery increasingly withdrew from active politics, and, although a voice in the Liberal League, he contented himself with speaking on a variety of diversified subjects. Rosebery was a capable writer of prose and produced studies of Peel, Napoleon, Pitt and Cromwell. He also enjoyed the rare distinction of being the first Prime Minister to run a Derby winner whilst in office.

SALISBURY, Lord: Robert Arthur Talbot Gascoyne-Cecil (1830–1903), 3rd Marquess of Salisbury; educated Eton and Oxford. First returned as Conservative MP for Stamford, Lord Salisbury gave his life to public service although, for some years, he used journalism to solve financial problems. He was three times Prime Minister: 1885–6; 1886–92, and 1895–1902. Salisbury was an aristocrat, disdainful of public adulation, and sensitive to the aristocrat's privileges whilst aware of his obligations. He stood for tradition, gravity and dignity. Salisbury lacked the magnetism of Gladstone and the colour of Disraeli, but he conveyed assurance, confidence and security to the British public. Caution, experience and level-headedness carried him far and earned him respect. Overburdened with work and in poor health, he resigned as Prime Minister in July 1902 and was succeeded by his nephew, Arthur Balfour.

TIPU SULTAN (1753–1799); Sultan of Mysore and also known as the 'Tiger of Mysore'. He was a particular enemy of the British. He fought in the Mahratta War of 1775–9 and in the Mysore War in which, in 1782, he defeated the British and at the same time succeeded his father as Sultan. Two years later he concluded a treaty with the British, but by ravaging the territories of Travancore in 1789 he provoked the Government anew. In the ensuing warfare Tipu was defeated by Cornwallis at Seringapatam in 1792, on which occasion he had to yield half his dominions and deliver his two sons as hostages. Tipu's dealings with the French enraged Lord Mornington, and Seringapatam was taken by storm by the English in May 1799; Tipu was killed there.

VANDERBILT, Consuelo (1877–1964). An American, she was married in 1895, at the age of eighteen, to the 9th Duke of Marlborough to whom she brought a dowry of some two and a half million dollars; in 1906 she separated from the Duke, for her marriage was wretchedly unhappy; and in 1921 – appropriately on 4 July – she married Jacques Balsan.

Reared in a world of immense privilege and wealth, Consuelo Vanderbilt plays a modest role in the Curzon letters; however, she is of interest both in herself and as a compatriot of the Vicereine for, like her, she never forfeited her essential American-ism. This is apparent in her crisply written autobiography *The Glitter and the Gold*, a penetrating and at times steely account of late-Victorian and Edwardian England. The book's chief value lies in its delineation of a society devoted to pleasure, extrava-gance and living off others. Her character studies – of Churchill, the Curzons, Balfour and others – are sharply etched and sometimes quite acerb. She strips away pre-tensions and reveals the hypocrisy and shoddiness so often lurking beneath the glitter and the gold. But she is neither blind nor deaf to the finer, nobler qualities sometimes found among the privileged. Unlike many memoirs of that age, Consuelo Vander-bilt's autobiography is perceptive and does not diminish into irrelevancy, watery anecdote or name-dropping. Over it all hovers a rather poignant sense of loneliness.

WELLDON, James Edward Cowell (1854–1937); educated Eton and Cambridge. Welldon had a full career both in the Church and in education. He was Headmaster of Dulwich, which he is said to have raised 'from a low ebb', and of Harrow. He was Metropolitan of the Anglican Church in India 1898–1902, and subsequently Canon of Westminster, Dean of Manchester and then of Durham. He translated Aristotle, edited Augustine and gave the Hulsean lectures at Cambridge.

A long-time friend of the Curzons, Welldon was a forthright man, an excellent host and an engaging raconteur. Such was his generous girth that he was once greeted in India as 'Honoured Enormity'. Unfortunately, Curzon did not consider Welldon suitable for his Indian post and particularly regretted his participation in secular affairs, as the letters of 1901 between the Curzons indicate. In his readable *Recollec-tions and Reflections* Welldon does little more than hint at differences, remarking on Curzon's lack of insight 'towards Christianity and especially towards Christian missions' and clouding his own resignation by denying the necessity to elaborate upon it. Nevertheless, Welldon is generous and charitable towards Lord Curzon in the *Recollections* and obviously respected his abilities; and he shows pronounced admiration for the Vicereine, questioning whether Anglo-India 'did her full justice'. Welldon conducted Lady Curzon's funeral service, of which he gives a moving account in his autobiography.

WYNDHAM, George (1863–1913); educated Eton and Sandhurst. Joined Coldstream Guards in 1883 and was subsequently Private Secretary to Balfour. Wyndham was Conservative MP for Dover 1889–1913 and also served as Parlia-mentary Under-Secretary in the War Office and as Chief Secretary for Ireland. In his privately printed *Letters* he left an enlightening account of Edward VII at work.

YOUNG, William Mackworth (1840–1924), KCSI 1897; educated Eton and Cam-bridge. Young entered the ICS in 1862 and spent many of his years in the Punjab, rising to Lieutenant-Governor (1897–1902). Although Young was an able, informed civil servant, he managed to lock horns with Curzon more than once. The quarrel that occupies a fair part of Curzon's letters to the Vicereine in 1901 centred upon his decision to separate the Frontier from the Punjab. The Lieutenant-Governor angrily claimed that he was neither consulted nor taken into the Viceroy's confidence over the matter; and he spoke out injudiciously in public upon this thorny subject. Of particular interest is Lady Curzon's response to the quarrel because, as her letters indicate, she assumed a firm, resolute stand and made it clear the Viceroy must do the same; thus her position is further refutation of the belief that she constantly deferred to her husband.

Selective Index